MW01106521

Add your opinion to our next book

Fill out a survey

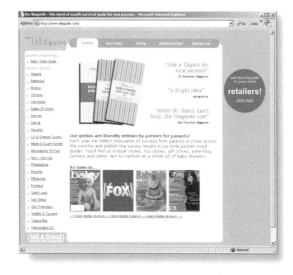

visit www.lilaguide.com

the lilaguide
by PARENTS *for* PARENTS

baby-friendly
miami & south fl

NEW PARENT SURVIVAL GUIDE TO SHOPPING,
ACTIVITIES, RESTAURANTS AND MORE...

2ND EDITION

LOCAL EDITOR: DANA KULVIN

PUBLISHED BY THE LILAGUIDE/OAM SOLUTIONS, INC.
SAN FRANCISCO, CA   WWW.LILAGUIDE.COM

Published by:
OAM Solutions, Inc.
139 Saturn Street
San Francisco, CA 94114, USA
415.252.1300
orders@lilaguide.com
www.lilaguide.com

ISBN. 1-932847-21-9
First Printing: 2005
Printed in the USA
Copyright © 2005 by OAM Solutions, Inc.

This book is designed to share parents' opinions regarding
baby-related products, services and activities. It is sold with the
understanding that the information contained in the book does
not represent the publisher's opinion or recommendations.
The reviews contained in this guide are based on public opinion
surveys and are therefore subjective in nature. The publisher
shall have neither liability nor responsibility to any person or
entity with respect to any loss or damage caused, or alleged to
have been caused, directly or indirectly, by the information
contained in this book.

If you do not wish to be bound by the above, you may return this
book to the publisher for a full refund.

table of contents

No, for the last time, the baby does not come with a handbook. And even if there were a handbook, you wouldn't read it. You'd fill out the warranty card, throw out the box, and start playing right away. Until a few hours passed and you were hit with the epiphany of, "Gee whiz honey, what in the wide, wide world of childcare are we doing here?"

Relax. We had that panicked thought when we had our daughter Delilah. And so did **all the parents** we talked to when they had their children. And while we all knew there was no handbook, there was, we found, a whole lot of **word-of-mouth information**. Everyone we talked to had some bit of child rearing advice about what baby gear store is the most helpful. Some **nugget of parenting wisdom** about which restaurant tolerates strained carrots on the floor. It all really seemed to help. Someone, we thought, should write this down.

And that's when, please pardon the pun, the lilaguide was born. The book you're now holding is a guide **written by local parents for local parents**. It's what happens when someone actually does write it down (and organizes it, calculates it, and presents it in an easy-to-use format).

Nearly 4,000 surveys have produced this first edition of **the lilaguide: Baby-Friendly Miami & South FL**. It provides a truly unique insider's view of over 900 "parent-friendly" stores, activities, restaurants, and service providers that are about to become a very big part of your life. And while this guide won't tell you how to change a diaper or how to get by on little or no sleep (that's what grandparents are for), it will tell you what other **local parents have learned** about the amazing things your city and neighborhood have to offer.

As you peruse these reviews, please remember that this guide is **not intended to be a comprehensive directory** since it does not contain every baby store or activity in the area. Rather, it is intended to provide a short-list of places that your neighbors and friends **deemed exciting and noteworthy**. If a place or business is not listed, it simply means that nobody (or not enough people) rated or submitted information about it to us. **Please let us know** about your favorite parent and baby-friendly businesses and service providers by participating in our online survey at **www.lilaguide.com**. We always want your opinions!

So there you have it. Now go make some phone calls, clean up the house, take a nap, or do something on your list before the baby arrives.

Enjoy!

Oli & Elysa

Oli Mittermaier & Elysa Marco, MD

PS

We love getting feedback (good and bad) so don't be bashful. Email us at **lila@lilaguide.com** with your thoughts, comments and suggestions. We'll be sure to try to include them in next year's edition!

We'd like to take a moment to offer a heart-felt thank you to all the **parents who participated in our survey** and took the time to share their thoughts and opinions. Without your participation, we would never have been able to create this unique guide.

Thanks to our extra helpful South Florida contributors **Debbie Adams**, **Nancy Bernstein**, **Andrea Cariglio**, **Jennifer Enlow**, **Debbie Falcone**, **Lori Fisher**, **Odette Hershkowitz**, **Susan Johnson**, **Tracy Kurzweil**, **Elizabeth Levine**, **Leslie Matus**, **Tamar Oppenheimer**, **Michele Rizzo**, **Maria Rubin**, and **Shari Silverman** for going above and beyond in the quest for hip tot spots.

Thanks also to **Lisa Barnes**, **Nora Borowsky**, **Todd Cooper**, **Amy Iannone**, **Katy Jacobson**, **Felicity John Odell**, **Shira Johnson**, **Kasia Kappes**, **Jen Krug**, **Dana Kulvin**, **Deborah Schneider**, **Kevin Schwall**, **April Stewart**, and **Nina Thompson** for their tireless editorial eyes, **Satoko Furuta** and **Paul D. Smith** for their beautiful sense of design, and **Lane Foard** for making the words yell.

Special thanks to **Paul D. Smith**, **Ken Miles**, and **Ali Wing** for their consistent support and overall encouragement in all things lilaguide, and of course **our parents** for their unconditional support in this and all our other endeavors.

And last, but certainly not least, thanks to **little Delilah** for inspiring us to embark on this challenging, yet incredibly fulfilling project.

participate in our survey at

ratings

Most listings have stars and numbers as part of their write-up. These symbols mean the following:

❺ / ★★★★★	extraordinary
❹ / ★★★★☆	very good
❸ / ★★★☆☆	good
❷ / ★★☆☆☆	fair
❶ / ★☆☆☆☆	poor
✓	available
✗	not available/relevant

If a ★ is listed instead of ★, it means that the rating is less reliable because a small number of parents surveyed the listing. Furthermore, if a listing has **no stars** or **criteria ratings**, it means that although the listing was rated, the number of surveys submitted was so low that we did not feel it justified an actual rating.

quotes & reviews

The quotes/reviews are taken directly from surveys submitted to us via our web site (**www.lilaguide.com**). Other than spelling and minor grammatical changes, they come to you as they came to us. Quotes were selected based on how well they appeared to represent the collective opinions of the surveys submitted.

fact checking

We have contacted all of the businesses listed to verify their address and phone number, as well as to inquire about their hours, class schedules and web site information. Since some of this information may change after this guide has been printed, we appreciate you letting us know of any errors by notifying us via email at **lila@lilaguide.com**.

baby basics & accessories

South Dade & Downtown

★ ★ ★ ★ ★

"lila picks"

- ★ Aleren
- ★ Babies R Us
- ★ Bellini
- ★ Charly & Hannah's
- ★ Genius Jones
- ★ Kate And Leo
- ★ Twinkle

Aleren ★ ★ ★ ★ ★

❝...a great little boutique with cute gifts and clothing for babies, toddlers and kids up to size 10... the customer service is fabulous and you can find unique outfits for children... the store's decor is beautiful, it feels good to be there... the staff (especially the owner) is always willing to help and accommodate your needs... ❞

Furniture, Bedding & Decor	✓	$$$	Prices
Gear & Equipment	✓	❸	Product availability
Nursing & Feeding	✗	❹	Staff knowledge
Safety & Babycare	✗	❹	Customer service
Clothing, Shoes & Accessories	✓	❹	Decor
Books, Toys & Entertainment	✓		

WWW.ALEREN.COM

PINECREST—8237 SW 124TH ST (AT S DIXIE HWY); 786.430.6000; M-SA 10-6

April Cornell

❝...beautiful, classic dresses and accessories for special occasions... I love the matching 'mommy and me' outfits... lots of fun knickknacks for sale... great selection of baby wear on their web site... rest assured your baby won't look like every other child in these adorable outfits... very frilly and girlie—beautiful... ❞

Furniture, Bedding & Decor	✗	$$$	Prices
Gear & Equipment	✗	❸	Product availability
Nursing & Feeding	✗	❹	Staff knowledge
Safety & Babycare	✗	❹	Customer service
Clothing, Shoes & Accessories	✓	❹	Decor
Books, Toys & Entertainment	✗		

WWW.APRILCORNELL.COM

MIAMI—8888 SW 136TH (AT THE FALLS SHOPPING CENTER); 305.254.2204; M-SA 10-9:30, SU 12-7

Babies R Us ★ ★ ★ ★ ★

❝...everything baby under one roof... they have a wide selection and carry most 'mainstream' items such as Graco, Fisher-Price, Avent and Britax... great customer service—given how big the stores are, I was pleasantly surprised at how attentive the staff was... easy return policy... super busy on weekends so try to visit on a weekday for the best service... keep an eye out for great coupons, deals and frequent

sales... easy and comprehensive registry... shopping here is so easy—you've got to check it out... "

Furniture, Bedding & Decor	✓	$$$	....	Prices
Gear & Equipment	✓	❹	....	Product availability
Nursing & Feeding	✓	❹	....	Staff knowledge
Safety & Babycare	✓	❹	....	Customer service
Clothing, Shoes & Accessories	✓	❹	....	Decor
Books, Toys & Entertainment	✓			

WWW.BABIESRUS.COM

MIAMI—15625 N KENDALL DR (AT SW 157TH AVE); 305.382.4060; M-SA 9:30-9:30, SU 11-7; PARKING IN FRONT OF BLDG

MIAMI—8755 SW 24TH ST (AT SW 87TH AVE); 305.226.8334; M-SA 9:30-9:30, SU 11-7; PARKING IN FRONT OF BLDG

Baby Bear Boutique ★★★★☆

" *...great to have a store like this close by... perfect when you need to pick up a little something...* "

Furniture, Bedding & Decor	✗	$$$$	....	Prices
Gear & Equipment	✗	❸	....	Product availability
Nursing & Feeding	✗	❹	....	Staff knowledge
Safety & Babycare	✗	❸	....	Customer service
Clothing, Shoes & Accessories	✓	❸	....	Decor
Books, Toys & Entertainment	✗			

KEY BISCAYNE—260 CRANDON BLVD (AT SONESTA DR); 305.361.2732

Baby Depot At Burlington Coat Factory ★★★⯪☆

" *...a large, 'super store' layout with a ton of baby gear... wide aisles, packed shelves, barely existent customer service and awesome prices... everything from bottles, car seats and strollers to gliders, cribs and clothes... I always find something worth getting... a little disorganized and hard to locate items you're looking for... the staff is not always knowledgeable about their merchandise... return policy is store credit only...* "

Furniture, Bedding & Decor	✓	$$	....	Prices
Gear & Equipment	✓	❸	....	Product availability
Nursing & Feeding	✓	❸	....	Staff knowledge
Safety & Babycare	✓	❸	....	Customer service
Clothing, Shoes & Accessories	✓	❸	....	Decor
Books, Toys & Entertainment	✓			

WWW.BABYDEPOT.COM

MIAMI—11301 NW 12TH ST (AT 14TH ST); 305.594.7776; M-SA 10-9:30, SU 11-7; MALL PARKING

BabyGap/GapKids ★★★★☆

" *...colorful baby and toddler clothing in clean, well-lit stores... great return policy... it's the Gap, so you know what you're getting—colorful, cute and well-made clothing... best place for baby hats... prices are reasonable especially since there's always a sale of some sort going on... sales, sales, sales—frequent and fantastic... everything I'm looking for in infant clothing—snap crotches, snaps up the front, all natural fabrics and great styling... fun seasonal selections—a great place to shop for gifts as well as for your own kids... although it can get busy, staff generally seem accommodating and helpful...* "

Furniture, Bedding & Decor	✗	$$$	....	Prices
Gear & Equipment	✗	❹	....	Product availability
Nursing & Feeding	✗	❹	....	Staff knowledge
Safety & Babycare	✗	❹	....	Customer service
Clothing, Shoes & Accessories	✓	❹	....	Decor
Books, Toys & Entertainment	✗			

WWW.GAP.COM

COCONUT GROVE—3015 GRAND AVE (AT MAYFAIR SHOPS); 305.529.9499;
F-SA 11-12, SU-TH 11-10; PARKING LOT

MIAMI—1455 NW 107TH AVE (AT MIAMI INTERNATIONAL MALL);
305.717.0985; M-SA 10-9, SU 11-7; MALL PARKING

MIAMI—401 BISCAYNE BLVD (AT NE 4TH ST); 305.539.9334; M-TH 10-10, F-
SA 10-11, SU 11-9; GARAGE PARKING

MIAMI—7521 N KENDALL DR (AT DADELAND MALL); 305.668.8886; M 0A 10-
9:30, SU 12-6; MALL PARKING

Bellini

❝...high-end furniture for a gorgeous nursery... if you're looking for
the kind of furniture you see in magazines then this is the place to go...
excellent quality... yes, it's pricey, but the quality is impeccable... free
delivery and setup... their furniture is built to withstand the abuse my
tots dish out... they sell very unique merchandise, ranging from cribs to
bedding and even some clothes... our nursery design was inspired by
their store decor... I wish they had more frequent sales... ❞

Furniture, Bedding & Decor	✓	$$$$	Prices
Gear & Equipment	✗	❹	Product availability
Nursing & Feeding	✗	❹	Staff knowledge
Safety & Babycare	✗	❹	Customer service
Clothing, Shoes & Accessories	✗	❹	Decor
Books, Toys & Entertainment	✓		

WWW.BELLINI.COM

CORAL GABLES—50 MIRACLE MILE (AT GALLANO ST); 305.460.9898; M-SA
10-6, SU 12-5; PARKING LOT

Books & Books

❝...wonderful independent bookstore where there is a wide selection
for parents to be, parents and babies and kids... beautiful settings...
Very knowledgeable staff... , big gorgeous high-quality illustrated
books abound, not your run of the mill chain books... they have
children's programming, but mostly geared toward adults.... ❞

Furniture, Bedding & Decor	✗	$$$	Prices
Gear & Equipment	✗	❹	Product availability
Nursing & Feeding	✗	❺	Staff knowledge
Safety & Babycare	✗	❺	Customer service
Clothing, Shoes & Accessories	✗	❹	Decor
Books, Toys & Entertainment	✓		

WWW.BOOKSANDBOOKS.COM

CORAL GABLES—265 ARAGON AVE (OFF MIRACLE MILE); 305.442.4408;
DAILY 9-11 ; PARKING LOT

Boy Meets Girl

❝...the owner makes a lot of the clothing herself... special, beautiful
baby outfits... a bit expensive for everyday wear, but perfect for a
special occasion... layette, infants, toddlers, and kids up to size 16...
shoes, hairbows and socks are also available... one-stop shop.... ❞

Furniture, Bedding & Decor	✗	$$$$	Prices
Gear & Equipment	✗	❹	Product availability
Nursing & Feeding	✗	❺	Staff knowledge
Safety & Babycare	✗	❺	Customer service
Clothing, Shoes & Accessories	✓	❹	Decor
Books, Toys & Entertainment	✗		

WWW.BMGKIDS.COM

MIAMI—357 MIRACLE MILE (AT S LE JEUNE RD); 305.445.9668; M-SA 10-6;
PARKING LOT

Bri Bri Children's Boutique ★★★★☆

"...very cute clothing, but the prices are up there... service is great, you get what you pay for... attentive staff..."

Furniture, Bedding & Decor	✗	$$$$ .... Prices
Gear & Equipment	✗	❸ .... Product availability
Nursing & Feeding	✗	❸ .... Staff knowledge
Safety & Babycare	✗	❸ .... Customer service
Clothing, Shoes & Accessories	✓	❹ .... Decor
Books, Toys & Entertainment	✗	

WWW.BRI-BRI.COM

MIAMI—7230 RED RD (AT 57TH AVE); 305.668.8210; M-SA 10-6; STREET PARKING

Canastilla Lavin Bay Center

Furniture, Bedding & Decor	✓	✓ .... Gear & Equipment
Nursing & Feeding	✓	✗ .... Safety & Babycare
Clothing, Shoes & Accessories	✓	✗ .... Books, Toys & Entertainment

WWW.LAVINBABYCENTER.COM

MIAMI—3604 NW 7TH ST (AT NW 37TH AVE); 305.649.0917; M-SA 10-8, SU 12-5

Carter's ★★★★☆

"...always a great selection of inexpensive baby basics—everything from clothing to linens... I always find something at 'giveaway prices' during one of their frequent sales... busy and crowded—it can be a chaotic shopping experience... 30 to 50 percent less than what you would pay at other boutiques... I bought five pieces of baby clothing for less than $40... durable, adorable and affordable... most stores have a small play area for kids in center of store so you can get your shopping done..."

Furniture, Bedding & Decor	✓	$$ .... Prices
Gear & Equipment	✗	❹ .... Product availability
Nursing & Feeding	✗	❹ .... Staff knowledge
Safety & Babycare	✗	❹ .... Customer service
Clothing, Shoes & Accessories	✓	❹ .... Decor
Books, Toys & Entertainment	✓	

WWW.CARTERS.COM

MIAMI—11401 NW 12TH ST (AT DOLPHIN MALL); 305.513.4557; M-SA 10-9; MALL PARKING

Charly & Hannah's ★★★★★

"...excellent old-fashioned toy store, unique in Miami... the owner and staff are pleasant and always willing to help you find the perfect toy... many unique toys you won't find in larger toy stores... they will wrap gifts with their signature brown paper and stickers... every kid gets excited when they see a gift from Charly and Hannah's coming... sweet products and nice educational toys, too..."

Furniture, Bedding & Decor	✗	$$$ .... Prices
Gear & Equipment	✗	❹ .... Product availability
Nursing & Feeding	✗	❹ .... Staff knowledge
Safety & Babycare	✗	❹ .... Customer service
Clothing, Shoes & Accessories	✗	❹ .... Decor
Books, Toys & Entertainment	✓	

WWW.CHARLYHANNAH.COM

CORAL GABLES—256 ANDALUSIA AVE (AT SALZEDO ST); 305.441.7677; M-F 10-6, SA 10-4; PARKING LOT

Children's Exchange, The

Furniture, Bedding & Decor	✗	✗ .... Gear & Equipment
Nursing & Feeding	✗	✗ .... Safety & Babycare

| Clothing, Shoes & Accessories | ...... ✓ | ✓ .... Books, Toys & Entertainment |

MIAMI—1415 SUNSET DR (AT 54TH AVE); 305.666.6235; M-TH 10-7, F-SA 10-5; PARKING LOT

Children's Place, The ★★★⯪☆

"...great bargains on cute clothing... shoes, socks, swimsuits, sunglasses and everything in between... lots of '3 for $20' type deals on sleepers, pants and mix-and-match separates... so much more affordable than the other 'big chains'... don't expect the most unique stuff here, but it wears and washes well... cheap clothing for cheap prices... you can leave the store with bags full of clothes without putting a huge dent in your wallet... **"**

Furniture, Bedding & Decor	✗	$$	Prices
Gear & Equipment	✗	❹	Product availability
Nursing & Feeding	✗	❹	Staff knowledge
Safety & Babycare	✗	❹	Customer service
Clothing, Shoes & Accessories	✓	❹	Decor
Books, Toys & Entertainment	✓		

WWW.CHILDRENSPLACE.COM

MIAMI—118 E FLAGLER ST (AT SE 1ST AVE); 305.416.6130; M-SA 10-9, SU 11-7; STREET PARKING

MIAMI—1455 NW 107TH AVE (AT JOSE CANSECO ST); 305.629.8156; M-SA 10-9, SU 11-7; PARKING LOT

Cinderella Boutique ★★★⯪☆

"...you must see for yourself... awesome store and beautiful clothing will make you cry... a must see!.. beautiful little store... pricey... **"**

Furniture, Bedding & Decor	✗	$$$	Prices
Gear & Equipment	✗	❸	Product availability
Nursing & Feeding	✗	❹	Staff knowledge
Safety & Babycare	✗	❹	Customer service
Clothing, Shoes & Accessories	✓	❸	Decor
Books, Toys & Entertainment	✗		

CORAL GABLES—329 MIRACLE MILE (AT S LE JEUME RD); 305.442.0379; M-SA 10-6; PARKING LOT

Consignment Corner

Furniture, Bedding & Decor	✓	✓	Gear & Equipment
Nursing & Feeding	✓	✓	Safety & Babycare
Clothing, Shoes & Accessories	✓	✓	Books, Toys & Entertainment

PINECREST—8267 SW 124TH ST (AT DIXIE HWY); 305.235.0958; M-F 10-6, SA 10-5

Costco ★★★⯪☆

"...dependable place for bulk diapers, wipes and formula at discount prices... clothing selection is very hit-or-miss... avoid shopping there during nights and weekends if possible, because parking and checkout lines are brutal... they don't have a huge selection of brands, but the brands they do have are almost always in stock and at a great price... lowest prices around for diapers and formula... kid's clothing tends to be picked through, but it's worth looking for great deals on name-brand items like Carter's... **"**

Furniture, Bedding & Decor	✓	$$	Prices
Gear & Equipment	✓	❸	Product availability
Nursing & Feeding	✓	❸	Staff knowledge
Safety & Babycare	✓	❸	Customer service
Clothing, Shoes & Accessories	✓	❷	Decor
Books, Toys & Entertainment	✓		

WWW.COSTCO.COM

MIAMI—16580 NW 59TH AVE (AT PALMETTO EXPY); 305.825.9818; M-F 11-8:30, SA 9:30-6, SU 10-6

MIAMI—8300 PARK BLVD (AT NW 84TH AVE); 305.267.0641; M-F 11-8:30, SA 9:30-6, SU 10-6

MIAMI—9194 SW 137TH AVE (AT N KENDALL DR); 305.382.1403; M-F 11-8:30, SA 9:30-6, SU 10-6

DIGS

"...gift and furniture shop with exclusive children's furniture lines like Maine Cottage and Finn and Hattie that I couldn't find anywhere else in Miami... great service and really knowledgeable decorators... created a lovely playroom for my friends kids, I can't wait to do mine..."

Furniture, Bedding & Decor	✓	$$$	Prices
Gear & Equipment	✗	❺	Product availability
Nursing & Feeding	✗	❺	Staff knowledge
Safety & Babycare	✗	❺	Customer service
Clothing, Shoes & Accessories	✗	❺	Decor
Books, Toys & Entertainment	✗		

WWW.DIGSMIAMI.COM

PINECREST—9525 S DIXIE HWY (AT SW 98TH ST); 305.667.3447; M-SA 11-5 ; PARKING LOT

Dillard's

"...this store has beautiful clothes, and if you catch a sale, you can get great quality clothes at super bargain prices... good customer service and helpful staff... a huge selection of merchandise for boys and girls... nice layette department... some furnishings like little tables and chairs... beautiful displays... the best part is that in addition to shopping for your kids, you can also shop for yourself..."

Furniture, Bedding & Decor	✓	$$$	Prices
Gear & Equipment	✗	❹	Product availability
Nursing & Feeding	✗	❸	Staff knowledge
Safety & Babycare	✗	❹	Customer service
Clothing, Shoes & Accessories	✓	❹	Decor
Books, Toys & Entertainment	✓		

WWW.DILLARDS.COM

MIAMI—1275 NW 107TH AVE (AT 12TH ST); 305.513.4007; M-SA 10-9, SU 12-6

El Dorado Furniture

"...pricey, but beautiful furniture... not baby friendly... super selection of furniture for tweens... great place to bring the family..."

Furniture, Bedding & Decor	✓	$$$	Prices
Gear & Equipment	✗	❹	Product availability
Nursing & Feeding	✗	❹	Staff knowledge
Safety & Babycare	✗	❹	Customer service
Clothing, Shoes & Accessories	✗	❹	Decor
Books, Toys & Entertainment	✗		

WWW.ELDORADOFURNITURE.COM

MIAMI—12650 N KENDALL DR (AT 127TH AVE); 305.752.3720; M-SA 10-9, SU 11-6; PARKING LOT

MIAMI—4200 SW 167TH ST (AT SW 162ND AVE); 305.624.9700; M-SA 9-9, SU 10-7; PARKING LOT

Five Cent Lemonade

"...I love everything Five Cent Lemonade sells... a great funky store to find a special gift for somebody with a baby... wonderful nursery and children's room decor and accessories... personal service by a mom who knows a lot... while expensive, the owner custom orders everything and

the quality is fabulous... the perfect store to find a special gift for someone with a baby... **"**

Furniture, Bedding & Decor	✓	$$$$	Prices
Gear & Equipment	✓	❹	Product availability
Nursing & Feeding	✗	❺	Staff knowledge
Safety & Babycare	✗	❹	Customer service
Clothing, Shoes & Accessories	✓	❺	Decor
Books, Toys & Entertainment	✓		

MIAMI—8816 SW 132ND ST (AT SW 88TH PL); 305.253.5666; M-F 10-4; STREET PARKING

Genius Jones ★★★★★

"...*specialty high-end store with an eye for well-designed products... only the best for the modern parent—Bugaboo, Dwell, Fleurville... they pick their merchandise carefully so you don't have to... the staff is great and will help you find anything or special order it... their displays are fun and will give you good ideas for your nursery...* **"**

Furniture, Bedding & Decor	✓	$$$$	Prices
Gear & Equipment	✓	❹	Product availability
Nursing & Feeding	✓	❹	Staff knowledge
Safety & Babycare	✓	❹	Customer service
Clothing, Shoes & Accessories	✓	❹	Decor
Books, Toys & Entertainment	✓		

WWW.GENIUSJONES.COM

MIAMI—49 NE 39TH ST (AT N MIAMI AVE); 305.571.2000; T-TH 12-8, F-SA 12-10, SU 12-8; PARKING LOT

Get Smart ★★★★☆

"...*you can't walk down their baby aisles without wanting to take one of everything... excellent educational materials—a jump start for school... every parent should invest... learning tools, games for parties, tooth fairy gifts... if they don't have what you want, they will get it for you... great shop for teachers and home schooling parents... no cheap plastic stuff, but good, high-quality games and toys...* **"**

Furniture, Bedding & Decor	✗	$$$	Prices
Gear & Equipment	✗	❹	Product availability
Nursing & Feeding	✗	❹	Staff knowledge
Safety & Babycare	✗	❹	Customer service
Clothing, Shoes & Accessories	✗	❹	Decor
Books, Toys & Entertainment	✓		

WWW.GETSMART.BIZ

MIAMI—8700 SW 137TH CT (AT N KENDALL DR); 305.385.8146; M-F 10-9, SA 10-6, SU 12-5; PARKING LOT

Gymboree ★★★★☆

"...*beautiful clothing and great quality... colorful and stylish baby and kids wear... lots of fun birthday gift ideas... easy exchange and return policy... items usually go on sale pretty quickly... save money with Gymbucks... many stores have a play area which makes shopping with my kids fun (let alone feasible)...* **"**

Furniture, Bedding & Decor	✗	$$$	Prices
Gear & Equipment	✗	❹	Product availability
Nursing & Feeding	✗	❹	Staff knowledge
Safety & Babycare	✗	❹	Customer service
Clothing, Shoes & Accessories	✓	❹	Decor
Books, Toys & Entertainment	✓		

WWW.GYMBOREE.COM

MIAMI—1455 NW 107 AVE (AT SW 14TH ST); 305.594.9800; M-F 10-9, SA 10-9, SU 11-7; PARKING LOT

MIAMI—7431 DADELAND MALL (AT N KENDALL DR); 305.665.3013; M-F 10-8, SA 10-7, SU 11-6; PARKING LOT

MIAMI—8888 SW 136 ST (AT SW 88TH PL); 305.234.2467; M-SA 10-9:30, SU 12-7; PARKING LOT

Hiho Batik ★★★★★

"...batik artist makes incredible baby clothes that are unique, colorful and fun... the owner, brings vibrancy and excitement to her store, real good energy... one of a kind clothing for your unique kid... I get stopped on the street with parents asking me where I got the cool clothes... **"**

Furniture, Bedding & Decor	✗	$$$	Prices
Gear & Equipment	✗	❺	Product availability
Nursing & Feeding	✗	❺	Staff knowledge
Safety & Babycare	✗	❺	Customer service
Clothing, Shoes & Accessories	✓	❺	Decor
Books, Toys & Entertainment	✗		

WWW.HIHOBATIK.COM

MIAMI—6909 BISCAYNE BLVD (AT 69TH ST); 305.754.8890; M-SA 11-6; PARKING LOT

Jacadi ★★★★☆

"...beautiful French clothes, baby bumpers and quilts... elegant and perfect for special occasions... quite expensive, but the clothing is hip and the quality really good... many handmade clothing and bedding items... take advantage of their sales... more of a store to buy gifts than practical, everyday clothes... beautiful, special clothing—especially for newborns and toddlers... velvet pajamas, coordinated nursery items... stores are as pretty as the clothes... they have a huge (half-off everything) sale twice a year that makes it very affordable... **"**

Furniture, Bedding & Decor	✓	$$$$	Prices
Gear & Equipment	✗	❹	Product availability
Nursing & Feeding	✗	❹	Staff knowledge
Safety & Babycare	✗	❹	Customer service
Clothing, Shoes & Accessories	✓	❹	Decor
Books, Toys & Entertainment	✓		

WWW.JACADIUSA.COM

SOUTH MIAMI—5872 SW 72ND ST (AT SW 72ND ST); 305.663.1407; M-SA 10-30-6; PARKING LOT

Janie And Jack ★★★★⯪

"...gorgeous clothing and some accessories (shoes, socks, etc.)... fun to look at, somewhat pricey, but absolutely adorable clothes for little ones... boutique-like clothes at non-boutique prices—especially on sale... high-quality infant and toddler clothes anyone would love—always good for a baby gift... I always check the clearance racks in the back of the store... their decor is darling—a really fun shopping experience... **"**

Furniture, Bedding & Decor	✗	$$$$	Prices
Gear & Equipment	✓	❹	Product availability
Nursing & Feeding	✗	❹	Staff knowledge
Safety & Babycare	✗	❹	Customer service
Clothing, Shoes & Accessories	✓	❹	Decor
Books, Toys & Entertainment	✗		

WWW.JANIEANDJACK.COM

CORAL GABLES—330 SAN LORENZO AVE (AT VILLAGE OF MERRICK PK); 305.447.0810; M-SA 10-9, SU 12-6; PARKING LOT

JCPenney

"...always a good place to find clothes and other baby basics... the registry process was seamless... staff is generally friendly but the lines always seem long and slow... they don't have the greatest selection of toddler clothes, but their baby section is great... we had some damaged furniture delivered but customer service was easy and accommodating... a pretty limited selection of gear, but what they have is priced right... **"**

Furniture, Bedding & Decor	✓	$$	Prices
Gear & Equipment	✓	❸	Product availability
Nursing & Feeding	✓	❸	Staff knowledge
Safety & Babycare	✓	❸	Customer service
Clothing, Shoes & Accessories	✓	❸	Decor
Books, Toys & Entertainment	✓		

WWW.JCPENNEY.COM

MIAMI—1603 NW 107TH AVE (AT MIAMI INTERNATIONAL MALL); 305.477.1786; M-SA 10-9, SU 12-6; MALL PARKING

MIAMI—7201 N KENDALL DR (AT DADELAND MALL); 305.666.1911; M-SA, 10-9, SU 12-6; MALL PARKING

MIAMI—8881 SW 107TH AVE (AT N KENDALL DR); 305.412.0912; M-SA 10-9, SU 12-6; MALL PARKING

Kate And Leo

"...beautiful boutique with hard to find, unique nursery decor... they will beautifully customize your baby's bedding... not a large clothing selection, but what they have is so beautiful... a pleasure to go there... perfect place for the fancy mom... very attentive staff that is willing to go above and beyond... **"**

Furniture, Bedding & Decor	✓	$$$$	Prices
Gear & Equipment	✗	❹	Product availability
Nursing & Feeding	✗	❺	Staff knowledge
Safety & Babycare	✗	❺	Customer service
Clothing, Shoes & Accessories	✓	❺	Decor
Books, Toys & Entertainment	✓		

WWW.KATEANDLEO.COM

MIAMI—293 MIRACLE MILE (AT SALZEDO ST); 305.441.7888; M-F 10-7, SA 10-6; PARKING LOT

KB Toys

"...hectic and always buzzing... wall-to-wall plastic and blinking lights... more Fisher-Price, Elmo and Sponge Bob than the eye can handle... a toy super store with discounted prices... they always have some kind of special sale going on... if you're looking for the latest and greatest popular toy, then look no further—not the place for unique or unusual toys... perfect for bulk toy shopping—especially around the holidays... **"**

Furniture, Bedding & Decor	✗	$$	Prices
Gear & Equipment	✗	❸	Product availability
Nursing & Feeding	✗	❸	Staff knowledge
Safety & Babycare	✗	❸	Customer service
Clothing, Shoes & Accessories	✗	❸	Decor
Books, Toys & Entertainment	✓		

WWW.KBTOYS.COM

MIAMI—11401 NW 12TH ST (AT DOLPHIN MALL); 305.513.0711; M-SA 10-9:30, SU 11-7; MALL PARKING

MIAMI—19575 BISCAYNE BLVD (AT AVENTURA MALL); 305.931.2347; M-SA 10-9:30, SU 12-8; MALL PARKING

MIAMI—20505 S DIXIE HWY (AT SOUTHLAND MALL); 305.253.3807; M-SA 10-9, SU 12-6; MALL PARKING

MIAMI—7795 W FLAGLER ST (AT MALL OF THE AMERICAS); 305.264.4225;
M-SA 10-9, SU 12-7; MALL PARKING

Kid's Foot Locker ★★★½☆

"...Nike, Reebok and Adidas for your little ones... hip, trendy and quite pricey... perfect for the sports addict dad who wants his kid sporting the latest NFL duds... shoes cost close to what the adult variety costs... generally good quality... they carry infant and toddler sizes... **"**

Furniture, Bedding & Decor	✗	$$$ .... Prices
Gear & Equipment	✗	❸ .... Product availability
Nursing & Feeding	✗	❸ .... Staff knowledge
Safety & Babycare	✗	❸ .... Customer service
Clothing, Shoes & Accessories	✓	❸ .... Decor
Books, Toys & Entertainment	✗	

WWW.KIDSFOOTLOCKER.COM

MIAMI—20505 S DIXIE HWY (AT CUTLER RIDGE RD); 305.259.7216; M-SA 10-9, SU 12-6

MIAMI—7573 N KENDALL DR (AT DADELAND MALL); 305.661.2845; M-SA 10-9:30, SU 12-7

MIAMI—7795 W FLAGLER ST (AT SW 78TH PL); 305.261.6011; M-SA 10-9, SU 12-7

Kidding Around ★★★★☆

"...great for dressy clothes which can be hard to find in south Florida... fancy and fun stuff... super kid friendly shoe department... high-end merchandise with a high-end price tag... **"**

Furniture, Bedding & Decor	✗	$$$ .... Prices
Gear & Equipment	✗	❹ .... Product availability
Nursing & Feeding	✗	❹ .... Staff knowledge
Safety & Babycare	✗	❹ .... Customer service
Clothing, Shoes & Accessories	✓	❹ .... Decor
Books, Toys & Entertainment	✗	

MIAMI—8888 HOWARD DR (AT SW 88TH PL); 305.253.0708; M-SA 10-9:30, 12-7; PARKING LOT

Kidz

Furniture, Bedding & Decor	✗	✗ .... Gear & Equipment
Nursing & Feeding	✗	✗ .... Safety & Babycare
Clothing, Shoes & Accessories	✓	✓ .... Books, Toys & Entertainment

MIAMI—19501 BISCAYNE BLVD (AT WILLIAM LEHMAN CSWY); 305.931.3559; M-SA 10-9:30, SU 12-8; MALL PARKING

La Ideal Baby Store ★★★½☆

"...large selection of high-end products... go during the week—the store is jam-packed on the weekends... they carry baby care products from A to Z... during their busy hours it can be hard to find help... difficult to return items... a place where you can find almost anything you need for your baby... a great family store... **"**

Furniture, Bedding & Decor	✓	$$$ .... Prices
Gear & Equipment	✓	❸ .... Product availability
Nursing & Feeding	✓	❸ .... Staff knowledge
Safety & Babycare	✓	❸ .... Customer service
Clothing, Shoes & Accessories	✓	❸ .... Decor
Books, Toys & Entertainment	✓	

WWW.IDEALBABY.COM

MIAMI—10613 NW 12TH ST (AT NW 107TH AVE); 305.716.1140; M-SA 10-9, SU 11-6

MIAMI—1143 W FLAGLER ST (AT SW 12TH AVE); 305.548.3296; M-F 9-8, SA 9-9, SU 10-5

Lavin Baby Center ★★★½☆

"...good variety and availability without the overwhelming volume and size of the 'mega' baby stores... beautiful selection... love the clothes from Spain... competitive prices... a bit outdated, didn't carry what they advertised on their website... Miami store hard to navigate with a stroller..."

Furniture, Bedding & Decor	✓	$$$	Prices
Gear & Equipment	✓	❹	Product availability
Nursing & Feeding	✓	❹	Staff knowledge
Safety & Babycare	✓	❸	Customer service
Clothing, Shoes & Accessories	✓	❸	Decor
Books, Toys & Entertainment	✓		

WWW.LAVINBABYCENTER.COM

MIAMI—8871 SW 132ND ST (AT SW 88TH PL); 305.251.2229; M-SA 10-8, SU 12-5; PARKING LOT

Little Feet ★★★★★

"...they really know kids' shoes here... for kids of all ages if you have a question this is a great spot... long standing store with quality customer service and products..."

Furniture, Bedding & Decor	✗	$$$	Prices
Gear & Equipment	✗	❺	Product availability
Nursing & Feeding	✗	❺	Staff knowledge
Safety & Babycare	✗	❹	Customer service
Clothing, Shoes & Accessories	✓	❹	Decor
Books, Toys & Entertainment	✗		

SOUTH MIAMI—7216 SW 57TH AVE (AT SUNSET DR); 305.666.9655; M-SA 10-6; STREET PARKING

Macy's ★★★½☆

"...Macy's has it all and I never leave empty-handed... if you time your visit right you can find some great deals... go during the week so you don't get overwhelmed with the weekend crowd... good for staples as well as beautiful party dresses for girls... lots of brand-names like Carter's, Guess, and Ralph Lauren... not much in terms of assistance... newspaper coupons and sales help keep the cost down... some stores are better organized and maintained than others... if you're going to shop at a department store for your baby, then Macy's is a safe bet..."

Furniture, Bedding & Decor	✓	$$$	Prices
Gear & Equipment	✗	❸	Product availability
Nursing & Feeding	✗	❸	Staff knowledge
Safety & Babycare	✗	❸	Customer service
Clothing, Shoes & Accessories	✓	❸	Decor
Books, Toys & Entertainment	✓		

WWW.MACYS.COM

MIAMI—13251 S DIXIE HWY (AT SW 132ND ST); 305.254.5700; M-SA 10-9, SU 12-6; PARKING LOT

MIAMI—1405 NW 107TH AVE (AT MIAMI INTERNATIONAL MALL); 305.594.6300; M-SA 10-9:30, SU 12-8; MALL PARKING

MIAMI—22 E FLAGLER ST (AT N PERIMETER AVE); 305.577.1500; M-SA 10-6, SU 11-5; PARKING LOT

MIAMI—7675 N KENDALL DR (AT DADELAND MALL); 305.662.3275; M-SA 10-9:30, SU 12-6; MALL PARKING

Magical Shoes For Children ★★★☆☆

"...nice selection, but high prices..."

Furniture, Bedding & Decor	✗	$$$$	Prices
Gear & Equipment	✗	❸	Product availability
Nursing & Feeding	✗	❸	Staff knowledge

Safety & Babycare	✗	❸	Customer service
Clothing, Shoes & Accessories	✓	❸	Decor
Books, Toys & Entertainment	✗		

CORAL GABLES—175 NAVARRE (AT S DOUGLAS RD); 305.448.2231; M-SA
10-6; STREET PARKING

Mommy Please
★★★½☆

66...good source of fancy outfits... beautiful linen baptismal outfits... I bought a linen bib for my son's baptism... it's expensive, but worth the money since the clothing is very good quality... sales are great... he owner is always willing to do what she can to make the customer happy... a nice place for Grandma to buy a gift... 99

Furniture, Bedding & Decor	✓	$$$$	Prices
Gear & Equipment	✗	❹	Product availability
Nursing & Feeding	✗	❹	Staff knowledge
Safety & Babycare	✗	❹	Customer service
Clothing, Shoes & Accessories	✓	❹	Decor
Books, Toys & Entertainment	✓		

SOUTH MIAMI—5840 SUNSET DR (AT SW 58TH AVE); 305.661.0978; CALL
FOR APPT; PARKING BEHIND BLDG

Mother Goose
★★★★☆

66...every expectant mother needs to go to this store... I promise you will not want to come out... lovely clothes, lovely staff... adorable clothing for the little ones in your life... good quality... perfect for a special occasion dresses... 99

Furniture, Bedding & Decor	✓	$$$	Prices
Gear & Equipment	✗	❹	Product availability
Nursing & Feeding	✗	❺	Staff knowledge
Safety & Babycare	✗	❺	Customer service
Clothing, Shoes & Accessories	✓	❹	Decor
Books, Toys & Entertainment	✓		

WWW.MOTHERGOOSE.COM

SOUTH MIAMI—5881 SUNSET DR (AT SW 59TH AVE); 305.665.3804; M-F 11-
6 SA 11-5; STREET PARKING

Nanitos Baby Store
★★★☆☆

66...nice store, good prices... staff very kind... 99

Furniture, Bedding & Decor	✓	$$	Prices
Gear & Equipment	✓	❸	Product availability
Nursing & Feeding	✓	❹	Staff knowledge
Safety & Babycare	✗	❸	Customer service
Clothing, Shoes & Accessories	✓	❹	Decor
Books, Toys & Entertainment	✗		

MIAMI—11401 NW 12TH ST (AT NW 11TH AVE); 305.470.7249; M-SA 10-
9:30, SU 11-7; PARKING LOT

Nordstrom
★★★★☆

66...quality service and quality clothes... awesome kids shoe department—almost as good as the one for adults... free balloons in the children's shoe area as well as drawing tables... in addition to their own brand, they carry a very nice selection of other high-end baby clothing including Ralph Lauren, Robeez, etc... adorable baby clothes— they make great shower gifts... such a wonderful shopping experience—their lounge is perfect for breastfeeding and for changing diapers... well-rounded selection of baby basics as well as fancy clothes for special events... 99

Furniture, Bedding & Decor	✓	$$$$	Prices
Gear & Equipment	✓	❹	Product availability
Nursing & Feeding	✗	❹	Staff knowledge
Safety & Babycare	✗	❹	Customer service

Clothing, Shoes & Accessories ...... ✓   **❹** .... , Decor

Books, Toys & Entertainment .... ✓

WWW.NORDSTROM.COM

CORAL GABLES—4310 PONCE DE LEON BLVD (AT VILLAGE OF MERRICK
PARK); 786.999.1313; M-SA 10-9:30, SU 12-7; PARKING LOT

MIAMI—7239 N KENDALL DR (OFF DIXIE HWY); 786.709.4100; M-SA 10-9:30,
SU 12-7

Old Navy ★★★★☆

❝...hip and 'in' clothes for infants and tots... plenty of steals on
clearance items... T-shirts and pants for $10 or less... busy, busy,
busy—long lines, especially on weekends... nothing fancy and you
won't mind when your kids get down and dirty in these clothes... easy
to wash, decent quality... you can shop for your baby, your toddler,
your teen and yourself all at the same time... clothes are especially
affordable when you hit their sales (post-holiday sales are
amazing!)... **❞**

Furniture, Bedding & Decor........... ✗	$$.. Prices	
Gear & Equipment .... ✗	❹ .... Product availability	
Nursing & Feeding .... ✗	❸ .... Staff knowledge	
Safety & Babycare .... ✗	❸ ....Customer service	
Clothing, Shoes & Accessories ...... ✓	❸ .... Decor	
Books, Toys & Entertainment .... ✗		

WWW.OLDNAVY.COM

MIAMI—11531 NW 12TH ST (AT DOLPHIN MALL); 305.468.3983; M-SA 10-9,
SU 11-7; MALL PARKING

MIAMI—13605 S DIXIE HWY (AT SW 136TH ST); 305.233.9930; M-SA 9-9, SU
11-7; PARKING LOT

MIAMI—1455 NW 107TH AVE (AT MIAMI INTERNATIONAL MALL);
305.463.0854; M-SA 9-9, SU 11-7; MALL PARKING

MIAMI—7220 N KENDALL DR (AT DADELAND MALL); 305.670.3417; M-SA 10-
9, SU 11-7; MALL PARKING

MIAMI—7795 W FLAGLER ST (AT MALL OF THE AMERICAS); 305.269.0809;
M-SA 10-9, SU 12-7; MALL PARKING

MIAMI—8715 SW 124TH AVE (AT N KENDALL DR); 305.271.2535; M-SA 9-9,
SU 11-7; PARKING LOT

Payless Shoe Source ★★★☆☆

❝...a good place for deals on children's shoes... staff is helpful with
sizing... the selection and prices for kids' shoes can't be beat, but the
quality isn't always spectacular... good leather shoes for cheap... great
variety of all sizes and widths... I get my son's shoes here and don't feel
like I'm wasting my money since he'll outgrow them in 3 months
anyway... **❞**

Furniture, Bedding & Decor........... ✗	$$.. Prices	
Gear & Equipment .... ✗	❸ .... Product availability	
Nursing & Feeding .... ✗	❸ .... Staff knowledge	
Safety & Babycare .... ✗	❸ ....Customer service	
Clothing, Shoes & Accessories ...... ✓	❸ .... Decor	
Books, Toys & Entertainment .... ✗		

WWW.PAYLESS.COM

CORAL GABLES—117 MIRACLE MILE (OFF DOUGLAS RD); 305.444.8773; M-
SA 10-8, SU 12-5

Peter Pan Children's Wear ★★★★☆

❝...selection is small, but breathtaking... after searching all around
town for a baptism dress for my daughter we went to this little store...
the selection was like nothing I had seen... I ended up buying her dress
at this great store... **❞**

Furniture, Bedding & Decor	✗	$$$$	Prices
Gear & Equipment	✗	❹	Product availability
Nursing & Feeding	✗	❺	Staff knowledge
Safety & Babycare	✗	❺	Customer service
Clothing, Shoes & Accessories	✓	❸	Decor
Books, Toys & Entertainment	✗		

MIAMI—2294 CORAL WAY (AT SW 23RD AVE); 305.858.5041; M-F 10-6, SA 10-4; STREET PARKING

Petit Amie

"...beautiful children's clothes... perfect for shower gifts... carries clothing for newborns up to size 6... **"**

Furniture, Bedding & Decor	✗	$$$$	Prices
Gear & Equipment	✗	❹	Product availability
Nursing & Feeding	✗	❹	Staff knowledge
Safety & Babycare	✗	❹	Customer service
Clothing, Shoes & Accessories	✓	❺	Decor
Books, Toys & Entertainment	✗		

SOUTH MIAMI—7241 SW 57TH CT (AT SW 72ND ST); 305.668.9563; M 11-5, T-F 10-6, SA 10-5; PARKING LOT

Pier 1 Kids ★★★★☆

"...everything from curtains and dressers to teddy bears and piggy banks... attractive furniture and prices are moderate to expensive... staff provided lots of help assembling a 'look' for my child's room... we had an excellent shopping experience here... the salesperson told my kids it was okay to touch everything because it's all kid friendly... takes you out of the crib stage and into the next step... **"**

Furniture, Bedding & Decor	✓	$$$	Prices
Gear & Equipment	✗	❸	Product availability
Nursing & Feeding	✗	❹	Staff knowledge
Safety & Babycare	✗	❹	Customer service
Clothing, Shoes & Accessories	✗	❹	Decor
Books, Toys & Entertainment	✗		

WWW.PIER1KIDS.COM

MIAMI—8655 SW 124TH AVE (AT N KENDALL DR); 305.271.6056; M-SA 9-9, SU 10-7; PARKING LOT

Pottery Barn Kids

"...stylish furniture, rugs, rockers and much more... they've found the right mix between quality and price... finally a company that stands behind what they sell—their customer service is great... gorgeous baby decor and furniture that will make your nursery to-die-for... the play area is so much fun—my daughter never wants to leave... a beautiful store with tons of ideas for setting up your nursery or kid's room... bright colors and cute patterns with basics to mix and match... if you see something in the catalog, but not in the store, just ask because they often have it in the back... **"**

Furniture, Bedding & Decor	✓	$$$$	Prices
Gear & Equipment	✗	❹	Product availability
Nursing & Feeding	✗	❹	Staff knowledge
Safety & Babycare	✗	❹	Customer service
Clothing, Shoes & Accessories	✗	❺	Decor
Books, Toys & Entertainment	✓		

WWW.POTTERYBARNKIDS.COM

CORAL GABLES—350 SAN LORENZO AVE (AT S LE JEUME RD); 305.446.6511; M-SA 10-9, SU 12-6; MALL PARKING

Rainbow Kids ★★⯪☆☆

"...fun clothing styles for infants and tots at low prices... the quality isn't the same as the more expensive brands, but the sleepers and play *outfits always hold up well... great place for basics... cute trendy shoe selection for your little walker... we love the prices... up-to-date selection...* **"**

Furniture, Bedding & Decor	✗	$$	Prices
Gear & Equipment	✓	❸	Product availability
Nursing & Feeding	✗	❸	Staff knowledge
Safety & Babycare	✗	❸	Customer service
Clothing, Shoes & Accessories	✓	❸	Decor
Books, Toys & Entertainment	✓		

WWW.RAINBOWSHOPS.COM

MIAMI—19189 S DIXIE HWY (AT MARLIN RD); 305.253.3653; M-SA 10-9, SU 11-6; PARKING LOT

MIAMI—20505 S DIXIE HWY (AT CUTLER RIDGE MALL); 305.235.1972; M-SA 10-9, SU 12-6; PARKING LOT

MIAMI—555 NE 79TH ST (AT BISCAYNE BLVD); 305.758.4136; M-SA 9-8, SU 11-5; PARKING LOT

Red Apple, The

"...*cute, specialty clothing store... fun place to find a gift or just to browse... not a lot of variety for younger children... somewhat limited choice of sizes...* **"**

Furniture, Bedding & Decor	✗	$$$$	Prices
Gear & Equipment	✗	❹	Product availability
Nursing & Feeding	✗	❹	Staff knowledge
Safety & Babycare	✗	❹	Customer service
Clothing, Shoes & Accessories	✓	❸	Decor
Books, Toys & Entertainment	✓		

WWW.REDAPPLECHILDRENS.COM

SOUTH MIAMI—7283 SW 57TH AV (AT SW 72ND ST); 305.669.6899; M-T 10-6, W-F 10-7, SA 10-6, SU 12-5

Ross Dress For Less

"...*if you're in the mood for bargain hunting and are okay with potentially coming up empty-handed, then Ross is for you... don't expect to get educated about baby products here... go early on a week day and you'll find an organized store and staff that is helpful and available—forget weekends... their selection is pretty inconsistent, but I have found some incredible bargains... a great place to stock up on birthday presents or stocking stuffers...* **"**

Furniture, Bedding & Decor	✗	$$	Prices
Gear & Equipment	✗	❸	Product availability
Nursing & Feeding	✗	❸	Staff knowledge
Safety & Babycare	✗	❸	Customer service
Clothing, Shoes & Accessories	✓	❸	Decor
Books, Toys & Entertainment	✓		

WWW.ROSSSTORES.COM

CORAL GABLES—2 MIRACLE MILE (AT S DOUGLAS RD); 305.446.8440; M-SA 9:30-9:30, SU 11-7; PARKING LOT

MIAMI—100 S BISCAYNE BLVD (AT 1ST ST); 305.379.5339; M-SA 9:30-9:30, SU 11-7; PARKING LOT

MIAMI—11321 NW 12TH ST (AT NW 11TH AVE); 305.477.3188; M-SA 9:30-9:30, SU 11-7

MIAMI—7795 W FLAGLER ST (AT MALL OF THE AMERICAS); 305.264.1203; M-SA 9:30-9:30, SU 11-7

MIAMI—8505 MILLS DR (AT SHERRI LN); 305.598.5753; M-SA 9:30-9:30, SU 11-7

MIAMI—8549 SW 24TH ST (AT SW 84TH AVE); 305.267.5304; M-SA 9:30-9:30, SU 11-7; PARKING LOT

MIAMI—8605 S DIXIE HWY (AT SW 58TH CT); 305.669.1691; M-SA 9:30-9:30,
SU 11-7; PARKING LOT

Running Around ★★★★☆

66...all you need from the first shoes through elementary school... all
the big brands—Stride-Rite, Elefanten, Jumping Jacks, Adidas,
Sketchers, Sam and Libby, Mimi and Kenneth Cole... their shoes run on
the pricier side, but they will last through a few kids and the staff takes
the time to find the right shoe for your child's foot... my kids love
coming here and I love the discounts they offer... bring your old shoes
to donate to a local charity... **99**

Furniture, Bedding & Decor	✗	$$$	Prices
Gear & Equipment	✗	❺	Product availability
Nursing & Feeding	✗	❺	Staff knowledge
Safety & Babycare	✗	❺	Customer service
Clothing, Shoes & Accessories	✓	❹	Decor
Books, Toys & Entertainment	✗		

MIAMI—8888 SW 136TH ST (AT SW 88TH PL); 305.253.3203; M-SA 10-9:30,
SU 12-7; PARKING IN FRONT OF BLDG

Sears ★★★☆☆

66...a decent selection of clothes and basic baby equipment... check
out the Kids Club program—it's a great way to save money... you go to
Sears to save money, not to be pampered... the quality of their
merchandise is better than Wal-Mart, but don't expect anything too
special or different... not much in terms of gear, but tons of well-priced
baby and toddler clothing... **99**

Furniture, Bedding & Decor	✓	$$	Prices
Gear & Equipment	✓	❸	Product availability
Nursing & Feeding	✓	❸	Staff knowledge
Safety & Babycare	✓	❸	Customer service
Clothing, Shoes & Accessories	✓	❸	Decor
Books, Toys & Entertainment	✓		

WWW.SEARS.COM

MIAMI—1625 NW 107TH AVE (AT 19TH ST); 305.470.7800; M-F 10-5, SA 10-
6, SU 11-5

MIAMI—20701 SW 112TH AVE (AT CUTLER RIDGE MALL); 305.378.5100; M-F
10-9, SA 8-9, SU 10-6

MIAMI—3655 CORAL WY (AT SW 22ND ST); 305.460.3400; M-SA 9:30-9, SU
11-6; PARKING LOT

MIAMI—8505 MILLS DR (OFF RT 94); 305.270.9200; M-F 10-9, SA 10-6, SU
11-5

Strasburg Children ★★★★☆

66...totally adorable special occasion outfits for babies and kids...
classic baby, toddler, and kids clothes... dress-up clothes for kids... if
you are looking for a flower girl or ring bearer outfit, look no further...
handmade clothes that will last through multiple kids or generations...
it's not cheap, but you can find great sales if you are patient... **99**

Furniture, Bedding & Decor	✗	$$$$	Prices
Gear & Equipment	✗	❹	Product availability
Nursing & Feeding	✗	❹	Staff knowledge
Safety & Babycare	✗	❹	Customer service
Clothing, Shoes & Accessories	✓	❹	Decor
Books, Toys & Entertainment	✗		

WWW.STRASBURGCHILDREN.COM

MIAMI—11401 NW 12TH ST (AT RT 107); 305.406.3973; M-SA 10-9:30, SU
11-7

Stride Rite Shoes

"...wonderful selection of baby and toddler shoes... sandals, sneakers, and even special-occasion shoes... decent quality shoes that last... they know a lot about kids' shoes and take the time to get it right—they always measure my son's feet before fittings... store sizes vary, but they always have something in stock that works... they've even special ordered shoes for my daughter... a fun 'first shoe' buying experience..."

Furniture, Bedding & Decor	✗	$$$	Prices
Gear & Equipment	✗	❹	Product availability
Nursing & Feeding	✗	❹	Staff knowledge
Safety & Babycare	✗	❹	Customer service
Clothing, Shoes & Accessories	✓	❹	Decor
Books, Toys & Entertainment	✗		

WWW.STRIDERITE.COM

MIAMI—406-8888 SW 136TH ST (AT THE FALLS SHOPPING CTR); 786.293.3970; M-SA 10-9:30, SU 12-7; MALL PARKING

MIAMI—7483 SW 88TH ST (AT DADELAND MALL); 305.666.0584; M-SA 10-9:30, SU 12-7; MALL PARKING

Target

"...our favorite place to shop for kids' stuff—good selection and very affordable... guilt-free shopping—kids grow so fast so I don't want to pay high department-store prices... everything from diapers and sippy cups to car seats and strollers... easy return policy... generally helpful staff, but you don't go for the service—you go for the prices... decent registry that won't freak your friends out with outrageous prices... easy, convenient shopping for well-priced items... all the big-box brands available—Graco, Evenflo, Eddie Bauer, etc...."

Furniture, Bedding & Decor	✓	$$	Prices
Gear & Equipment	✓	❹	Product availability
Nursing & Feeding	✓	❸	Staff knowledge
Safety & Babycare	✓	❸	Customer service
Clothing, Shoes & Accessories	✓	❸	Decor
Books, Toys & Entertainment	✓		

WWW.TARGET.COM

MIAMI—15005 SW 88TH ST (AT SW 151ST AVE); 305.386.1244; M-SA 8-10, SU 8-9; PARKING LOT

MIAMI—20500 SW 112TH AVE (AT CUTLER RIDGE MALL); 305.235.0839; M-SA 8-10, SU 8-9; PARKING LOT

MIAMI—7795 SW 40TH ST (AT SW 79TH AVE); 305.262.5767; M-SA 8-10, SU 8-9; PARKING LOT

MIAMI—8350 S DIXIE HWY (AT SW 70TH AVE); 305.668.0262; M-SA 8-10, SU 8-9; PARKING LOT

Toy Town

Furniture, Bedding & Decor	✗	✓	Gear & Equipment
Nursing & Feeding	✗	✗	Safety & Babycare
Clothing, Shoes & Accessories	✗	✓	Books, Toys & Entertainment

WWW.TOYTOWNONLINE.COM

KEY BISCAYNE—260 CRANDON BLVD (AT EAST DR); 305.361.5501; M-SA 10-6; PARKING LOT

Toys R Us

"...not just toys, but also tons of gear and supplies including diapers and formula... a hectic shopping experience but the prices make it all worthwhile... I've experienced good and bad service at the same store on the same day... the stores are huge and can be overwhelming...

participate in our survey at

most big brand-names available... leave the kids at home unless you want to end up with a cart full of toys... **"**

Furniture, Bedding & Decor .... ✓	$$$ .... Prices	
Gear & Equipment .... ✓	❹ .... Product availability	
Nursing & Feeding .... ✓	❸ .... Staff knowledge	
Safety & Babycare .... ✓	❸ .... Customer service	
Clothing, Shoes & Accessories .... ✓	❸ .... Decor	
Books, Toys & Entertainment .... ✓		

WWW.TOYSRUS.COM

CUTLER RIDGE—19525 S DIXIE HWY (AT MARIN RD); 305.233.6122; M-SA 9:30-9:30, SU 11-7; PARKING LOT

MIAMI—1645 NW 107TH AVE (AT MIAMI INTERNATIONAL MALL); 305.593.1517; M-SA 10-9, SU 11-6; MALL PARKING

MIAMI—8621 CORAL WY (AT SW 87TH AVE); 305.264.1991; M-SA 9:30-9:30, SU 11-7; PARKING LOT

MIAMI—8789 SW 117TH AVE (AT N KENDALL DR); 305.273.9311; M-SA 9:30-9:30, SU 11-7; PARKING LOT

Twinkle ★★★★★

"...*this store has everything one could want for their baby—my daughter's clothes are nicer than mine... the latest trendy fashions for the hipster kid (Dwell Baby, Skip Hop, Bugaboo)... they carry good brands like Bugaboo and Oeuf... it will cost you a little more than at a big box store, but their merchandise is better than the 'standard' stuff you find elsewhere... the staff is more than willing to help... this place is fantastic...* **"**

Furniture, Bedding & Decor .... ✓	$$$$ .... Prices	
Gear & Equipment .... ✓	❹ .... Product availability	
Nursing & Feeding .... ✓	❺ .... Staff knowledge	
Safety & Babycare .... ✓	❺ .... Customer service	
Clothing, Shoes & Accessories .... ✓	❹ .... Decor	
Books, Toys & Entertainment .... ✓		

WWW.TWINKLEKID.COM

COCONUT GROVE—3115 COMMODORE PLZ (AT MAIN HWY); 305.448.9966; M-SA 10-7, SU 12-5

Veronique Fine Linen ★★★⯪☆

"...*Veronique is known for being able to hand embroider any theme for a crib set, bassinet, placemats etc... wonderful hand embroidered christening gowns, hand smocked dresses and linen outfits for babies... unique personalized embroidery services ...* **"**

Furniture, Bedding & Decor .... ✓	$$$$ .... Prices	
Gear & Equipment .... ✓	❸ .... Product availability	
Nursing & Feeding .... ✗	❹ .... Staff knowledge	
Safety & Babycare .... ✗	❹ .... Customer service	
Clothing, Shoes & Accessories .... ✓	❹ .... Decor	
Books, Toys & Entertainment .... ✗		

CORAL GABLES—345 ARAGON AVE (AT S LE JEUNE RD); 305.461.3466; M 11-5, T-F 10-5:30; STREET PARKING

North Dade & Beaches

★★★★★

"lila picks"

★ Babies R Us   ★ Genius Jones

★ Bellini   ★ Twinkles of Bay Harbor

A To Z Toys ★★★★☆

❝...enjoyable shopping experience... with few toy stores in the area, it's refreshing to have this one so centrally located... great selection of wooden and high-end intellectually stimulating toys—like the old mom and pop toy stores... phenomenal... great educational toys!.. **❞**

Furniture, Bedding & Decor	✗	$$$	Prices
Gear & Equipment	✗	❹	Product availability
Nursing & Feeding	✗	❹	Staff knowledge
Safety & Babycare	✗	❹	Customer service
Clothing, Shoes & Accessories	✗	❹	Decor
Books, Toys & Entertainment	✓		

MIAMI BEACH—728 ARTHUR GODFREY RD (AT CHASE AVE); 305.532.5250; M-TH 9-7, F 9-6:30, SU 9-6:30; STREET PARKING

Babies R Us ★★★★★

❝...everything baby under one roof... they have a wide selection and carry most 'mainstream' items such as Graco, Fisher-Price, Avent and Britax... great customer service—given how big the stores are, I was pleasantly surprised at how attentive the staff was... easy return policy... super busy on weekends so try to visit on a weekday for the best service... keep an eye out for great coupons, deals and frequent sales... easy and comprehensive registry... shopping here is so easy—you've got to check it out... **❞**

Furniture, Bedding & Decor	✓	$$$	Prices
Gear & Equipment	✓	❹	Product availability
Nursing & Feeding	✓	❹	Staff knowledge
Safety & Babycare	✓	❹	Customer service
Clothing, Shoes & Accessories	✓	❹	Decor
Books, Toys & Entertainment	✓		

WWW.BABIESRUS.COM

NORTH MIAMI—2745 NE 193RD ST (AT BISCAYNE BLVD); 305.705.9893; M-SA 9:30-9:30, SU 11-7 ; PARKING LOT

Baby Depot At Burlington Coat Factory ★★★½☆

❝...a large, 'super store' layout with a ton of baby gear... wide aisles, packed shelves, barely existent customer service and awesome prices... everything from bottles, car seats and strollers to gliders, cribs and clothes... I always find something worth getting... a little disorganized and hard to locate items you're looking for... the staff is not always *knowledgeable about their merchandise... return policy is store credit only...* **"**

Furniture, Bedding & Decor	✓	$$	Prices
Gear & Equipment	✓	❸	Product availability
Nursing & Feeding	✓	❸	Staff knowledge
Safety & Babycare	✓	❸	Customer service
Clothing, Shoes & Accessories	✓	❸	Decor
Books, Toys & Entertainment	✓		

WWW.BABYDEPOT.COM

HIALEAH—590 W 49TH ST (AT W 6TH AVE); 305.820.9997; M-SA 10-9, SU 11-6; PARKING LOT

BabyGap/GapKids ★★★★☆

"...*colorful baby and toddler clothing in clean, well-lit stores... great return policy... it's the Gap, so you know what you're getting—colorful, cute and well-made clothing... best place for baby hats... prices are reasonable especially since there's always a sale of some sort going on... sales, sales, sales—frequent and fantastic... everything I'm looking for in infant clothing—snap crotches, snaps up the front, all natural fabrics and great styling... fun seasonal selections—a great place to shop for gifts as well as for your own kids... although it can get busy, staff generally seem accommodating and helpful...* **"**

Furniture, Bedding & Decor	✗	$$$	Prices
Gear & Equipment	✗	❹	Product availability
Nursing & Feeding	✗	❹	Staff knowledge
Safety & Babycare	✗	❹	Customer service
Clothing, Shoes & Accessories	✓	❹	Decor
Books, Toys & Entertainment	✗		

WWW.GAP.COM

AVENTURA—19575 BISCAYNE BLVD (AT WILLIAM LEHMAN CSWY); 305.932.2009; M-SA 10-9, SU 11-8; PARKING LOT

BAL HARBOUR—9700 COLLINS AVE (AT 96TH ST); 305.865.6595; M-SA 10-9, SU 12-6; PARKING LOT

Bellini ★★★★★

"...*high-end furniture for a gorgeous nursery... if you're looking for the kind of furniture you see in magazines then this is the place to go... excellent quality... yes, it's pricey, but the quality is impeccable... free delivery and setup... their furniture is built to withstand the abuse my tots dish out... they sell very unique merchandise, ranging from cribs to bedding and even some clothes... our nursery design was inspired by their store decor... I wish they had more frequent sales...* **"**

Furniture, Bedding & Decor	✓	$$$$	Prices
Gear & Equipment	✗	❹	Product availability
Nursing & Feeding	✗	❹	Staff knowledge
Safety & Babycare	✗	❹	Customer service
Clothing, Shoes & Accessories	✗	❹	Decor
Books, Toys & Entertainment	✓		

WWW.BELLINI.COM

AVENTURA—2782 NE 187TH ST (AT LOEMAN'S FASHION ISLAND); 305.931.1515; M-SA 10-5:30, SU 12-5; MALL PARKING

Bloomingdale's ★★★½☆

"...*a wide selection of baby and toddler clothing... they carry all the major brands... some stores have a smaller selection than others so call ahead to double check... well organized racks and good quality merchandise... good for special occasion clothing and gifts... if you shop at the right time you can get some great deals...* **"**

Furniture, Bedding & Decor	✗	$$$	Prices
Gear & Equipment	✗	❹	Product availability

Nursing & Feeding	✗	❸ .... Staff knowledge
Safety & Babycare	✗	❹ ....Customer service
Clothing, Shoes & Accessories	✓	❹ .... Decor
Books, Toys & Entertainment	✓	

WWW.BLOOMINGDALES.COM

AVENTURA—19555 BISCAYNE BLVD (AT AVENTURA MALL); 305.792.1000; M-SA 10-9; FREE PARKING

Books & Books ★★★★★

❝...wonderful independent bookstore where there is a wide selection for parents to be, parents and babies and kids... beautiful settings... Very knowledgeable staff... ,big gorgeous high-quality illustrated books abound, not your run of the mill chain books... they have children's programming, but mostly geared toward adults... brand new store in Bal Harbour, it was worth the wait for a local book shop... **❞**

Furniture, Bedding & Decor	✗	$$$...Prices
Gear & Equipment	✗	❹ ....Product availability
Nursing & Feeding	✗	❺ .... Staff knowledge
Safety & Babycare	✗	❺ ....Customer service
Clothing, Shoes & Accessories	✗	❹ .... Decor
Books, Toys & Entertainment	✓	

WWW.BOOKANDBOOKS.COM

BAL HARBOUR—9700 COLLINS AVE (AT 96TH ST); 305.864.4241; M-SA 10-9, SU 12-6; MALL PARKING

Camille's Lollipops & Rainbows ★★★★☆

❝...has at least one of everything... consignment store... the owner only accepts items that are in excellent condition... nice selection, great deals... packed with items some of which are brand new... salesperson knew exactly where to look for what I wanted, but you can not negotiate on price... **❞**

Furniture, Bedding & Decor	✗	$$..Prices
Gear & Equipment	✓	❸ ....Product availability
Nursing & Feeding	✗	❸ .... Staff knowledge
Safety & Babycare	✗	❹ ....Customer service
Clothing, Shoes & Accessories	✓	❸ .... Decor
Books, Toys & Entertainment	✓	

NORTH MIAMI—809 NE 125TH ST (AT NE 8TH AVE); 305.891.5437; M-F 10-5:30, SA 10-5; PARKING LOT

Cheeky Baby & Kids ★★★★☆

❝...great easy to wear clothing... very affordable and great looking Argentine clothing line... terrific shoe selection... **❞**

Furniture, Bedding & Decor	✓	$$..Prices
Gear & Equipment	✓	❺ ....Product availability
Nursing & Feeding	✗	❹ .... Staff knowledge
Safety & Babycare	✗	❺ ....Customer service
Clothing, Shoes & Accessories	✓	❺ .... Decor
Books, Toys & Entertainment	✓	

WWW.CHEEKYPLANET.COM

AVENTURA—19501 BISCANE BLVD (AT AVENTURA MALL); 786.428.0133; M-SA 10-9:30, SU 12-8; FREE PARKING

Chewing Gum Kids

Furniture, Bedding & Decor	✗	✗ ....Gear & Equipment
Nursing & Feeding	✗	✗ ....Safety & Babycare
Clothing, Shoes & Accessories	✓	✓ ....Books, Toys & Entertainment

MIAMI BEACH—548 41ST ST; 305.672.3008

participate in our survey at

Chocolate Milk

"...brand new children's furniture and accessory shop:.. what a unique store for kids and parents... gorgeous high-end items... the most beautiful linens... antique and contemporary furniture, which you can have customized in other finishes... great baby gifts—the toys and clothes are super... loved the whole concept—a welcome addition to the hood..."

Furniture, Bedding & Decor	✓	$$$$	Prices
Gear & Equipment	✗	❺	Product availability
Nursing & Feeding	✗	❺	Staff knowledge
Safety & Babycare	✗	❺	Customer service
Clothing, Shoes & Accessories	✗	❺	Decor
Books, Toys & Entertainment	✗		

NORTH MIAMI—2172 NE 123RD ST (AT BISCAYNE BLVD); 305.893.0026;
CALL FOR HOURS

Costco

"...dependable place for bulk diapers, wipes and formula at discount prices... clothing selection is very hit-or-miss... avoid shopping there during nights and weekends if possible, because parking and checkout lines are brutal... they don't have a huge selection of brands, but the brands they do have are almost always in stock and at a great price... lowest prices around for diapers and formula... kid's clothing tends to be picked through, but it's worth looking for great deals on name-brand items like Carter's..."

Furniture, Bedding & Decor	✓	$$	Prices
Gear & Equipment	✓	❸	Product availability
Nursing & Feeding	✓	❸	Staff knowledge
Safety & Babycare	✓	❸	Customer service
Clothing, Shoes & Accessories	✓	❷	Decor
Books, Toys & Entertainment	✓		

WWW.COSTCO.COM

NORTH MIAMI—14585 BISCAYNE BLVD (AT NE 146TH ST); 305.944.8711; M-F 11-8:30, SA 9:30-6, SU 10-6

Genius Jones

"...specialty high-end store with an eye for well-designed products... only the best for the modern parent—Bugaboo, Dwell, Fleurville... they pick their merchandise carefully so you don't have to... the staff is great and will help you find anything or special order it... their displays are fun and will give you good ideas for your nursery..."

Furniture, Bedding & Decor	✓	$$$$	Prices
Gear & Equipment	✓	❹	Product availability
Nursing & Feeding	✓	❹	Staff knowledge
Safety & Babycare	✓	❹	Customer service
Clothing, Shoes & Accessories	✓	❹	Decor
Books, Toys & Entertainment	✓		

WWW.GENIUSJONES.COM

MIAMI BEACH—1661 MICHIGAN AVE (AT LINCOLN RD MALL); 305.534.7622; T-TH 12-8, F-SA 12-10, SU 12-8; GARAGE AT 1675 MICHIGAN AVE

Jacadi

"...beautiful French clothes, baby bumpers and quilts... elegant and perfect for special occasions... quite expensive, but the clothing is hip and the quality really good... many handmade clothing and bedding items... take advantage of their sales... more of a store to buy gifts than practical, everyday clothes... beautiful, special clothing—especially for newborns and toddlers... velvet pajamas, coordinated nursery items... stores are as pretty as the clothes... they have a huge (half-off everything) sale twice a year that makes it very affordable..."

Furniture, Bedding & Decor	✓	$$$$	Prices
Gear & Equipment	✗	❹	Product availability
Nursing & Feeding	✗	❹	Staff knowledge
Safety & Babycare	✗	❹	Customer service
Clothing, Shoes & Accessories	✓	❹	Decor
Books, Toys & Entertainment	✓		

WWW.JACADIUSA.COM

AVENTURA—19501 BISCAYNE BLVD (AT GATE (KEY) ACCESS); 305.705.0770; M-SA 10-9:30, SU 12-8; PARKING LOT

Janie And Jack ★★★★⯪

"...gorgeous clothing and some accessories (shoes, socks, etc.)... fun to look at, somewhat pricey, but absolutely adorable clothes for little ones... boutique-like clothes at non-boutique prices—especially on sale... high-quality infant and toddler clothes anyone would love—always good for a baby gift... I always check the clearance racks in the back of the store... their decor is darling—a really fun shopping experience... **"**

Furniture, Bedding & Decor	✗	$$$$	Prices
Gear & Equipment	✓	❹	Product availability
Nursing & Feeding	✗	❹	Staff knowledge
Safety & Babycare	✗	❹	Customer service
Clothing, Shoes & Accessories	✓	❹	Decor
Books, Toys & Entertainment	✗		

WWW.JANIEANDJACK.COM

AVENTURA—19501 BISCAYNE BLVD (AT AVENTURA MALL); 305.466.1253; M-SA 10-9:30, SU 12-8; PARKING LOT

JCPenney ★★★⯪☆

"...always a good place to find clothes and other baby basics... the registry process was seamless... staff is generally friendly but the lines always seem long and slow... they don't have the greatest selection of toddler clothes, but their baby section is great... we had some damaged furniture delivered but customer service was easy and accommodating... a pretty limited selection of gear, but what they have is priced right... **"**

Furniture, Bedding & Decor	✓	$$	Prices
Gear & Equipment	✓	❸	Product availability
Nursing & Feeding	✓	❸	Staff knowledge
Safety & Babycare	✓	❸	Customer service
Clothing, Shoes & Accessories	✓	❸	Decor
Books, Toys & Entertainment	✓		

WWW.JCPENNEY.COM

AVENTURA—19252 BISCAYNE BLVD (AT AVENTURA MALL); 305.937.0022; M-SA 10-9:30, SU 11-6; PARKING LOT

KB Toys ★★★☆☆

"...hectic and always buzzing... wall-to-wall plastic and blinking lights... more Fisher-Price, Elmo and Sponge Bob than the eye can handle... a toy super store with discounted prices... they always have some kind of special sale going on... if you're looking for the latest and greatest popular toy, then look no further—not the place for unique or unusual toys... perfect for bulk toy shopping—especially around the holidays... **"**

Furniture, Bedding & Decor	✗	$$	Prices
Gear & Equipment	✗	❸	Product availability
Nursing & Feeding	✗	❸	Staff knowledge
Safety & Babycare	✗	❸	Customer service
Clothing, Shoes & Accessories	✗	❸	Decor
Books, Toys & Entertainment	✓		

WWW.KBTOYS.COM

participate in our survey at

HIALEAH—1705 W 49TH ST (AT WESTLAND MALL); 305.822.1569; M-SA 10-9, SU 11-6; MALL PARKING

La Ideal Baby Store ★★★⯪☆

❝...large selection of high-end products... go during the week—the store is jam-packed on the weekends... they carry baby care products from A to Z... during their busy hours it can be hard to find help... difficult to return items... a place where you can find almost anything you need for your baby... a great family store... **❞**

Furniture, Bedding & Decor	✓	$$$	Prices
Gear & Equipment	✓	❸	Product availability
Nursing & Feeding	✓	❸	Staff knowledge
Safety & Babycare	✓	❸	Customer service
Clothing, Shoes & Accessories	✓	❸	Decor
Books, Toys & Entertainment	✓		

WWW.IDEALBABY.COM

HIALEAH—1170 W 49TH ST (AT W 12TH AVE); 305.826.2021; M-SA 10-9, SU 11-6

Le Petit Choux

Furniture, Bedding & Decor	✗	✗	Gear & Equipment
Nursing & Feeding	✗	✗	Safety & Babycare
Clothing, Shoes & Accessories	✓	✓	Books, Toys & Entertainment

WWW.LEPETITCHOUX.COM

BAY HARBOR ISLANDS—1052 96TH ST (AT BAY HARBOUR TER); 305.864.4666; CALL FOR HRS

Macy's ★★★⯪☆

❝...Macy's has it all and I never leave empty-handed... if you time your visit right you can find some great deals... go during the week so you don't get overwhelmed with the weekend crowd... good for staples as well as beautiful party dresses for girls... lots of brand-names like Carter's, Guess, and Ralph Lauren... not much in terms of assistance... newspaper coupons and sales help keep the cost down... some stores are better organized and maintained than others... if you're going to shop at a department store for your baby, then Macy's is a safe bet... **❞**

Furniture, Bedding & Decor	✓	$$$	Prices
Gear & Equipment	✗	❸	Product availability
Nursing & Feeding	✗	❸	Staff knowledge
Safety & Babycare	✗	❸	Customer service
Clothing, Shoes & Accessories	✓	❸	Decor
Books, Toys & Entertainment	✓		

WWW.MACYS.COM

HIALEAH—1777 W 49TH ST (AT WESTLAND MALL); 305.825.7300; M-SA 10-9, SU 12-6; MALL PARKING

MIAMI BEACH—1675 MERIDIAN AVE (AT LINCOLN LN N); 305.674.6300; M-SA 10-9, SU 12-6; PARKING LOT

Marshalls ★★⯪☆☆

❝...the ultimate hit or miss... you can generally find all the basics—pajamas, onesies, and booties for a fraction of the regular price... I love to browse the toy aisle for inexpensive shower and birthday gifts... I only go when I am feeling patient and persistent... the aisles are crammed with goods... **❞**

Furniture, Bedding & Decor	✗	$$	Prices
Gear & Equipment	✗	❸	Product availability
Nursing & Feeding	✗	❷	Staff knowledge
Safety & Babycare	✗	❷	Customer service
Clothing, Shoes & Accessories	✓	❸	Decor
Books, Toys & Entertainment	✓		

WWW.MARSHALLS.COM

AVENTURA—20515 BISCAYNE BLVD (AT HWY 854); 305.937.2525; DAILY
9:30-9:30

Old Navy

❝...hip and 'in' clothes for infants and tots... plenty of steals on
clearance items... T-shirts and pants for $10 or less... busy, busy,
busy—long lines, especially on weekends... nothing fancy and you
won't mind when your kids get down and dirty in these clothes... easy
to wash, decent quality... you can shop for your baby, your toddler,
your teen and yourself all at the same time... clothes are especially
affordable when you hit their sales (post-holiday sales are
amazing!)... **❞**

Furniture, Bedding & Decor	✗	$$	Prices
Gear & Equipment	✗	❹	Product availability
Nursing & Feeding	✗	❸	Staff knowledge
Safety & Babycare	✗	❸	Customer service
Clothing, Shoes & Accessories	✓	❸	Decor
Books, Toys & Entertainment	✗		

WWW.OLDNAVY.COM

AVENTURA—19225 BISCAYNE BLVD (AT WILLIAM LEHAM CSWY);
305.931.6545; M-SA 9-9, SU 11-7; PARKING LOT

NORTH MIAMI BEACH—3885 NE 163RD ST (AT NE 35TH AVE); 305.940.4640;
M-SA 10-9:30, SU 11-7; PARKING IN FRONT OF BLDG

Pier 1 Kids

❝...everything from curtains and dressers to teddy bears and piggy
banks... attractive furniture and prices are moderate to expensive...
staff provided lots of help assembling a 'look' for my child's room... we
had an excellent shopping experience here... the salesperson told my
kids it was okay to touch everything because it's all kid friendly... takes
you out of the crib stage and into the next step... **❞**

Furniture, Bedding & Decor	✓	$$$	Prices
Gear & Equipment	✗	❸	Product availability
Nursing & Feeding	✗	❹	Staff knowledge
Safety & Babycare	✗	❹	Customer service
Clothing, Shoes & Accessories	✗	❹	Decor
Books, Toys & Entertainment	✗		

WWW.PIER1KIDS.COM

DORAL—10610 NW 19TH ST (AT NW 107TH AVE); 305.468.8630; M-SA 9-9,
SU 10-7

Premaman

❝...this place is great for a special occasion outfit... it has that special
European look... also has sets for twins... European maternity, baby and
kids store has finally made it to the US... you feel like you have been
transported to Belgium... fun shopping, cool clothes, decent prices... **❞**

Furniture, Bedding & Decor	✗	$$$$	Prices
Gear & Equipment	✗	❹	Product availability
Nursing & Feeding	✗	❹	Staff knowledge
Safety & Babycare	✗	❹	Customer service
Clothing, Shoes & Accessories	✓	❺	Decor
Books, Toys & Entertainment	✗		

WWW.PREMAMAN.COM

AVENTURA—19575 BISCAYNE BLVD (AT AVENTURA MALL); 305.935.5155;
M-SA 10-9:30, SU 12-8; MALL PARKING

Rainbow Kids

❝...fun clothing styles for infants and tots at low prices... the quality
isn't the same as the more expensive brands, but the sleepers and play

outfits always hold up well... great place for basics... cute trendy shoe selection for your little walker... we love the prices... up-to-date selection... **"**

Furniture, Bedding & Decor	✗	$$	Prices
Gear & Equipment	✓	❸	Product availability
Nursing & Feeding	✗	❸	Staff knowledge
Safety & Babycare	✗	❸	Customer service
Clothing, Shoes & Accessories	✓	❸	Decor
Books, Toys & Entertainment	✓		

WWW.RAINBOWSHOPS.COM

HIALEAH—1253 E 10TH AVE (AT E 9TH ST); 305.883.1007; M-SA 210-7, SU 11-5; PARKING LOT

HIALEAH—500 W 49TH ST (AT RED RD); 305.828.6011; M-SA 9-9, SU 11-6; PARKING LOT

NORTH MIAMI—MALL AT 163RD ST (AT NE 15TH AVE); 305.940.6353; M-SA 10-9, SU 12-6; PARKING LOT

Ross Dress For Less ★★★☆☆

"...*if you're in the mood for bargain hunting and are okay with potentially coming up empty-handed, then Ross is for you... don't expect to get educated about baby products here... go early on a week day and you'll find an organized store and staff that is helpful and available—forget weekends... their selection is pretty inconsistent, but I have found some incredible bargains... a great place to stock up on birthday presents or stocking stuffers...* **"**

Furniture, Bedding & Decor	✗	$$	Prices
Gear & Equipment	✗	❸	Product availability
Nursing & Feeding	✗	❸	Staff knowledge
Safety & Babycare	✗	❸	Customer service
Clothing, Shoes & Accessories	✓	❸	Decor
Books, Toys & Entertainment	✓		

WWW.ROSSSTORES.COM

HIALEAH—449 W 49TH ST (AT PALM SPRINGS MILE SHOPPING CTR); 305.512.8625; M-SA 9:30-9:30, SU 11-7

HIALEAH—5780 NW 183RD ST (AT MIAMI GARDENS SHOPPING CTR); 305.557.9933; M-SA 9:30-9:30, SU 11-7

NORTH MIAMI BEACH—12115 BISCAYNE BLVD (OFF NE 18TH AVE); 305.891.2412; M-SA 9:30-9:30, SU 11-7; PARKING IN FRONT OF BLDG

Saks Fifth Avenue ★★★⯪☆

"...*if you have the cash for high-end baby items, then this is the place for you... all top quality... expensive, but lovely... the place to go for special occasion clothing... fairly frequent sales during which you can get some amazing deals...* **"**

Furniture, Bedding & Decor	✗	$$$$	Prices
Gear & Equipment	✗	❹	Product availability
Nursing & Feeding	✗	❹	Staff knowledge
Safety & Babycare	✗	❹	Customer service
Clothing, Shoes & Accessories	✓	❹	Decor
Books, Toys & Entertainment	✗		

WWW.SAKSFIFTHAVENUE.COM

BAL HARBOUR—9700 COLLINS AVE (AT BAL HARBOUR BLVD); 305.865.1100; M-SA 10-9, SU 12-7

Sears ★★★☆☆

"...*a decent selection of clothes and basic baby equipment... check out the Kids Club program—it's a great way to save money... you go to Sears to save money, not to be pampered... the quality of their merchandise is better than Wal-Mart, but don't expect anything too*

special or different... not much in terms of gear, but tons of well-priced baby and toddler clothing... **"**

Furniture, Bedding & Decor	✓	$$	Prices
Gear & Equipment	✓	❸	Product availability
Nursing & Feeding	✓	❸	Staff knowledge
Safety & Babycare	✓	❸	Customer service
Clothing, Shoes & Accessories	✓	❸	Decor
Books, Toys & Entertainment	✓		

WWW.SEARS.COM

HIALEAH —1625 W 49TH ST (AT WESTLAND MALL); 305.364.3800; M-F 10-9, SA 10-6, SU 11-5

HIALEAH —5750 NW 183RD ST (AT RED RD); 305.907.2400; M-SA 8-10, SU 8-8

Stride Rite Shoes

"*...wonderful selection of baby and toddler shoes... sandals, sneakers, and even special-occasion shoes... decent quality shoes that last... they know a lot about kids' shoes and take the time to get it right—they always measure my son's feet before fittings... store sizes vary, but they always have something in stock that works... they've even special ordered shoes for my daughter... a fun 'first shoe' buying experience...* **"**

Furniture, Bedding & Decor	✗	$$$	Prices
Gear & Equipment	✗	❹	Product availability
Nursing & Feeding	✗	❹	Staff knowledge
Safety & Babycare	✗	❹	Customer service
Clothing, Shoes & Accessories	✓	❹	Decor
Books, Toys & Entertainment	✗		

WWW.STRIDERITE.COM

AVENTURA—1341-19575 BISCAYNE BLVD (AT AVENTURA MALL); 305.935.1746; M-SA 9:30-10, SU 12-8; MALL PARKING

Target

"*...our favorite place to shop for kids' stuff—good selection and very affordable... guilt-free shopping—kids grow so fast so I don't want to pay high department-store prices... everything from diapers and sippy cups to car seats and strollers... easy return policy... generally helpful staff, but you don't go for the service—you go for the prices... decent registry that won't freak your friends out with outrageous prices... easy, convenient shopping for well-priced items... all the big-box brands available—Graco, Evenflo, Eddie Bauer, etc....* **"**

Furniture, Bedding & Decor	✓	$$	Prices
Gear & Equipment	✓	❹	Product availability
Nursing & Feeding	✓	❸	Staff knowledge
Safety & Babycare	✓	❸	Customer service
Clothing, Shoes & Accessories	✓	❸	Decor
Books, Toys & Entertainment	✓		

WWW.TARGET.COM

AVENTURA—21265 BISCAYNE BLVD (AT NE 213TH ST); 305.933.4616; M-SA 8-10, SU 8-9; PARKING IN FRONT OF BLDG

NORTH MIAMI—14075 BISCAYNE BLVD (AT NE 135TH ST); 305.944.5341; M-SA 8-10, SU 8-9; PARKING IN FRONT OF BLDG

Toys R Us

"*...not just toys, but also tons of gear and supplies including diapers and formula... a hectic shopping experience but the prices make it all worthwhile... I've experienced good and bad service at the same store on the same day... the stores are huge and can be overwhelming... most big brand-names available... leave the kids at home unless you want to end up with a cart full of toys...* **"**

participate in our survey at

Furniture, Bedding & Decor .... ✓	$$$ .... Prices
Gear & Equipment .... ✓	❹ .... Product availability
Nursing & Feeding .... ✓	❸ .... Staff knowledge
Safety & Babycare .... ✓	❸ .... Customer service
Clothing, Shoes & Accessories .... ✓	❸ .... Decor
Books, Toys & Entertainment .... ✓	

WWW.TOYSRUS.COM

HIALEAH—500 W 49TH ST (AT RED RD); 305.557.6704; M-SA 10-9, SU 11-7

NORTH MIAMI BEACH—551 NE 167TH ST (OFF RT 826); 305.653.8697; M-SA 10-9, SU 10-7; PARKING IN FRONT OF BLDG

Twinkles of Bay Harbor ★★★★★

❝...Twinkles is the best thing that could have ever happened to the beach... an excellent store with a cool, eclectic mix of toys for all ages... the owners are in all the time and give you personalized care... they explain, teach, and help choose that perfect gift or build that perfect basket... great toy shop for kids... some clothes—also can have birthday parties... ❞

Furniture, Bedding & Decor .... ✗	$$$ .... Prices
Gear & Equipment .... ✗	❹ .... Product availability
Nursing & Feeding .... ✗	❺ .... Staff knowledge
Safety & Babycare .... ✗	❺ .... Customer service
Clothing, Shoes & Accessories .... ✓	❹ .... Decor
Books, Toys & Entertainment .... ✓	

BAY HARBOR ISLANDS—1075 KANE CONCOURSE (AT BAY HARBOR TER); 305.864.1558; M-F 10-6, SA 10-4; PARKING IN FRONT OF BLDG

Vera Baby

Furniture, Bedding & Decor .... ✗	✗ .... Gear & Equipment
Nursing & Feeding .... ✗	✗ .... Safety & Babycare
Clothing, Shoes & Accessories .... ✓	✗ .... Books, Toys & Entertainment

BAL HARBOUR—9700 COLLINS AV (AT BAL HARBOUR SHOPS); 305.868.0960; M-SA 10-9, SU 12-6; PARKING LOT

Broward County

$\bigstar\bigstar\bigstar\bigstar\bigstar$

"lila picks"

★Babies R Us   ★Over The Moon

★Baby Love

Babies R Us ★★★★★

"...*everything baby under one roof... they have a wide selection and carry most 'mainstream' items such as Graco, Fisher-Price, Avent and Britax... great customer service—given how big the stores are, I was pleasantly surprised at how attentive the staff was... easy return policy... super busy on weekends so try to visit on a weekday for the best service... keep an eye out for great coupons, deals and frequent sales... easy and comprehensive registry... shopping here is so easy—you've got to check it out...* **"**

Furniture, Bedding & Decor .... ✓	$$$ .... Prices	
Gear & Equipment .... ✓	❹ .... Product availability	
Nursing & Feeding .... ✓	❹ .... Staff knowledge	
Safety & Babycare .... ✓	❹ .... Customer service	
Clothing, Shoes & Accessories ..... ✓	❹ .... Decor	
Books, Toys & Entertainment .... ✓		

WWW.BABIESRUS.COM

LAUDERHILL—7350 W COMMERCIAL BLVD (AT UNIVERSITY DR); 954.749.2229; M-SA 9:30-9:30, SU 11-7; PARKING IN FRONT OF BLDG

PEMBROKE PINES—11930 PINES BLVD (AT PEMBROKE LAKES MALL); 954.441.8600; M-SA 9:30-9:30, SU 11-7; MALL PARKING

Baby Depot At Burlington Coat Factory ★★★⯪☆

"...*a large, 'super store' layout with a ton of baby gear... wide aisles, packed shelves, barely existent customer service and awesome prices... everything from bottles, car seats and strollers to gliders, cribs and clothes... I always find something worth getting... a little disorganized and hard to locate items you're looking for... the staff is not always knowledgeable about their merchandise... return policy is store credit only...* **"**

Furniture, Bedding & Decor .... ✓	$$ .... Prices	
Gear & Equipment .... ✓	❸ .... Product availability	
Nursing & Feeding .... ✓	❸ .... Staff knowledge	
Safety & Babycare .... ✓	❸ .... Customer service	
Clothing, Shoes & Accessories ..... ✓	❸ .... Decor	
Books, Toys & Entertainment .... ✓		

WWW.BABYDEPOT.COM

CORAL SPRINGS—6251 W SAMPLE RD (AT NW 62ND AVE); 954.227.0274; M-SA 10-9, SU 11-6; PARKING LOT

SUNRISE—12801 W SUNRISE BLVD (AT SATIN LEAF WY); 954.846.7977; M-SA 10-9:30, SU 11-8; PARKING LOT

Baby Love ★★★★★

"...this store is a staple for any new parents—a huge display of every possible baby product you might need... staff is very knowledgeable and willing to help you figure out what you need... they carry many hard to find items that you don't see at the big chains... prices are reasonable... it can be a little overwhelming on your first visit so don't feel like you need to buy everything... good registry service...**"**

Furniture, Bedding & Decor	✓	$$$	Prices
Gear & Equipment	✓	❹	Product availability
Nursing & Feeding	✓	❺	Staff knowledge
Safety & Babycare	✓	❺	Customer service
Clothing, Shoes & Accessories	✓	❸	Decor
Books, Toys & Entertainment	✓		

WWW.BABYLOVE.COM

SUNRISE—8100 W OAKLAND PARK BLVD (AT N UNIVERSITY DR); 954.741.2227; M-SA 10-9, SU 10-6; PARKING IN FRONT OF BLDG

BabyGap/GapKids ★★★★☆

"...colorful baby and toddler clothing in clean, well-lit stores... great return policy... it's the Gap, so you know what you're getting—colorful, cute and well-made clothing... best place for baby hats... prices are reasonable especially since there's always a sale of some sort going on... sales, sales, sales—frequent and fantastic... everything I'm looking for in infant clothing—snap crotches, snaps up the front, all natural fabrics and great styling... fun seasonal selections—a great place to shop for gifts as well as for your own kids... although it can get busy, staff generally seem accommodating and helpful...**"**

Furniture, Bedding & Decor	✗	$$$	Prices
Gear & Equipment	✗	❹	Product availability
Nursing & Feeding	✗	❹	Staff knowledge
Safety & Babycare	✗	❹	Customer service
Clothing, Shoes & Accessories	✓	❹	Decor
Books, Toys & Entertainment	✗		

WWW.GAP.COM

FORT LAUDERDALE—321 N UNIVERSITY DR (AT NW 2ND PL); 954.753.7802; M-SA 10-9, SU 12-6; PARKING LOT

PEMBROKE PINES—11401 PINES BLVD (AT N HAITUS RD); 954.433.0900; M-SA 10-9, SU 12-7; PARKING LOT

Carter's ★★★★☆

"...always a great selection of inexpensive baby basics—everything from clothing to linens... I always find something at 'giveaway prices' during one of their frequent sales... busy and crowded—it can be a chaotic shopping experience... 30 to 50 percent less than what you would pay at other boutiques... I bought five pieces of baby clothing for less than $40... durable, adorable and affordable... most stores have a small play area for kids in center of store so you can get your shopping done...**"**

Furniture, Bedding & Decor	✓	$$	Prices
Gear & Equipment	✗	❹	Product availability
Nursing & Feeding	✗	❹	Staff knowledge
Safety & Babycare	✗	❹	Customer service
Clothing, Shoes & Accessories	✓	❹	Decor
Books, Toys & Entertainment	✓		

WWW.CARTERS.COM

SUNRISE—12801 W SUNRISE BLVD (AT SAWGRASS MILLS); 954.846.2688; M-SA 10-9:30, SU 11-7; PARKING LOT

Children's Place, The ★★★⯪☆

"...great bargains on cute clothing... shoes, socks, swimsuits, sunglasses and everything in between... lots of '3 for $20' type deals on sleepers, pants and mix-and-match separates... so much more affordable than the other 'big chains'... don't expect the most unique stuff here, but it wears and washes well... cheap clothing for cheap prices... you can leave the store with bags full of clothes without putting a huge dent in your wallet..."

Furniture, Bedding & Decor	✗	$$	Prices
Gear & Equipment	✗	❹	Product availability
Nursing & Feeding	✗	❹	Staff knowledge
Safety & Babycare	✗	❹	Customer service
Clothing, Shoes & Accessories	✓	❹	Decor
Books, Toys & Entertainment	✓		

WWW.CHILDRENSPLACE.COM

CORAL SPRINGS—9357 W ATLANTIC BLVD (AT N UNIVERSITY DR); 954.345.8283; M-SA 10-9, SU 11-7; PARKING LOT

HOLLYWOOD—5087 SHERIDAN ST (AT N 56TH AVE); 954.987.0220; M-SA 10-9, SU 11-6; PARKING LOT

PEMBROKE PINES—11401 PINES BLVD (AT S HIATUS MALL); 954.450.9497; M-SA 10-9, SU 11-7; PARKING LOT

PLANTATION—8000 W BROWARD BLVD (AT N UNIVERSITY DR); 954.474.4747; M-SA 10-9, SU 11-6; PARKING LOT

SUNRISE—12801 W SUNRISE BLVD (AT NW 136TH AVE); 954.835.1122; M-SA 10-9:30, SU 11-8; PARKING LOT

Chuckle Patch ★★★⯪☆

"...my favorite clothing shop for the kids... unique items so your child stands out just a bit... super friendly staff... good pricing..."

Furniture, Bedding & Decor	✗	$$$	Prices
Gear & Equipment	✗	❸	Product availability
Nursing & Feeding	✗	❹	Staff knowledge
Safety & Babycare	✗	❹	Customer service
Clothing, Shoes & Accessories	✓	❹	Decor
Books, Toys & Entertainment	✗		

POMPANO BEACH—7011 N STATE RD 7 (AT HOLMBERG RD); 954.757.5437; M-SA 9:30-5:30; PARKING LOT

Costco ★★★⯪☆

"...dependable place for bulk diapers, wipes and formula at discount prices... clothing selection is very hit-or-miss... avoid shopping there during nights and weekends if possible, because parking and checkout lines are brutal... they don't have a huge selection of brands, but the brands they do have are almost always in stock and at a great price... lowest prices around for diapers and formula... kid's clothing tends to be picked through, but it's worth looking for great deals on name-brand items like Carter's..."

Furniture, Bedding & Decor	✓	$$	Prices
Gear & Equipment	✓	❸	Product availability
Nursing & Feeding	✓	❸	Staff knowledge
Safety & Babycare	✓	❸	Customer service
Clothing, Shoes & Accessories	✓	❷	Decor
Books, Toys & Entertainment	✓		

WWW.COSTCO.COM

DAVIE—1980 S UNIVERSITY DR (OFF W SR 84); 954.370.8990; M-F 11-8:30, SA 9:30-6, SU 10-6

POMPANO BEACH—1800 W SAMPLE RD (AT N POWERLINE RD); 954.968.7114; M-F 11-8:30, SA 9:30-6, SU 10-6

Dillard's ★★★★☆

"...this store has beautiful clothes, and if you catch a sale, you can get great quality clothes at super bargain prices... good customer service and helpful staff... a huge selection of merchandise for boys and girls... nice layette department... some furnishings like little tables and chairs... beautiful displays... the best part is that in addition to shopping for your kids, you can also shop for yourself..."

Furniture, Bedding & Decor .... ✓	$$$ .... Prices
Gear & Equipment .... ✗	❹ .... Product availability
Nursing & Feeding .... ✗	❸ .... Staff knowledge
Safety & Babycare .... ✗	❹ .... Customer service
Clothing, Shoes & Accessories .... ✓	❹ .... Decor
Books, Toys & Entertainment .... ✓	

WWW.DILLARDS.COM

CORAL SPRINGS—9001 W ATLANTIC BLVD (AT CORAL SQ MALL);
954.341.4122; M-SA 10-9, SU 12-6

PEMBROKE PINES—11945 PINES BLVD (AT PEMBROKE LAKES MALL);
954.450.8661; M-SA 10-9, SU 12-6

Flora Ottimer Children's
Boutique ★★★★☆

"...fun shop if you are willing to spend a little extra... nice for a special occassion or for for special gift... great selection of shoes for both boys and girls..."

Furniture, Bedding & Decor .... ✗	$$$$ .... Prices
Gear & Equipment .... ✗	❸ .... Product availability
Nursing & Feeding .... ✗	❹ .... Staff knowledge
Safety & Babycare .... ✗	❹ .... Customer service
Clothing, Shoes & Accessories .... ✓	❺ .... Decor
Books, Toys & Entertainment .... ✗	

WWW.FLORAOTTIMER.COM

FORT LAUDERDALE—713B-E LAS OLAS BLVD (AT 8TH AVE); 954.463.2292; M
10-6, T-TH 10-9, F-SA 10-11, SU 12-8; PARKING LOT

Get Smart ★★★★☆

"...you can't walk down their baby aisles without wanting to take one of everything... excellent educational materials—a jump start for school... every parent should invest... learning tools, games for parties, tooth fairy gifts... if they don't have what you want, they will get it for you... great shop for teachers and home schooling parents... no cheap plastic stuff, but good, high-quality games and toys..."

Furniture, Bedding & Decor .... ✗	$$$ .... Prices
Gear & Equipment .... ✗	❹ .... Product availability
Nursing & Feeding .... ✗	❹ .... Staff knowledge
Safety & Babycare .... ✗	❹ .... Customer service
Clothing, Shoes & Accessories .... ✗	❹ .... Decor
Books, Toys & Entertainment .... ✓	

WWW.GETSMART.BIZ

PEMBROKE PINES—8507 PINES BLVD (AT NW 86TH AVE); 954.431.5052; M-F
10-9, SA 10-6, SU 12-5; PARKING LOT

Gifted Child

Furniture, Bedding & Decor .... ✗	✗ .... Gear & Equipment
Nursing & Feeding .... ✗	✗ .... Safety & Babycare
Clothing, Shoes & Accessories .... ✗	✓ .... Books, Toys & Entertainment

WESTON—1721 MAIN ST (AT COUNTRY ISLES PLAZA); 954.389.7301; CALL
FOR HRS

Growing Steps To Childrens Shoes

"...I bought my son's first pair of shoes there and I was very happy... Too pricey for me to go on a regular basis, but a good place to go when you need something special or for sizing... "

Furniture, Bedding & Decor	✗	$$$$	Prices
Gear & Equipment	✗	❹	Product availability
Nursing & Feeding	✗	❺	Staff knowledge
Safety & Babycare	✗	❺	Customer service
Clothing, Shoes & Accessories	✓	❹	Decor
Books, Toys & Entertainment	✗		

FORT LAUDERDALE—853 N NOB HILL RD (AT CLEARY BLVD); 954.472.7463; M-SA 10-6; FREE PARKING

Gymboree

"...beautiful clothing and great quality... colorful and stylish baby and kids wear... lots of fun birthday gift ideas... easy exchange and return policy... items usually go on sale pretty quickly... save money with Gymbucks... many stores have a play area which makes shopping with my kids fun (let alone feasible)... "

Furniture, Bedding & Decor	✗	$$$	Prices
Gear & Equipment	✗	❹	Product availability
Nursing & Feeding	✗	❹	Staff knowledge
Safety & Babycare	✗	❹	Customer service
Clothing, Shoes & Accessories	✓	❹	Decor
Books, Toys & Entertainment	✓		

WWW.GYMBOREE.COM

CORAL SPRINGS—9153 W ATLANTIC BLVD (AT CORAL SQUARE MALL); 954.346.1088; M-F 10-8, SA 10-7, SU 11-6; PARKING IN FRONT OF BLDG

PEMBROKE PINES—11401 PINES BLVD (AT N HAITUS RD); 954.430.4007; M-F 10-8, SA 10-7, SU 11-6; PARKING IN FRONT OF BLDG

PLANTATION—8000 W BROWARD BLVD (AT BROWARD MALL); 954.370.3345; M-SA 10-9, SU 11-6; PARKING IN FRONT OF BLDG

JCPenney

"...always a good place to find clothes and other baby basics... the registry process was seamless... staff is generally friendly but the lines always seem long and slow... they don't have the greatest selection of toddler clothes, but their baby section is great... we had some damaged furniture delivered but customer service was easy and accommodating... a pretty limited selection of gear, but what they have is priced right... "

Furniture, Bedding & Decor	✓	$$	Prices
Gear & Equipment	✓	❸	Product availability
Nursing & Feeding	✓	❸	Staff knowledge
Safety & Babycare	✓	❸	Customer service
Clothing, Shoes & Accessories	✓	❸	Decor
Books, Toys & Entertainment	✓		

WWW.JCPENNEY.COM

CORAL SPRINGS—9303 W ATLANTIC BLVD (AT CORAL SQUARE MALL); 954.752.8116; M-SA 10-9, SU 11-6; MALL PARKING

PEMBROKE PINES—11401 PINES BLVD (AT PEMBROKE LAKES MALL); 954.433.2445; M-SA 10-9, SU 12-6; MALL PARKING

PEMBROKE PINES—13650 PINES BLVD (AT NW 136TH AVE); 954.442.8171; M-SA 10-9, SU 12-7

PLANTATION—8000 W BROWARD BLVD (AT BROWARD MALL); 954.472.2500; M-SA 10-9, SU 11-6; MALL PARKING

participate in our survey at

KB Toys

"...hectic and always buzzing... wall-to-wall plastic and blinking lights... more Fisher-Price, Elmo and Sponge Bob than the eye can handle... a toy super store with discounted prices... they always have some kind of special sale going on... if you're looking for the latest and greatest popular toy, then look no further—not the place for unique or unusual toys... perfect for bulk toy shopping—especially around the holidays... **"**

Furniture, Bedding & Decor	✗	$$	Prices
Gear & Equipment	✗	❸	Product availability
Nursing & Feeding	✗	❸	Staff knowledge
Safety & Babycare	✗	❸	Customer service
Clothing, Shoes & Accessories	✗	❸	Decor
Books, Toys & Entertainment	✓		

WWW.KBTOYS.COM

PEMBROKE PINES—11401 PINES BLVD (AT PEMBROKE LAKES); 954.437.8605; M-SA 10-9, SU 12-8; PARKING LOT

SUNRISE—12801 W SUNRISE BLVD (AT SAWGRASS MILLS); 954.846.0917; M-SA 10-9:30, SU 11-8; PARKING LOT

Kid's Foot Locker

"...Nike, Reebok and Adidas for your little ones... hip, trendy and quite pricey... perfect for the sports addict dad who wants his kid sporting the latest NFL duds... shoes cost close to what the adult variety costs... generally good quality... they carry infant and toddler sizes... **"**

Furniture, Bedding & Decor	✗	$$$	Prices
Gear & Equipment	✗	❸	Product availability
Nursing & Feeding	✗	❸	Staff knowledge
Safety & Babycare	✗	❸	Customer service
Clothing, Shoes & Accessories	✓	❸	Decor
Books, Toys & Entertainment	✗		

WWW.KIDSFOOTLOCKER.COM

FORT LAUDERDALE—8000 W BROWARD BLVD (AT BROWARD MALL); 954.452.3366; M-SA 10-9, SU 12-6

La Ideal Baby Store

"...large selection of high-end products... go during the week—the store is jam-packed on the weekends... they carry baby care products from A to Z... during their busy hours it can be hard to find help... difficult to return items... a place where you can find almost anything you need for your baby... a great family store... **"**

Furniture, Bedding & Decor	✓	$$$	Prices
Gear & Equipment	✓	❸	Product availability
Nursing & Feeding	✓	❸	Staff knowledge
Safety & Babycare	✓	❸	Customer service
Clothing, Shoes & Accessories	✓	❸	Decor
Books, Toys & Entertainment	✓		

WWW.IDEALBABY.COM

PEMBROKE PINES—12151 PINES BLVD (AT N FLAMINGO RD); 954.620.2229; M-SA 10-9, SU 11-6

Learning Express

"...a great toy store with a lot of educational toys and a great selection... quality toys that engage kids and teach concepts... great artistic and hands on toys... will personalize small furniture for the room... a wonderful family owned business that caters to customer service, they make your shopping experience easy... Coral Springs store is tight with a stroller, but is the only store that delivers balloons in town... The best for unique toys and are always well-stocked... my favorite!... **"**

Furniture, Bedding & Decor	✗	$$$	Prices
Gear & Equipment	✗	❹	Product availability
Nursing & Feeding	✗	❹	Staff knowledge
Safety & Babycare	✗	❹	Customer service
Clothing, Shoes & Accessories	✗	❹	Decor
Books, Toys & Entertainment	✓		

WWW.LEARNINGEXPRESS.COM

CORAL SPRINGS—2067 UNIVERSITY DR (AT ROYAL PALM); 954.344.1270; M-SA 10-8, SU 10-5; PARKING LOT

Macy's ★★★⯪☆

66...Macy's has it all and I never leave empty-handed... if you time your visit right you can find some great deals... go during the week so you don't get overwhelmed with the weekend crowd... good for staples as well as beautiful party dresses for girls... lots of brand-names like Carter's, Guess, and Ralph Lauren... not much in terms of assistance... newspaper coupons and sales help keep the cost down... some stores are better organized and maintained than others... if you're going to shop at a department store for your baby, then Macy's is a safe bet... **99**

Furniture, Bedding & Decor	✓	$$$	Prices
Gear & Equipment	✗	❸	Product availability
Nursing & Feeding	✗	❸	Staff knowledge
Safety & Babycare	✗	❸	Customer service
Clothing, Shoes & Accessories	✓	❸	Decor
Books, Toys & Entertainment	✓		

WWW.MACYS.COM

CORAL SPRINGS—9129 W ATLANTIC BLVD (AT CORAL SQUARE MALL); 954.345.3300; M-SA 10-9, SU 12-6; MALL PARKING

FORT LAUDERDALE—2314 E SUNRISE BLVD (AT THE GALLERIA); 954.537.2300; M-SA 10-9, SU 12-6 ; PARKING LOT

FORT LAUDERDALE—4501 N FEDERAL HWY (AT FLORANANDA RD); 954.567.6500; M-SA 10-9, SU 12-6; PARKING LOT

POMPANO BEACH—1200 NE 23RD ST (AT POMPANO SQ); 954.786.6300; M-SA 10-9, SU 12-6; FREE PARKING

Mimo & Company ★★★★☆

66...Very cute clothing store... great place for a gift... love the outfits... adorable clothing from infants to children's... friendly atmosphere... **99**

Furniture, Bedding & Decor	✗	$$$	Prices
Gear & Equipment	✗	❹	Product availability
Nursing & Feeding	✗	❹	Staff knowledge
Safety & Babycare	✗	❹	Customer service
Clothing, Shoes & Accessories	✓	❺	Decor
Books, Toys & Entertainment	✗		

DAVIE—1636 TOWN CENTER CIR (AT BELL TOWER LN); 954.384.1323; M-SA 10-7; PARKING LOT

Miss Katie's Charm School ★★★★☆

66...super cute, girly shop... jewelry, clothes and other pretty knick knacks for my little girl's room... They also have a party room that seems like so much fun for little girls... you feel like you've entered another age when you step into this store... **99**

Furniture, Bedding & Decor	✗	$$$$	Prices
Gear & Equipment	✗	❹	Product availability
Nursing & Feeding	✗	❺	Staff knowledge
Safety & Babycare	✗	❺	Customer service
Clothing, Shoes & Accessories	✓	❺	Decor
Books, Toys & Entertainment	✓		

WWW.CHARMSCHOOL.COM

FORT LAUDERDALE—2474 E SUNRISE BLVD (AT GALLERIA MALL); 954.564.4144; M-SA 10-9, SU 12-6; MALL PARKING

PLANTATION—801 S UNIVERSITY DR (OFF SW 10TH ST); 954.474.7733; M-TH 10-7, F-SA 10-6 ; PARKING IN FRONT OF BLDG

Mona's Kids Clothes ★★★★☆

"...start here if you're searching for a special occasion dress for your little one... cute little boutique... unique clothes that will get lots of comments from your friends... expensive, but gorgeous... "

Furniture, Bedding & Decor	✗	$$$$	Prices
Gear & Equipment	✗	❺	Product availability
Nursing & Feeding	✗	❺	Staff knowledge
Safety & Babycare	✗	❺	Customer service
Clothing, Shoes & Accessories	✓	❺	Decor
Books, Toys & Entertainment	✗		

CORAL SPRINGS—9709 W SAMPLE RD (AT CORAL HILLS DR); 954.346.0805; M-SA 9:30-5:30, SU 11-4

Old Navy ★★★★☆

"...hip and 'in' clothes for infants and tots... plenty of steals on clearance items... T-shirts and pants for $10 or less... busy, busy, busy—long lines, especially on weekends... nothing fancy and you won't mind when your kids get down and dirty in these clothes... easy to wash, decent quality... you can shop for your baby, your toddler, your teen and yourself all at the same time... clothes are especially affordable when you hit their sales (post-holiday sales are amazing!)... "

Furniture, Bedding & Decor	✗	$$	Prices
Gear & Equipment	✗	❹	Product availability
Nursing & Feeding	✗	❸	Staff knowledge
Safety & Babycare	✗	❸	Customer service
Clothing, Shoes & Accessories	✓	❸	Decor
Books, Toys & Entertainment	✗		

WWW.OLDNAVY.COM

CORAL SPRINGS—9197 W ATLANTIC BLVD (AT CORAL SQUARE MALL); 954.255.2901; M-SA 10-9, SU 11-6; PARKING LOT

DAVIE—2100 S UNIVERSITY DR (AT HWY 595); 954.370.9660; M-SA 9-9, SU 10-7; PARKING LOT

FORT LAUDERDALE—3200 N FEDERAL HWY (AT E OAKLAND PARK BLVD); 954.566.4648; M-SA 9-9, SU 11-6; PARKING LOT

HOLLYWOOD—3801 OAKWOOD BLVD (AT STIRLING RD); 954.927.4256; M-SA 9-9, SU 11-6; PARKING LOT

PEMBROKE PINES—11830 PINES BLVD (AT PEMBROKE LAKES MALL); 954.441.9322; M-SA 9-9, SU 11-6; MALL PARKING

OshKosh B'Gosh ★★★★☆

"...cute, sturdy clothes for infants and toddlers... frequent sales make their high-quality merchandise a lot more affordable... doesn't every American kid have to get a pair of their overalls?.. great selection of cute clothes for boys... you can't go wrong here—their clothing is fun and worth the price... customer service is pretty hit-or-miss from store to store... we always walk out of here with something fun and colorful... "

Furniture, Bedding & Decor	✗	$$$	Prices
Gear & Equipment	✗	❹	Product availability
Nursing & Feeding	✗	❹	Staff knowledge
Safety & Babycare	✗	❹	Customer service
Clothing, Shoes & Accessories	✓	❹	Decor
Books, Toys & Entertainment	✗		

WWW.OSHKOSHBGOSH.COM

SUNRISE—12801 W SUNRISE BLVD (AT WHITE SEAHORSE WAY);
954.846.7953; M-SA 10-9:30, SU 11-8:30 ; PARKING LOT

Over The Moon

❝...this is a must go store for any new mother... just the decor alone is amazing... very helpful... awesome gifts, beautiful bedding... Over The Moon is over the top beautiful!.. unique baby items, custom dreamy linens... I feel like a 'Hollywood Mom' every time I go in here... a must—not to be believed... **❞**

Furniture, Bedding & Decor	✓	$$$$ .... Prices
Gear & Equipment	✗	❹ .... Product availability
Nursing & Feeding	✗	❺ .... Staff knowledge
Safety & Babycare	✗	❺ ....Customer service
Clothing, Shoes & Accessories	✗	❺ .... Decor
Books, Toys & Entertainment	✗	

HOLLYWOOD—2036 HARRISON ST (AT S 20TH AVE); 954.924.0066; M-F 10-6, SA-SU 10-5

Pier 1 Kids ★★★★☆

❝...everything from curtains and dressers to teddy bears and piggy banks... attractive furniture and prices are moderate to expensive... staff provided lots of help assembling a 'look' for my child's room... we had an excellent shopping experience here... the salesperson told my kids it was okay to touch everything because it's all kid friendly... takes you out of the crib stage and into the next step... **❞**

Furniture, Bedding & Decor	✓	$$$ .... Prices
Gear & Equipment	✗	❸ .... Product availability
Nursing & Feeding	✗	❹ .... Staff knowledge
Safety & Babycare	✗	❹ ....Customer service
Clothing, Shoes & Accessories	✗	❹ .... Decor
Books, Toys & Entertainment	✗	

WWW.PIER1KIDS.COM

FORT LAUDERDALE—1800 N FEDERAL HWY (AT NE 18TH ST); 954.564.9152; M-SA 9-9, SU 10-7

PEMBROKE PINES—11926 PINES BLVD (AT N FLAMINGO RD); 954.499.9450; M-SA 9-9, SU 10-7; PARKING LOT

Rainbow Kids ★★⯪☆☆

❝...fun clothing styles for infants and tots at low prices... the quality isn't the same as the more expensive brands, but the sleepers and play outfits always hold up well... great place for basics... cute trendy shoe selection for your little walker... we love the prices... up-to-date selection... **❞**

Furniture, Bedding & Decor	✗	$$ .... Prices
Gear & Equipment	✓	❸ .... Product availability
Nursing & Feeding	✗	❸ .... Staff knowledge
Safety & Babycare	✗	❸ ....Customer service
Clothing, Shoes & Accessories	✓	❸ .... Decor
Books, Toys & Entertainment	✓	

WWW.RAINBOWSHOPS.COM

HOLLYWOOD—6721 TAFT ST (AT NW 66TH AVE); 954.961.7437; M-SA 10-9, SU 11-5; PARKING LOT

PEMBROKE PINES—448 N UNIVERSITY DR (AT PINES BLVD); 954.499.3330; M-SA 10-9, SU 11-6

Sears ★★★☆☆

❝...a decent selection of clothes and basic baby equipment... check out the Kids Club program—it's a great way to save money... you go to Sears to save money, not to be pampered... the quality of their merchandise is better than Wal-Mart, but don't expect anything too

participate in our survey at

special or different... not much in terms of gear, but tons of well-priced baby and toddler clothing... **"**

Furniture, Bedding & Decor	✓	$$	Prices
Gear & Equipment	✓	❸	Product availability
Nursing & Feeding	✓	❸	Staff knowledge
Safety & Babycare	✓	❸	Customer service
Clothing, Shoes & Accessories	✓	❸	Decor
Books, Toys & Entertainment	✓		

WWW.SEARS.COM

PEMBROKE PINES—12055 PINES BLVD (AT RTE 823); 954.438.3100; M-F 10-9, SA 10-6, SU 11-5

Spider And The Fly   ★★★☆☆

"*...very cool children's boutique... great place to buy a gift—owner is the artist and does beautiful work... adorable store with cute products, but it's a bit pricey... great place to treat your kids to something special or if you want to buy a special gift for someone ...* **"**

Furniture, Bedding & Decor	✓	$$$$	Prices
Gear & Equipment	✓	❹	Product availability
Nursing & Feeding	✓	❺	Staff knowledge
Safety & Babycare	✗	❺	Customer service
Clothing, Shoes & Accessories	✓	❺	Decor
Books, Toys & Entertainment	✗		

WWW.SPIDERANDTHEFLY.COM

WESTON—2402 WESTON RD (AT ARVIDA PKWY); 954.659.9244; M-TH 10-6, F 10-8, SA 10-6, SU 11-5; PARKING IN FRONT OF BLDG

Stride Rite Shoes   ★★★½☆

"*...wonderful selection of baby and toddler shoes... sandals, sneakers, and even special-occasion shoes... decent quality shoes that last... they know a lot about kids' shoes and take the time to get it right—they always measure my son's feet before fittings... store sizes vary, but they always have something in stock that works... they've even special ordered shoes for my daughter... a fun 'first shoe' buying experience...* **"**

Furniture, Bedding & Decor	✗	$$$	Prices
Gear & Equipment	✗	❹	Product availability
Nursing & Feeding	✗	❹	Staff knowledge
Safety & Babycare	✗	❹	Customer service
Clothing, Shoes & Accessories	✓	❹	Decor
Books, Toys & Entertainment	✗		

WWW.STRIDERITE.COM

PEMBROKE PINES—246-11401 PINES BLVD (AT PEMBROKE LAKES MALL); 954.433.5504; M-SA 10-9, SU 12-7; MALL PARKING

Target   ★★★★☆

"*...our favorite place to shop for kids' stuff—good selection and very affordable... guilt-free shopping—kids grow so fast so I don't want to pay high department-store prices... everything from diapers and sippy cups to car seats and strollers... easy return policy... generally helpful staff, but you don't go for the service—you go for the prices... decent registry that won't freak your friends out with outrageous prices... easy, convenient shopping for well-priced items... all the big-box brands available—Graco, Evenflo, Eddie Bauer, etc....* **"**

Furniture, Bedding & Decor	✓	$$	Prices
Gear & Equipment	✓	❹	Product availability
Nursing & Feeding	✓	❸	Staff knowledge
Safety & Babycare	✓	❸	Customer service
Clothing, Shoes & Accessories	✓	❸	Decor
Books, Toys & Entertainment	✓		

WWW.TARGET.COM

FORT LAUDERDALE—3200 N FEDERAL HWY (AT E OAKLAND PARK BLVD);
954.390.7992; M-SA 8-10, SU 8-9; PARKING IN FRONT OF BLDG

HOLLYWOOD—300 HOLLYWOOD MALL (AT N PARK RD); 954.963.1200; M-SA
8-10, SU 8-9; PARKING IN FRONT OF BLDG

MIRAMAR—16901 MIRAMAR PKWY (AT SW 172ND AVE); 954.435.2571; M-SA
8-10, SU 8-9; PARKING IN FRONT OF BLDG

PEMBROKE PINES—11235 PINES BLVD (AT N HIATUS RD); 954.435.3161; M-
SA 8-10, SU 8-9; PARKING IN FRONT OF BLDG

PLANTATION—8201 FEDERATED W (AT W BROWARD BLVD); 954.377.0085;
M-SA 8-10, SU 8-9; PARKING IN FRONT OF BLDG

Toys R Us

❝...not just toys, but also tons of gear and supplies including diapers
and formula... a hectic shopping experience but the prices make it all
worthwhile... I've experienced good and bad service at the same store
on the same day... the stores are huge and can be overwhelming...
most big brand-names available... leave the kids at home unless you
want to end up with a cart full of toys...**❞**

Furniture, Bedding & Decor	✓	$$$	Prices
Gear & Equipment	✓	❹	Product availability
Nursing & Feeding	✓	❸	Staff knowledge
Safety & Babycare	✓	❸	Customer service
Clothing, Shoes & Accessories	✓	❸	Decor
Books, Toys & Entertainment	✓		

WWW.TOYSRUS.COM

CORAL SPRINGS—650 UNIVERSITY DR (AT W ATLANTIC BLVD);
954.752.6100; M-SA 10-9, SU 11-6; PARKING IN FRONT OF BLDG

FORT LAUDERDALE—1600 N FEDERAL HWY (AT NE15TH ST); 954.564.3571;
M-SA 10-9, SU 11-6; PARKING IN FRONT OF BLDG

PEMBROKE PINES—12235 PINES BLVD (AT PEMBROKE LAKES MALL);
954.433.0308; M-SA 9:30-9:30, SU 11-7; MALL PARKING

PLANTATION—8101 W BROWARD BLVD (AT BROWARD MALL); 954.474.1404;
M-SA 10-9, SU 11-6; MALL PARKING

USA Baby

❝...they carry an extensive selection of high-end nursery products such
as furniture, bedding, accessories and highchairs... popular place to do
all the shopping for your nursery... the staff knows their products well
and can help you sort through their vast selection... allow plenty of
time for your products to arrive, especially the big-ticket items (they
offer loaners while you wait for your order to arrive)... they have great
sales a few times a year and will match competitor prices... good
selection, especially if you're getting ready to set up your nursery...**❞**

Furniture, Bedding & Decor	✓	$$$$	Prices
Gear & Equipment	✓	❹	Product availability
Nursing & Feeding	✓	❹	Staff knowledge
Safety & Babycare	✓	❹	Customer service
Clothing, Shoes & Accessories	✗	❹	Decor
Books, Toys & Entertainment	✓		

WWW.USABABY.COM

HOLLYWOOD—4923 SHERIDAN ST (AT N 52ND AVE); 954.985.6464; M TH SA
10-8, T-W 10-5:30, F 10-6, SU 11:30-6

Wee Feet

❝...great store for getting the right size shoe... staff is wonderful in
sizing children's feet and they won't sell you a shoe that doesn't fit...
where we go for all our shoes... staff knowledgeable and friendly...
only place I can find my son's Tevas...**❞**

Furniture, Bedding & Decor	✗	$$$	Prices
Gear & Equipment	✗	❹	Product availability
Nursing & Feeding	✗	❹	Staff knowledge
Safety & Babycare	✗	❹	Customer service
Clothing, Shoes & Accessories	✓	❹	Decor
Books, Toys & Entertainment	✗		

COOPER CITY—2595 N HIATUS RD (AT SHERIDAN ST); 954.450.0150; M-F 10-6, SA 10-5, SU 12-4; PARKING IN FRONT OF BLDG

PEMBROKE PINES—2204 N FLAMINGO RD (AT SHERIDAN ST); 954.450.0150; M-F 10-6, SA 10-5, SU 10-4

Welfit Kids Shoes

"...I am always impressed with the helpful and friendly sales associates.. they are so patient with children... honest enough to tell you whether your child actually needs a new pair of shoes... they send reminder cards about coming in for a fitting and there are toys for the kids to play with if you have to wait... I will only buy my baby's shoes from here... **"**

Furniture, Bedding & Decor	✗	$$$	Prices
Gear & Equipment	✗	❸	Product availability
Nursing & Feeding	✗	❹	Staff knowledge
Safety & Babycare	✗	❹	Customer service
Clothing, Shoes & Accessories	✓	❸	Decor
Books, Toys & Entertainment	✗		

CORAL SPRINGS—9112 WILES RD (AT CYPRESS DR); 954.345.9677; M-F 10-6

Widenskys Children's Clothing

Furniture, Bedding & Decor	✗	✗	Gear & Equipment
Nursing & Feeding	✗	✗	Safety & Babycare
Clothing, Shoes & Accessories	✓	✓	Books, Toys & Entertainment

POMPANO BEACH—4659 N UNIVERSITY DR (AT WILES RD); 954.341.2813; CALL FOR HRS; STREET PARKING

Palm Beach County

"lila picks"

- ★ Babies R Us
- ★ Baby Alexandra
- ★ Bellini
- ★ Oilily

April Cornell

"...beautiful, classic dresses and accessories for special occasions... I love the matching 'mommy and me' outfits... lots of fun knickknacks for sale... great selection of baby wear on their web site... rest assured your baby won't look like every other child in these adorable outfits... very frilly and girlie—beautiful..."

Category		Rating	
Furniture, Bedding & Decor	✗	$$$	Prices
Gear & Equipment	✗	❸	Product availability
Nursing & Feeding	✗	❹	Staff knowledge
Safety & Babycare	✗	❹	Customer service
Clothing, Shoes & Accessories	✓	❹	Decor
Books, Toys & Entertainment	✗		

WWW.APRILCORNELL.COM

PALM BEACH GARDENS—3101 PGA BLVD (AT THE GARDENS OF THE PALM BEACHES); 561.625.6979; M-SA 10-9, SU 12-5

Arthurs Shoes

Furniture, Bedding & Decor	✗	✗	Gear & Equipment
Nursing & Feeding	✗	✗	Safety & Babycare
Clothing, Shoes & Accessories	✓	✗	Books, Toys & Entertainment

BOCA RATON—21073 POWERLINE RD (AT VERDE TRL); 561.451.1476; M-SA 10-6, SU 11-2:30

Babies R Us

"...everything baby under one roof... they have a wide selection and carry most 'mainstream' items such as Graco, Fisher-Price, Avent and Britax... great customer service—given how big the stores are, I was pleasantly surprised at how attentive the staff was... easy return policy... super busy on weekends so try to visit on a weekday for the best service... keep an eye out for great coupons, deals and frequent sales... easy and comprehensive registry... shopping here is so easy—you've got to check it out..."

Category		Rating	
Furniture, Bedding & Decor	✓	$$$	Prices
Gear & Equipment	✓	❹	Product availability
Nursing & Feeding	✓	❹	Staff knowledge
Safety & Babycare	✓	❹	Customer service
Clothing, Shoes & Accessories	✓	❹	Decor
Books, Toys & Entertainment	✓		

WWW.BABIESRUS.COM

BOCA RATON—21697 STATE RD 7 (AT CENTRAL PARK BLVD); 561.477.3337; M-SA 9:30-9:30, SU 11-7; PARKING IN FRONT OF BLDG

WEST PALM BEACH—4895 OKEECHOBEE BLVD (AT HAVERHILL RD N); 561.478.9400; M-SA 9:30-9:30, SU 11-7; PARKING LOT

Baby Alexandra ★★★★★

"...a wonderful boutique chock full of stuff and ideas to create a little paradise for your tot... decor, bedding, accessories... you can get any type of crib bedding possible... kind of expensive, but the merchandise is really nice... a really nice shopping excursion... **"**

Furniture, Bedding & Decor	✓	$$$$	Prices
Gear & Equipment	✓	❹	Product availability
Nursing & Feeding	✗	❹	Staff knowledge
Safety & Babycare	✗	❹	Customer service
Clothing, Shoes & Accessories	✓	❺	Decor
Books, Toys & Entertainment	✓		

WWW.BABYALEXANDRA.COM

PALM BEACH GARDENS—105-4550 PGA BLVD (AT N MILITARY TRL); 561.626.4466; M-SA 10-6; PARKING LOT

BabyGap/GapKids ★★★★☆

"...colorful baby and toddler clothing in clean, well-lit stores... great return policy... it's the Gap, so you know what you're getting—colorful, cute and well-made clothing... best place for baby hats... prices are reasonable especially since there's always a sale of some sort going on... sales, sales, sales—frequent and fantastic... everything I'm looking for in infant clothing—snap crotches, snaps up the front, all natural fabrics and great styling... fun seasonal selections—a great place to shop for gifts as well as for your own kids... although it can get busy, staff generally seem accommodating and helpful... **"**

Furniture, Bedding & Decor	✗	$$$	Prices
Gear & Equipment	✗	❹	Product availability
Nursing & Feeding	✗	❹	Staff knowledge
Safety & Babycare	✗	❹	Customer service
Clothing, Shoes & Accessories	✓	❹	Decor
Books, Toys & Entertainment	✗		

WWW.GAP.COM

BOCA RATON—329 TOWN CTR (AT TOWN CTR AT BOCA RATON); 561.361.9640; M-SA 10-9, SU 12-6; PARKING LOT

BOCA RATON—401 TOWN CTR (AT TOWN CTR AT BOCA RATON); 561.391.2224; M-SA 10-9, SU 12-6

PALM BEACH GARDENS—3101 PGA BLVD (AT CAMPUS DR); 561.624.1814; M-SA 10-9, SU 12-6; PARKING LOT

Bellini ★★★★★

"...high-end furniture for a gorgeous nursery... if you're looking for the kind of furniture you see in magazines then this is the place to go... excellent quality... yes, it's pricey, but the quality is impeccable... free delivery and setup... their furniture is built to withstand the abuse my tots dish out... they sell very unique merchandise, ranging from cribs to bedding and even some clothes... our nursery design was inspired by their store decor... I wish they had more frequent sales... **"**

Furniture, Bedding & Decor	✓	$$$$	Prices
Gear & Equipment	✗	❹	Product availability
Nursing & Feeding	✗	❹	Staff knowledge
Safety & Babycare	✗	❹	Customer service
Clothing, Shoes & Accessories	✗	❹	Decor
Books, Toys & Entertainment	✓		

WWW.BELLINI.COM

BOCA RATON—5050 TOWN CTR CIR (AT S MILITARY TRL); 561.392.7444; M-SA 10-6, SU 12-4 ; MALL PARKING

Bloomingdale's

"...a wide selection of baby and toddler clothing... they carry all the major brands... some stores have a smaller selection than others so call ahead to double check... well organized racks and good quality merchandise... good for special occasion clothing and gifts... if you shop at the right time you can get some great deals... "

Furniture, Bedding & Decor	✗	$$$	Prices
Gear & Equipment	✗	❹	Product availability
Nursing & Feeding	✗	❸	Staff knowledge
Safety & Babycare	✗	❹	Customer service
Clothing, Shoes & Accessories	✓	❹	Decor
Books, Toys & Entertainment	✓		

WWW.BLOOMINGDALES.COM

BOCA RATON—5840 GLADES RD (AT ST ANDREWS BLVD); 561.394.2000; M-SA 10-9, SU 12-7

PALM BEACH GARDENS—3105 PGA BLVD (AT THE GARDENS MALL); 561.625.2000; M-TH 10-9, F 10-10, SA 9-10, SU 12-6; PARKING LOT

Bombay Kids

"...the kids section of this furniture store carries out-of-the-ordinary items... whimsical, pastel grandfather clocks... zebra bean bags... perfect for my eclectic taste... I now prefer my daughter's room to my own... clean bathroom with changing area and wipes... they have a little table with crayons and coloring books for the kids... easy and relaxed shopping destination... "

Furniture, Bedding & Decor	✓	$$$	Prices
Gear & Equipment	✗	❹	Product availability
Nursing & Feeding	✗	❹	Staff knowledge
Safety & Babycare	✗	❹	Customer service
Clothing, Shoes & Accessories	✗	❹	Decor
Books, Toys & Entertainment	✗		

WWW.BOMBAYKIDS.COM

PALM BEACH GARDENS—2841 PGA BLVD (AT MINSK GARDENS AVE); 561.630.4070; M-SA 10-9, SU 12-6

Bonpoint

"...stylish, elegant clothes for the trendy toddler and child... gorgeous European workmanship... a great splurge for your little one... make sure you get the right size as they run small... black silk dresses for girls, as well as tailored pants and jumpers for boys... good for the oohs and aahs... "

Furniture, Bedding & Decor	✗	$$$$	Prices
Gear & Equipment	✗	❹	Product availability
Nursing & Feeding	✗	❹	Staff knowledge
Safety & Babycare	✗	❹	Customer service
Clothing, Shoes & Accessories	✓	❹	Decor
Books, Toys & Entertainment	✓		

WWW.BONPOINT.COM

PALM BEACH—246 WORTH AVE (AT HIBISCUS AVE); 561.659.2119; M-SA 10-6

Breastfeeding Boutique

"...Jennifer is absolutely amazing—she helped me survive the first 3 months... don't miss her free group that is held at her home once a week. Best in the business... the nursing super store, help make that transition to nursing so much more comfortable... knowledgeable service... "

Furniture, Bedding & Decor	✗	$$$	Prices
Gear & Equipment	✗	❺	Product availability
Nursing & Feeding	✓	❺	Staff knowledge

participate in our survey at

Safety & Babycare	✗	❺	Customer service
Clothing, Shoes & Accessories	✓	❺	Decor
Books, Toys & Entertainment	✗		

WWW.BREASTFEEDINGBOUTIQUE.COM

BOCA RATON—1575 SW 4TH CIR (AT SW 15TH AVE); 561.338.3322; M-F 8-3; NA

Children's Place, The ★★★½☆

"...great bargains on cute clothing... shoes, socks, swimsuits, sunglasses and everything in between... lots of '3 for $20' type deals on sleepers, pants and mix-and-match separates... so much more affordable than the other 'big chains'... don't expect the most unique stuff here, but it wears and washes well... cheap clothing for cheap prices... you can leave the store with bags full of clothes without putting a huge dent in your wallet..."

Furniture, Bedding & Decor	✗	$$	Prices
Gear & Equipment	✗	❹	Product availability
Nursing & Feeding	✗	❹	Staff knowledge
Safety & Babycare	✗	❹	Customer service
Clothing, Shoes & Accessories	✓	❹	Decor
Books, Toys & Entertainment	✓		

WWW.CHILDRENSPLACE.COM

BOYNTON BEACH—801 N CONGRESS AVE (AT BOYNTON BEACH MALL); 561.742.9106; M-SA 10-9, SU 12-6; MALL PARKING

Children's Wearhouse ★★½☆☆

"...large selection of clothing items, although it is more everyday clothing and a few specialty items... store is a little crowded... store can be hard to find..."

Furniture, Bedding & Decor	✗	$$$	Prices
Gear & Equipment	✗	❸	Product availability
Nursing & Feeding	✗	❹	Staff knowledge
Safety & Babycare	✗	❹	Customer service
Clothing, Shoes & Accessories	✓	❸	Decor
Books, Toys & Entertainment	✓		

WWW.CHILDRENSWEARHOUSEINC.COM

JUPITER—661 MAPLEWOOD DR (AT TONNEY PENNA DR); 561.741.1001; T-F10-5, SA 10-4; PARKING LOT

Childrens Cottage Consignment

Furniture, Bedding & Decor	✗	✗	Gear & Equipment
Nursing & Feeding	✗	✗	Safety & Babycare
Clothing, Shoes & Accessories	✓	✗	Books, Toys & Entertainment

JUPITER—661 MAPLEWOOD DR (AT COMMERCE LN); 561.741.4600; CALL FOR HRS

Cloud 10 ★★★½☆

"...a little bit of France right here in Miami... great place to buy little French dresses and French pre-made bows for little girls hair..."

Furniture, Bedding & Decor	✗	$$$$	Prices
Gear & Equipment	✗	❺	Product availability
Nursing & Feeding	✗	❺	Staff knowledge
Safety & Babycare	✗	❺	Customer service
Clothing, Shoes & Accessories	✓	❹	Decor
Books, Toys & Entertainment	✗		

PALM BEACH—450 S COUNTY RD (BTWN WORTH & HAMMON AVES); 561.835.9110; M-SA 10-5:15 ; STREET PARKING

Costco

❝...dependable place for bulk diapers, wipes and formula at discount prices... clothing selection is very hit-or-miss... avoid shopping there during nights and weekends if possible, because parking and checkout lines are brutal... they don't have a huge selection of brands, but the brands they do have are almost always in stock and at a great price... lowest prices around for diapers and formula... kid's clothing tends to be picked through, but it's worth looking for great deals on name-brand items like Carter's... ❞

Furniture, Bedding & Decor	✓	$$	Prices
Gear & Equipment	✓	❸	Product availability
Nursing & Feeding	✓	❸	Staff knowledge
Safety & Babycare	✓	❸	Customer service
Clothing, Shoes & Accessories	✓	❷	Decor
Books, Toys & Entertainment	✓		

WWW.COSTCO.COM

BOCA RATON—17800 CONGRESS AVE (AT CLINT MOORE RD); 561.981.5004; M-F 10-8:30, SA 9:30-6, SU 10-6

LAKE PARK—3250 NORTHLAKE BLVD (AT OLD DIXIE HWY); 561.776.3052; M-F 11-8:30, SA 9:30-6, SU 10-6

LANTANA—1873 W LANTANA RD (AT ANDREW REDDING RD); 561.533.0958; M-F 11-8:30, SA 9:30-6, SU 10-6

Dillard's

❝...this store has beautiful clothes, and if you catch a sale, you can get great quality clothes at super bargain prices... good customer service and helpful staff... a huge selection of merchandise for boys and girls... nice layette department... some furnishings like little tables and chairs... beautiful displays... the best part is that in addition to shopping for your kids, you can also shop for yourself... ❞

Furniture, Bedding & Decor	✓	$$$	Prices
Gear & Equipment	✗	❹	Product availability
Nursing & Feeding	✗	❸	Staff knowledge
Safety & Babycare	✗	❹	Customer service
Clothing, Shoes & Accessories	✓	❹	Decor
Books, Toys & Entertainment	✓		

WWW.DILLARDS.COM

WEST PALM BEACH—1801 PALM BEACH LAKES BLVD (AT PALM BEACH MALL); 561.478.7789; M-SA 10-9, SU 12-6

Disney Store, The

❝...everything Disney you could possibly want—toys, books, videos, clothes, lithographs and loud Disney music as you shop through the store with your ecstatic tot... giant movie screens show classic Disney movies... perky, friendly staff... can be really busy during weekends and holidays... the best selection of Halloween costumes... ❞

Furniture, Bedding & Decor	✗	$$$	Prices
Gear & Equipment	✗	❹	Product availability
Nursing & Feeding	✗	❹	Staff knowledge
Safety & Babycare	✗	❹	Customer service
Clothing, Shoes & Accessories	✓	❹	Decor
Books, Toys & Entertainment	✓		

WWW.DISNEYSTORE.COM

BOYNTON BEACH—801 N CONGRESS AV (AT BOYNTON BEACH MALL); 561.369.2332; M-SA 10-9, SU 12-6

Gymboree

❝...beautiful clothing and great quality... colorful and stylish baby and kids wear... lots of fun birthday gift ideas... easy exchange and return policy... items usually go on sale pretty quickly... save money with

Gymbucks... many stores have a play area which makes shopping with my kids fun (let alone feasible)... "

Furniture, Bedding & Decor	✗	$$$	Prices
Gear & Equipment	✗	❹	Product availability
Nursing & Feeding	✗	❹	Staff knowledge
Safety & Babycare	✗	❹	Customer service
Clothing, Shoes & Accessories	✓	❹	Decor
Books, Toys & Entertainment	✓		

WWW.GYMBOREE.COM

BOCA RATON—6000 W GLADES RD (AT ST ANDREWS BLVD); 561.368.0802; M-SA 10-9, SU 12-6; PARKING IN FRONT OF BLDG

JCPenney ★★★½☆

" *...always a good place to find clothes and other baby basics... the registry process was seamless... staff is generally friendly but the lines always seem long and slow... they don't have the greatest selection of toddler clothes, but their baby section is great... we had some damaged furniture delivered but customer service was easy and accommodating... a pretty limited selection of gear, but what they have is priced right...* "

Furniture, Bedding & Decor	✓	$$	Prices
Gear & Equipment	✓	❸	Product availability
Nursing & Feeding	✓	❸	Staff knowledge
Safety & Babycare	✓	❸	Customer service
Clothing, Shoes & Accessories	✓	❸	Decor
Books, Toys & Entertainment	✓		

WWW.JCPENNEY.COM

WELLINGTON—10308 W FOREST HILL BLVD (AT WELLINGTON EDGE BLVD); 561.333.3399; M-SA 10-9, SU 12-6; PARKING LOT

WEST PALM BEACH—1801 PALM BEACH LAKES BLVD (NEAR PALM BEACH MALL); 561.683.5710; M-SA 10-9, SU 12-6; PARKING LOT

Kangaroo's Pouch

Furniture, Bedding & Decor	✗	✓	Gear & Equipment
Nursing & Feeding	✗	✗	Safety & Babycare
Clothing, Shoes & Accessories	✓	✓	Books, Toys & Entertainment

JUPITER—1695 W INDIANTOWN RD (OFF MAPLEWOOD DR); 561.743.1182; T-F 10-5, SA 10-4; PARKING IN FRONT OF BLDG

KB Toys ★★★☆☆

" *...hectic and always buzzing... wall-to-wall plastic and blinking lights... more Fisher-Price, Elmo and Sponge Bob than the eye can handle... a toy super store with discounted prices... they always have some kind of special sale going on... if you're looking for the latest and greatest popular toy, then look no further—not the place for unique or unusual toys... perfect for bulk toy shopping—especially around the holidays...* "

Furniture, Bedding & Decor	✗	$$	Prices
Gear & Equipment	✗	❸	Product availability
Nursing & Feeding	✗	❸	Staff knowledge
Safety & Babycare	✗	❸	Customer service
Clothing, Shoes & Accessories	✗	❸	Decor
Books, Toys & Entertainment	✓		

WWW.KBTOYS.COM

PALM BEACH GARDENS—3101 PGA BLVD (AT THE GARDENS MALL); 561.624.1546; M-SA 9-9, SU 10-6; MALL PARKING

Kid's Kloset Of Jupiter

Furniture, Bedding & Decor	✗	✗	Gear & Equipment
Nursing & Feeding	✗	✗	Safety & Babycare

Clothing, Shoes & Accessories ...... ✓   ✗ .... Books, Toys & Entertainment
JUPITER—651 W INDIANTOWN RD (AT COLONIAL PLAZA); 561.743.7716; T-F
  10-5, SA 10-2; PARKING IN FRONT OF BLDG

Kids Kastle

Furniture, Bedding & Decor	✗	✗ Gear & Equipment
Nursing & Feeding	✗	✗ Safety & Babycare
Clothing, Shoes & Accessories	✓	✓ Books, Toys & Entertainment

DELRAY BEACH—16850 JOG RD (AT MORIKAMI PARK RD); 561.865.2720; M-
  SA 10-5; PARKING LOT

Kids Konnection

Furniture, Bedding & Decor	✓	✗ Gear & Equipment
Nursing & Feeding	✗	✗ Safety & Babycare
Clothing, Shoes & Accessories	✗	✓ Books, Toys & Entertainment

BOCA RATON—8903 GLADES RD (AT LYONS); 561.483.9799; M-F 10-6, SA
  10-5 ; PARKING LOT

Kidz To Kidz   ★★☆☆☆

"...good for second-hand clothes... the value is definitely there, you just might need to dig a little... don't try to shop there with a stroller—it gets very crowded... "

Furniture, Bedding & Decor	✗	$ Prices
Gear & Equipment	✗	❸ Product availability
Nursing & Feeding	✗	❸ Staff knowledge
Safety & Babycare	✗	❸ Customer service
Clothing, Shoes & Accessories	✓	❶ Decor
Books, Toys & Entertainment	✗	

BOCA RATON—23020 SANDALFOOT PLAZA DR (AT MARINA BLVD);
  561.883.0905; M-SA 10-6, SU 11-5; PARKING LOT

Learning Express   ★★★★☆

"...A great toy store with a lot of educational toys and a great selection... Quality toys that engage kids and teach concepts... great artistic and hands on toys... will personalize small furniture for the room... A wonderful family owned business that caters to customer service, they make your shopping experience easy... Coral Springs store is tight with a stroller, but is the only store that delivers Balloons in town!.. The best for unique toys and are always well-stocked. My favorite!..... "

Furniture, Bedding & Decor	✗	$$$ Prices
Gear & Equipment	✗	❹ Product availability
Nursing & Feeding	✗	❹ Staff knowledge
Safety & Babycare	✗	❹ Customer service
Clothing, Shoes & Accessories	✗	❹ Decor
Books, Toys & Entertainment	✓	

WWW.LEARNINGEXPRESS.COM

PALM BEACH GARDENS—10941 N MILITARY TR (AT PGA BLVD);
  561.799.2869; M-W SA 9:30-6, TH-F 9:30-8, SU 12-5; PARKING LOT

Macy's   ★★★½☆

"...Macy's has it all and I never leave empty-handed... if you time your visit right you can find some great deals... go during the week so you don't get overwhelmed with the weekend crowd... good for staples as well as beautiful party dresses for girls... lots of brand-names like Carter's, Guess, and Ralph Lauren... not much in terms of assistance... newspaper coupons and sales help keep the cost down... some stores are better organized and maintained than others... if you're going to shop at a department store for your baby, then Macy's is a safe bet... "

Furniture, Bedding & Decor	✓	$$$ Prices
Gear & Equipment	✗	❸ Product availability

Nursing & Feeding	✗	❸ .... Staff knowledge
Safety & Babycare	✗	❸ .... Customer service
Clothing, Shoes & Accessories	✓	❸ .... Decor
Books, Toys & Entertainment	✓	

WWW.MACYS.COM

BOCA RATON—5700 W GLADES RD (AT ST ANDREWS BLVD); 561.393.4400;
M-SA 10-9; SU 12-6; PARKING LOT

BOCA RATON—9339 GLADES RD (AT ST ANDREWS BLVD); 561.620.4500;
DAILY 10-9; FREE PARKING

BOYNTON BEACH—801 N CONGRESS AVE (AT BOYTON BEACH MALL);
561.738.4200; M-SA 10-9, SU 12-6; MALL PARKING

NORTH PALM BEACH—3101 PGA BLVD (AT KEW GARDEN AVE);
561.625.2985; M-SA 10-9, SU 12-6; FREE PARKING

Meant To Bee

Furniture, Bedding & Decor	✓	✗ .... Gear & Equipment
Nursing & Feeding	✗	✗ .... Safety & Babycare
Clothing, Shoes & Accessories	✗	✓ .... Books, Toys & Entertainment

WWW.MEANTTOBEE.COM

JUNO BEACH—873 DONALD ROSS RD (AT ELLISON WILSON RD);
561.626.9977; M-SA 10-5; PARKING LOT

New Beginning Consignment Boutique, A

Furniture, Bedding & Decor	✗	✗ .... Gear & Equipment
Nursing & Feeding	✗	✗ .... Safety & Babycare
Clothing, Shoes & Accessories	✓	✗ .... Books, Toys & Entertainment

LAKE PARK—1441 10TH ST (AT NOTHLAKE BLVD); 561.882.9719; CALL FOR
HRS

Nordstrom ★★★★☆

"...quality service and quality clothes... awesome kids shoe department—almost as good as the one for adults... free balloons in the children's shoe area as well as drawing tables... in addition to their own brand, they carry a very nice selection of other high-end baby clothing including Ralph Lauren, Robeez, etc... adorable baby clothes—they make great shower gifts... such a wonderful shopping experience—their lounge is perfect for breastfeeding and for changing diapers... well-rounded selection of baby basics as well as fancy clothes for special events... "

Furniture, Bedding & Decor	✓	$$$$ .... Prices
Gear & Equipment	✓	❹ .... Product availability
Nursing & Feeding	✗	❹ .... Staff knowledge
Safety & Babycare	✗	❹ .... Customer service
Clothing, Shoes & Accessories	✓	❹ .... Decor
Books, Toys & Entertainment	✓	

WWW.NORDSTROM.COM

BOCA RATON—5820 GLADES RD (AT TOWN CTR RD); 561.620.5555; M-SA
10-9, SU 12-6; PARKING LOT

WELLINGTON—10320 W FOREST HILLS BLVD (AT TOWN CTR AT BOCA
RATON); 561.227.3000; M-SA 10-9, SU 12-6

Oilily ★★★★★

"...exclusive shop with fun, colorful clothing... prices are a bit steep, but if you value unique, well-designed clothes, this is the place... better selection for girls than boys but there are special items for either sex... your tot will definitely stand out from the crowd in these unique pieces... my kids love wearing their 'cool' clothes... whimsical items for mom, too... "

Furniture, Bedding & Decor	✗	$$$$ .... Prices
Gear & Equipment	✗	❹ .... Product availability
Nursing & Feeding	✗	❹ .... Staff knowledge
Safety & Babycare	✗	❹ .... Customer service
Clothing, Shoes & Accessories	✓	❹ .... Decor
Books, Toys & Entertainment	✗	

WWW.OILILYUSA.COM

WEST PALM BEACH—701 S ROSEMARY AVE (AT PALLADIUM); 561.805.5884; M-SA 10-9, SU 12-6

Old Navy ★★★★☆

❝...hip and 'in' clothes for infants and tots... plenty of steals on clearance items... T-shirts and pants for $10 or less... busy, busy, busy—long lines, especially on weekends... nothing fancy and you won't mind when your kids get down and dirty in these clothes... easy to wash, decent quality... you can shop for your baby, your toddler, your teen and yourself all at the same time... clothes are especially affordable when you hit their sales (post-holiday sales are amazing!)... ❞

Furniture, Bedding & Decor	✗	$$ .... Prices
Gear & Equipment	✗	❹ .... Product availability
Nursing & Feeding	✗	❸ .... Staff knowledge
Safety & Babycare	✗	❸ .... Customer service
Clothing, Shoes & Accessories	✓	❸ .... Decor
Books, Toys & Entertainment	✗	

WWW.OLDNAVY.COM

BOCA RATON—6000 GLADES RD (AT ST ANDREWS BLVD); 561.417.8324; M-SA 9-9, SU 11-6; PARKING LOT

BOYNTON BEACH—373 N CONGRESS AVE (AT W BOYNTON BEACH BLVD); 561.733.4449; M-SA 9-9, SU 11-7; PARKING LOT

ROYAL PALM BEACH—550 N STATE RD 7 (AT BELLA TERRA WAY); 561.753.6539; M-SA 9-9, SU 11-7; PARKING IN FRONT OF BLDG

WEST PALM BEACH—2497 OKEECHOBEE BLVD (AT LOXAHATCHEE DR); 561.689.2180; M-SA 9-9, SU 11-7; PARKING IN FRONT OF BLDG

Patty Cakes Boutique

Furniture, Bedding & Decor	✗	✗ .... Gear & Equipment
Nursing & Feeding	✗	✗ .... Safety & Babycare
Clothing, Shoes & Accessories	✓	✗ .... Books, Toys & Entertainment

WEST PALM BEACH—9091 N MILITARY TR (AT SUNNY PLAZA); 561.776.8543; T-F 10-6, SA 8-5

Pier 1 Kids ★★★★☆

❝...everything from curtains and dressers to teddy bears and piggy banks... attractive furniture and prices are moderate to expensive... staff provided lots of help assembling a 'look' for my child's room... we had an excellent shopping experience here... the salesperson told my kids it was okay to touch everything because it's all kid friendly... takes you out of the crib stage and into the next step... ❞

Furniture, Bedding & Decor	✓	$$$ .... Prices
Gear & Equipment	✗	❸ .... Product availability
Nursing & Feeding	✗	❹ .... Staff knowledge
Safety & Babycare	✗	❹ .... Customer service
Clothing, Shoes & Accessories	✗	❹ .... Decor
Books, Toys & Entertainment	✗	

WWW.PIER1KIDS.COM

BOCA RATON—1400 GLADES RD (AT RT 95); 561.391.4988; M-SA 9-9, SU 10-7; PARKING LOT

participate in our survey at

Purple Turtle, The

Furniture, Bedding & Decor .... ✗	✗ .... Gear & Equipment
Nursing & Feeding .... ✗	✗ .... Safety & Babycare
Clothing, Shoes & Accessories .... ✓	✗ .... Books, Toys & Entertainment

PALM BEACH—150 WORTH AVE (AT S COUNTY RD); 561.655.1625; M-SA 10-5:30

Skadoodles Children's Boutique

Furniture, Bedding & Decor .... ✓	✗ .... Gear & Equipment
Nursing & Feeding .... ✓	✗ .... Safety & Babycare
Clothing, Shoes & Accessories .... ✓	✓ .... Books, Toys & Entertainment

WWW.SKADOODLES.COM

DELRAY BEACH—422 E ATLANTIC AVE (AT FED HWY 1); 561.272.0828; M-F 10:30-5:30, SA 10-9, SU 12-4; PARKING IN FRONT OF BLDG

Snappy Turtle ★★★☆☆

"...so cute... very Palm Beach—Lilly Pulitzer-esque... better selection for girls than boys... **"**

Furniture, Bedding & Decor .... ✗	$$$$$ .... Prices
Gear & Equipment .... ✗	❷ .... Product availability
Nursing & Feeding .... ✗	❹ .... Staff knowledge
Safety & Babycare .... ✗	❷ .... Customer service
Clothing, Shoes & Accessories .... ✓	❺ .... Decor
Books, Toys & Entertainment .... ✗	

DELRAY BEACH—1038 E ATLANTIC AVE (AT SEABREEZE AVE); 561.276.8088; M-F 10-6, SA 10-5:30, SU 12-5

Strasburg Children ★★★★☆

"...totally adorable special occasion outfits for babies and kids... classic baby, toddler, and kids clothes... dress-up clothes for kids... if you are looking for a flower girl or ring bearer outfit, look no further... handmade clothes that will last through multiple kids or generations... it's not cheap, but you can find great sales if you are patient... **"**

Furniture, Bedding & Decor .... ✗	$$$$ .... Prices
Gear & Equipment .... ✗	❹ .... Product availability
Nursing & Feeding .... ✗	❹ .... Staff knowledge
Safety & Babycare .... ✗	❹ .... Customer service
Clothing, Shoes & Accessories .... ✓	❹ .... Decor
Books, Toys & Entertainment .... ✗	

WWW.STRASBURGCHILDREN.COM

WELLINGTON—10300 W FOREST HILL BLVD (AT RT 441); 561.784.1505; M-SA 10-9 SU11-6

Stride Rite Shoes ★★★⯪☆

"...wonderful selection of baby and toddler shoes... sandals, sneakers, and even special-occasion shoes... decent quality shoes that last... they know a lot about kids' shoes and take the time to get it right—they always measure my son's feet before fittings... store sizes vary, but they always have something in stock that works... they've even special ordered shoes for my daughter... a fun 'first shoe' buying experience... **"**

Furniture, Bedding & Decor .... ✗	$$$ .... Prices
Gear & Equipment .... ✗	❹ .... Product availability
Nursing & Feeding .... ✗	❹ .... Staff knowledge
Safety & Babycare .... ✗	❹ .... Customer service
Clothing, Shoes & Accessories .... ✓	❹ .... Decor
Books, Toys & Entertainment .... ✗	

WWW.STRIDERITE.COM

WELLINGTON—116-10300 W FOREST HILL BLVD (AT WELLINGTON GREEN MALL); 561.798.4552; M-SA 10-9, SU 11-6; MALL PARKING

Toys R Us

"...not just toys, but also tons of gear and supplies including diapers and formula... a hectic shopping experience but the prices make it all worthwhile... I've experienced good and bad service at the same store on the same day... the stores are huge and can be overwhelming... most big brand-names available... leave the kids at home unless you want to end up with a cart full of toys... **"**

Furniture, Bedding & Decor .... ✓	$$$ .... Prices
Gear & Equipment .... ✓	❹ .... Product availability
Nursing & Feeding .... ✓	❸ .... Staff knowledge
Safety & Babycare .... ✓	❸ .... Customer service
Clothing, Shoes & Accessories ..... ✓	❸ .... Decor
Books, Toys & Entertainment .... ✓	

WWW.TOYSRUS.COM

BOCA RATON—20429 STATE RD 7 (AT GLADES RD); 561.451.0464; M-SA 10-9, SU 11-7

PALM BEACH GARDENS—3195 PGA BLVD (AT KEW GARDENS AVE); 561.624.8905; M-SA 10-9, SU 11-6; PARKING LOT

participate in our survey at

The Keys

Bayshore Clothing

"...tropical clothing and toys for infants and young children..."

Furniture, Bedding & Decor	✗	$$ .... Prices
Gear & Equipment	✗	❸ .... Product availability
Nursing & Feeding	✗	❹ .... Staff knowledge
Safety & Babycare	✗	❸ .... Customer service
Clothing, Shoes & Accessories	✓	❸ .... Decor
Books, Toys & Entertainment	✗	

WWW.BAYSHORECLOTHING.COM

MARATHON—12650 OVERSEES HWY (AT SADOWSKI CSWY); 305.743.8430; M-SA 10-5:30, SU 12-4; PARKING LOT

Chicken Store, The

"...a fun place to take the kids, all sorts of chickens for sale—ceramic chickens, plastic chickens, chicken art, bumper stickers, tee shirts and more... also many wild chickens running loose and usually has dozens waiting for adoption-really fun for the kids..."

Furniture, Bedding & Decor	✗	$$$ .... Prices
Gear & Equipment	✗	❸ .... Product availability
Nursing & Feeding	✗	❸ .... Staff knowledge
Safety & Babycare	✗	❸ .... Customer service
Clothing, Shoes & Accessories	✓	❸ .... Decor
Books, Toys & Entertainment	✗	

WWW.THECHICKENSTORE.COM

KEY WEST—1229 DUVAL ST (AT UNITED ST); 305.294.0070; M-SA 10-5 ; PARKING LOT

Down To Earth

"...boutique clothing, gifts, layette, with earthy, island feel... great shop!.."

Furniture, Bedding & Decor	✗	$$$$ .... Prices
Gear & Equipment	✗	❺ .... Product availability
Nursing & Feeding	✗	❺ .... Staff knowledge
Safety & Babycare	✗	❺ .... Customer service
Clothing, Shoes & Accessories	✗	❺ .... Decor
Books, Toys & Entertainment	✓	

WWW.DOWNTOEARTHBYSUMMER.COM

ISLAMORADA—82205 OVERSEAS HWY (AT MM 822); 305.664.9828; M-SA 10-5:30 ; PARKING LOT

Imagination Station

"...baby accessories and gifts... children's educational, creative, and developmental toys, puzzles, balloons, games..."

Furniture, Bedding & Decor	✗	$$$ .... Prices
Gear & Equipment	✗	❹ .... Product availability
Nursing & Feeding	✗	❹ .... Staff knowledge
Safety & Babycare	✗	❹ .... Customer service
Clothing, Shoes & Accessories	✗	❹ .... Decor
Books, Toys & Entertainment	✓	

WWW.IMAGINATIONSYSTEM.COM

KEY WEST—3302 N ROOSEVELT BLVD (AT SEARS TOWN SHOPPING PLAZA); 305.294.1852; M-SA 10-7:30, SU 11-5; PARKING LOT

Lilly Pulitzer

"...colorful Florida inspired clothing for the family..."

Furniture, Bedding & Decor	✗	$$$	Prices
Gear & Equipment	✗	❸	Product availability
Nursing & Feeding	✗	❸	Staff knowledge
Safety & Babycare	✗	❸	Customer service
Clothing, Shoes & Accessories	✓	❸	Decor
Books, Toys & Entertainment	✗		

WWW.LILLYPULITZER.COM

KEY WEST—600 FRONT ST (AT SIMONTON ST); 305 296.0995; CALL FOR HRS

Mystic Isle ★★★★★

"...*eclectic shop with great herbal kid vitamins, handcrafted toys, natural products, and great books!...* **"**

Furniture, Bedding & Decor	✗	$$	Prices
Gear & Equipment	✗	❺	Product availability
Nursing & Feeding	✗	❺	Staff knowledge
Safety & Babycare	✗	❺	Customer service
Clothing, Shoes & Accessories	✗	❺	Decor
Books, Toys & Entertainment	✓		

ISLAMORADA—82205 OVERSEAS HWY (AT LIST ST); 305.664.1020; T-SA 11-6; PARKING LOT

Sears ★★★☆☆

"...*a decent selection of clothes and basic baby equipment... check out the Kids Club program—it's a great way to save money... you go to Sears to save money, not to be pampered... the quality of their merchandise is better than Wal-Mart, but don't expect anything too special or different... not much in terms of gear, but tons of well-priced baby and toddler clothing...* **"**

Furniture, Bedding & Decor	✓	$$	Prices
Gear & Equipment	✓	❸	Product availability
Nursing & Feeding	✓	❸	Staff knowledge
Safety & Babycare	✓	❸	Customer service
Clothing, Shoes & Accessories	✓	❸	Decor
Books, Toys & Entertainment	✓		

WWW.SEARS.COM

KEY WEST—3202 N ROOSEVELT BL (AT PRESS KENNEDY DR); 305.294.4621; M-F 10-9, SA 8-9, SU 11-5; PARKING LOT

participate in our survey at

Online

★★★★★

"lila picks"

★ babycenter.com   ★ babystyle.com
★ babyuniverse.com   ★ joggingstroller.com

ababy.com

Furniture, Bedding & Decor .... ✓   ✓ .... Gear & Equipment
Nursing & Feeding .... ✗   ✓ .... Safety & Babycare
Clothing, Shoes & Accessories .... ✓   ✗ .... Books, Toys & Entertainment

aikobaby.com   ★★★☆☆

❝...high end clothes that are so cute... everything from Catamini to Jack and Lily... you can find super expensive infant and baby clothes at discounted prices... amazing selection of diaper bags so you don't have to look like a frumpy mom (or dad)... ❞

Furniture, Bedding & Decor .... ✗   ✓ .... Gear & Equipment
Nursing & Feeding .... ✗   ✗ .... Safety & Babycare
Clothing, Shoes & Accessories .... ✓   ✗ .... Books, Toys & Entertainment

albeebaby.com   ★★★★☆

❝...they offer a really comprehensive selection of baby gear... their prices are some of the best online... great discounts on Maclarens before the new models come out... good product availability—fast shipping and easy transactions... the site is pretty easy to use... the prices are surprisingly great... ❞

Furniture, Bedding & Decor .... ✓   ✓ .... Gear & Equipment
Nursing & Feeding .... ✓   ✓ .... Safety & Babycare
Clothing, Shoes & Accessories .... ✓   ✓ .... Books, Toys & Entertainment

amazon.com   ★★★★☆

❝...unless you've been living under a rock, you know that in addition to books, Amazon carries an amazing amount of baby stuff too... they have the best prices and offer free shipping on bigger purchases... you can even buy used items for dirt cheap... I always read the comments written by others—they're very useful in helping make my decisions... I love Amazon for just about everything, but their baby selection only carries the big box standards... ❞

Furniture, Bedding & Decor .... ✗   ✓ .... Gear & Equipment
Nursing & Feeding .... ✓   ✓ .... Safety & Babycare
Clothing, Shoes & Accessories .... ✓   ✓ .... Books, Toys & Entertainment

arunningstroller.com   ★★★★☆

❝...the prices are very competitive and the customer service is great... I talked to them on the phone for a while and they totally hooked me up with the right model... if you're looking for a new stroller, look no further... talk to Marilyn—she's the best... shipping costs are reasonable and their prices overall are good... ❞

Furniture, Bedding & Decor.......... ✓   ✓ ....Gear & Equipment
Nursing & Feeding .... ✗   ✗ ....Safety & Babycare
Clothing, Shoes & Accessories .... ✗   ✗ ....Books, Toys & Entertainment

babiesinthesun.com   ★★★★☆

❝...one-stop shopping for cloth diapers... run by a fantastic woman who had 3 cloth diapered babies herself and is a wealth of knowledge... if you live in South Florida, the owner will let you into her home to see the merchandise and ask questions... great selection and the customer service is the best... ❞

Furniture, Bedding & Decor.......... ✗   ✓ ....Gear & Equipment
Nursing & Feeding .... ✗   ✓ ....Safety & Babycare
Clothing, Shoes & Accessories .... ✗   ✗ ....Books, Toys & Entertainment

babiesrus.com   ★★★★☆

❝...terrific web site with all the baby gear you'll need... registering online made it easy for my family and friends... getting the registry activated was a bit tricky... super convenient and ideal for the moms-to-be who are on bedrest... web site prices are comparable to in-store prices... shipping is usually free... a very efficient way to buy and send baby gifts... our local Babies R Us said they will accept returns if they carry the same item... not all online items are available in your local store... ❞

Furniture, Bedding & Decor.......... ✓   ✓ ....Gear & Equipment
Nursing & Feeding .... ✓   ✓ ....Safety & Babycare
Clothing, Shoes & Accessories ...... ✓   ✓ ....Books, Toys & Entertainment

babiestravellite.com   ★★★★½

❝...caters to traveling families... they deliver baby items to your hotel room anywhere in the country... all of the different baby supplies you will need when you travel with a baby or a toddler... they sell almost every major brand for each product and their prices are sometimes cheaper than you would find at your local store... ❞

Furniture, Bedding & Decor.......... ✓   ✗ ....Gear & Equipment
Nursing & Feeding .... ✓   ✓ ....Safety & Babycare
Clothing, Shoes & Accessories .... ✗   ✓ ....Books, Toys & Entertainment

babyage.com   ★★★★☆

❝...fast shipping and the best prices around... flat rate shipping is great after the baby has arrived and you don't have time to go to the store... very attentive customer service... clearance items are a great deal (regular items are very competitive too)... ordering and delivery were super smooth... I usually check this web site before I purchase any baby gear... sign up for their newsletter and they'll notify you when they are having a sale... ❞

Furniture, Bedding & Decor.......... ✓   ✓ ....Gear & Equipment
Nursing & Feeding .... ✓   ✓ ....Safety & Babycare
Clothing, Shoes & Accessories ...... ✓   ✓ ....Books, Toys & Entertainment

babyant.com   ★★★★☆

❝...wide variety of brands and products available through their site... super easy to navigate... fun, whimsical ideas... nice people and helpful... easy to return items and you can call them with questions... often has the best prices and low shipping costs... ❞

Furniture, Bedding & Decor.......... ✓   ✓ ....Gear & Equipment
Nursing & Feeding .... ✓   ✓ ....Safety & Babycare
Clothing, Shoes & Accessories ...... ✓   ✓ ....Books, Toys & Entertainment

participate in our survey at

babybazaar.com

"...high-end baby stuff available on an easy-to-use web site... lots of European styles... quick processing and shipping... mom's tips, educational toys, exclusive favorites Bugaboo and Stokke..."

Furniture, Bedding & Decor ....✓	✓ .... Gear & Equipment
Nursing & Feeding ....✓	✓ .... Safety & Babycare
Clothing, Shoes & Accessories.......✓	✓ .... Books, Toys & Entertainment

babybestbuy.com

Furniture, Bedding & Decor ....✓	✓ .... Gear & Equipment
Nursing & Feeding ....✓	✓ .... Safety & Babycare
Clothing, Shoes & Accessories.......✓	✓ .... Books, Toys & Entertainment

babycatalog.com ★★★★☆

"...great deals on many essentials... wide selection of rockers but fewer options in other categories... the web site could be more user-friendly... customer service and delivery was fast and efficient... check out their seasonal specials... the baby club is a great way to save additional money... sign up for their wonderful pregnancy/new baby email newsletter... check this web site before you buy anywhere else..."

Furniture, Bedding & Decor ....✓	✓ .... Gear & Equipment
Nursing & Feeding ....✓	✓ .... Safety & Babycare
Clothing, Shoes & Accessories.......✓	✓ .... Books, Toys & Entertainment

babycenter.com ★★★★★

"...a terrific selection of all things baby, plus quick shipping... free shipping on big orders... makes shopping convenient for new parents... web site is very user friendly... they always email you about sale items and special offers... lots of useful information for parents... carries everything you may need... online registry is simple, easy and a great way to get what you need... includes helpful products ratings by parents... they've created a nice online community in addition to their online store..."

Furniture, Bedding & Decor ....✓	✓ .... Gear & Equipment
Nursing & Feeding ....✓	✓ .... Safety & Babycare
Clothing, Shoes & Accessories.......✓	✓ .... Books, Toys & Entertainment

babydepot.com ★★★☆☆

"...carries everything you'll find in a big department store but at cheaper prices and with everything all in one place... be certain you know what you want because returns can be difficult... site could be more user-friendly... online selection can differ from instore selection... love the online registry..."

Furniture, Bedding & Decor ....✓	✓ .... Gear & Equipment
Nursing & Feeding ....✓	✓ .... Safety & Babycare
Clothing, Shoes & Accessories.......✓	✓ .... Books, Toys & Entertainment

babygeared.com

Furniture, Bedding & Decor ....✓	✓ .... Gear & Equipment
Nursing & Feeding ....✓	✓ .... Safety & Babycare
Clothing, Shoes & Accessories.......✓	✓ .... Books, Toys & Entertainment

babyphd.com

Furniture, Bedding & Decor ....✓	✗ .... Gear & Equipment
Nursing & Feeding ....✗	✗ .... Safety & Babycare
Clothing, Shoes & Accessories.......✓	✓ .... Books, Toys & Entertainment

babystyle.com ★★★★★

"...their web site is just like their stores—terrific... an excellent source for everything a parent needs... fantastic maternity and baby clothes...

they always respond quickly by email... their site seems to have even more merchandise than their stores... I started shopping on their site after receiving a gift card—very easy and convenient... wonderful selection... 〞

Furniture, Bedding & Decor	✓	✓ .... Gear & Equipment
Nursing & Feeding	✓	✓ .... Safety & Babycare
Clothing, Shoes & Accessories	✓	✓ .... Books, Toys & Entertainment

babysupermall.com

Furniture, Bedding & Decor	✓	✓ .... Gear & Equipment
Nursing & Feeding	✓	✓ .... Safety & Babycare
Clothing, Shoes & Accessories	✓	✓ .... Books, Toys & Entertainment

babyuniverse.com ★★★★★

〝*...nice large selection of specialty and basic items... easy-to-use web site with decent prices... carries Carter's clothes and many other popular brands... great bedding selection - they're one of the few places with the Kidsline bedding I wanted... adorable backpacks for toddlers and preschoolers... check out the site for strollers and car seats... this was my first online shopping experience and they made it so easy, convenient and fast, I was hooked... fine customer service... flat rate (if not free) shipping takes the 'ouch' factor out of those big ticket purchases...* 〞

Furniture, Bedding & Decor	✓	✓ .... Gear & Equipment
Nursing & Feeding	✓	✓ .... Safety & Babycare
Clothing, Shoes & Accessories	✓	✓ .... Books, Toys & Entertainment

barebabies.com

Furniture, Bedding & Decor	✓	✓ .... Gear & Equipment
Nursing & Feeding	✓	✓ .... Safety & Babycare
Clothing, Shoes & Accessories	✓	✓ .... Books, Toys & Entertainment

birthandbaby.com ★★★★☆

〝*...incredible site for buying a nursing bra... there is more information about different manufacturers than you can imagine... I've even received a phone call from the owner after placing an order to clarify something... free shipping, so it's easy to buy multiple sizes and send back the ones that don't fit... their selection of nursing bras is better than any other place I've found... if you are a hard to fit size, this is the place to go...* 〞

Furniture, Bedding & Decor	✗	✓ .... Gear & Equipment
Nursing & Feeding	✓	✓ .... Safety & Babycare
Clothing, Shoes & Accessories	✗	✓ .... Books, Toys & Entertainment

blueberrybabies.com

Furniture, Bedding & Decor	✓	✓ .... Gear & Equipment
Nursing & Feeding	✓	✓ .... Safety & Babycare
Clothing, Shoes & Accessories	✓	✓ .... Books, Toys & Entertainment

buybuybaby.com ★★★★⯪

〝*...this is the web site for the popular New York-based baby retailer... you name it, they've got it... all the items in their store can also be found on their web site... prices are fair - especially since things get shipped right to your door... we had some items that were damaged and their online customer service took care of it without any problems...* 〞

Furniture, Bedding & Decor	✓	✓ .... Gear & Equipment
Nursing & Feeding	✓	✓ .... Safety & Babycare
Clothing, Shoes & Accessories	✓	✓ .... Books, Toys & Entertainment

childcarriers.com

Furniture, Bedding & Decor	✗	✓ .... Gear & Equipment

Nursing & Feeding	✗	✗ .... Safety & Babycare
Clothing, Shoes & Accessories	✗	✗ .... Books, Toys & Entertainment

clothdiaper.com

Furniture, Bedding & Decor	✗	✓ .... Gear & Equipment
Nursing & Feeding	✓	✓ .... Safety & Babycare
Clothing, Shoes & Accessories	✗	✗ .... Books, Toys & Entertainment

cocoacrayon.com

Furniture, Bedding & Decor	✓	✓ .... Gear & Equipment
Nursing & Feeding	✓	✓ .... Safety & Babycare
Clothing, Shoes & Accessories	✓	✓ .... Books, Toys & Entertainment

cvs.com ★★★★☆

"...super convenient web site for any 'drug store' items... items are delivered in a reasonable amount of time... decent selection of baby products... prices are competitive and ordering online definitely beats making the trip out to the drugstore... order a bunch of stuff at a time so shipping is free... I used them for my baby announcements and everyone loved them... super easy to refill prescriptions... it was a real relief to order all my formula, baby wipes and diapers online... **"**

Furniture, Bedding & Decor	✗	✗ .... Gear & Equipment
Nursing & Feeding	✓	✓ .... Safety & Babycare
Clothing, Shoes & Accessories	✗	✗ .... Books, Toys & Entertainment

dreamtimebaby.com

Furniture, Bedding & Decor	✓	✓ .... Gear & Equipment
Nursing & Feeding	✓	✓ .... Safety & Babycare
Clothing, Shoes & Accessories	✓	✓ .... Books, Toys & Entertainment

drugstore.com ★★★★☆

Furniture, Bedding & Decor	✗	✗ .... Gear & Equipment
Nursing & Feeding	✓	✓ .... Safety & Babycare
Clothing, Shoes & Accessories	✗	✗ .... Books, Toys & Entertainment

ebay.com ★★★★☆

"...great way to save money on everything from maternity clothes to breast pumps... be careful with whom you do business... it's always worth checking out what's available... I picked up a brand new jogger for dirt cheap... great deals to be had if you have patience to browse and be willing to resell or exchange what you don't like... baby stuff is easily found and often reasonably priced... keep an eye on shipping costs when you're bidding... **"**

Furniture, Bedding & Decor	✓	✓ .... Gear & Equipment
Nursing & Feeding	✓	✓ .... Safety & Babycare
Clothing, Shoes & Accessories	✓	✓ .... Books, Toys & Entertainment

egiggle.com ★★★★☆

"...nice selection—not overwhelming... don't expect the big box store brands here—they carry higher-end, specialty items that you won't find elsewhere... smooth shopping experience... nice site—convenient and easy to use... **"**

Furniture, Bedding & Decor	✓	✓ .... Gear & Equipment
Nursing & Feeding	✓	✓ .... Safety & Babycare
Clothing, Shoes & Accessories	✓	✓ .... Books, Toys & Entertainment

gagagifts.com ★★★★☆

"...great online store that carries fun clothes and unique gifts and toys for kids and adults... unique and special gifts like designer diaper bags, Whoozit learning toys and handmade quilts... this site makes gift buying incredibly easy—I'm done in less than 5 minutes... prices are high but products are special... **"**

Furniture, Bedding & Decor .... ✓	✓ .... Gear & Equipment
Nursing & Feeding .... ✓	✓ .... Safety & Babycare
Clothing, Shoes & Accessories ...... ✓	✓ .... Books, Toys & Entertainment

gap.com ★★★★☆

"...I love the Gap's online store—all the cool things in their stores available via my computer... terrific selection of boys and girls clothes plus cute shoes.., you can find awesome deals and return online purchases to Gap stores... their clothes are very durable... it's easy to purchase items online and delivery is prompt... a very practical and affordable way to shop... site makes it easy to quickly find what you need... sign up for the weekly newsletter and you'll find out about online sales... **"**

Furniture, Bedding & Decor .... ✓	✓ .... Gear & Equipment
Nursing & Feeding .... ✗	✗ .... Safety & Babycare
Clothing, Shoes & Accessories ...... ✓	✓ .... Books, Toys & Entertainment

geniusbabies.com ★★★☆☆

"...the best selection available of developmental toys and gifts... the only place to order real puppets from the Baby Einstein video series... cool place for unique baby shower and birthday gifts... their site navigation could use an upgrade... **"**

Furniture, Bedding & Decor .... ✗	✗ .... Gear & Equipment
Nursing & Feeding .... ✗	✗ .... Safety & Babycare
Clothing, Shoes & Accessories .... ✗	✓ .... Books, Toys & Entertainment

gymboree.com ★★★★☆

"...beautiful clothing and great quality... colorful and stylish baby and kids wear... lots of fun birthday gift ideas... easy exchange and return policy... items usually go on sale pretty quickly... save money with gymbucks... many stores have a play area which makes shopping with my kids fun (let alone feasible)... **"**

Furniture, Bedding & Decor .... ✗	✗ .... Gear & Equipment
Nursing & Feeding .... ✗	✗ .... Safety & Babycare
Clothing, Shoes & Accessories ...... ✓	✓ .... Books, Toys & Entertainment

hannaandersson.com

Furniture, Bedding & Decor .... ✓	✗ .... Gear & Equipment
Nursing & Feeding .... ✓	✗ .... Safety & Babycare
Clothing, Shoes & Accessories ...... ✓	✓ .... Books, Toys & Entertainment

jcpenney.com

Furniture, Bedding & Decor .... ✓	✗ .... Gear & Equipment
Nursing & Feeding .... ✗	✓ .... Safety & Babycare
Clothing, Shoes & Accessories ...... ✓	✗ .... Books, Toys & Entertainment

joggingstroller.com ★★★★★

"...an excellent resource when you're choosing a jogging stroller... the entire site is devoted to joggers... very helpful information that's worth checking whether you plan to buy from them or not... the best online guide for researching jogging strollers... includes helpful comparisons and parent reviews on the top strollers... **"**

Furniture, Bedding & Decor .... ✗	✓ .... Gear & Equipment
Nursing & Feeding .... ✗	✗ .... Safety & Babycare
Clothing, Shoes & Accessories .... ✗	✗ .... Books, Toys & Entertainment

kidsurplus.com

Furniture, Bedding & Decor .... ✓	✗ .... Gear & Equipment
Nursing & Feeding .... ✓	✗ .... Safety & Babycare
Clothing, Shoes & Accessories ...... ✓	✓ .... Books, Toys & Entertainment

participate in our survey at

landofnod.com ★★★★☆

"...cool site with adorable and unique furnishings... hip kid style art work... fabulous furniture and bedding... the catalog is amusing and nicely laid out... lots of sweet selections for both boys and girls... good customer service... fun but small selection of music, books, toys and more... a great way to get ideas for putting rooms together..."

Furniture, Bedding & Decor ✓	✗	Gear & Equipment
Nursing & Feeding ✗	✗	Safety & Babycare
Clothing, Shoes & Accessories ✗	✓	Books, Toys & Entertainment

landsend.com ★★★★☆

"...carries the best quality in children's wear—their stuff lasts forever... durable and adorable clothing, shoes and bedding... they offer a huge variety of casual clothing and awesome pajamas... not as inexpensive as other sites, but you can't beat the quality... the very best diaper bags... site is easy to navigate and has great finds for the entire family... love the flannel sheets, maternity clothes and shoes for mom..."

Furniture, Bedding & Decor ✓	✗	Gear & Equipment
Nursing & Feeding ✗	✗	Safety & Babycare
Clothing, Shoes & Accessories ✓	✗	Books, Toys & Entertainment

letsgostrolling.com

Furniture, Bedding & Decor ✓	✓	Gear & Equipment
Nursing & Feeding ✓	✗	Safety & Babycare
Clothing, Shoes & Accessories ✓	✓	Books, Toys & Entertainment

llbean.com ★★★★☆

"...high quality clothing for babies, toddlers and kids at reasonable prices... the clothes are extremely durable and stand up to wear and tear very well... a great site for winter clothing and gear shopping... wonderful selection for older kids, too... fewer options for infants... an awesome way to shop for clothing basics... you can't beat the diaper bags..."

Furniture, Bedding & Decor ✗	✗	Gear & Equipment
Nursing & Feeding ✗	✗	Safety & Babycare
Clothing, Shoes & Accessories ✓	✗	Books, Toys & Entertainment

modernseed.com ★★★★½

"...it was fun finding many unique items for my son's nursery... I wanted a contemporary theme and they had lots of wonderful items including crib linens, wall art and lighting... the place to find super cool baby and kid stuff and the best place for modern nursery decor... they also carry children and adult clothing and furniture and toys... not cheap but one of my favorite places..."

Furniture, Bedding & Decor ✓	✓	Gear & Equipment
Nursing & Feeding ✓	✓	Safety & Babycare
Clothing, Shoes & Accessories ✓	✓	Books, Toys & Entertainment

naturalbaby-catalog.com ★★★★☆

"...all natural products—clothes, toys, herbal medicines, bathing, etc... fine quality and a great alternative to the usual products... site is fairly easy to navigate and has a good selection... dealing with returns is pretty painless... love the catalogue and the products... excellent customer service... lots of organic clothing made with natural materials... high quality shoes in a range of prices..."

Furniture, Bedding & Decor ✓	✓	Gear & Equipment
Nursing & Feeding ✓	✓	Safety & Babycare
Clothing, Shoes & Accessories ✓	✓	Books, Toys & Entertainment

netkidswear.com

Furniture, Bedding & Decor .... ✓	✓ .... Gear & Equipment
Nursing & Feeding .... ✓	✓ .... Safety & Babycare
Clothing, Shoes & Accessories ...... ✓	✓ .... Books, Toys & Entertainment

nordstrom.com ★★★★☆

❝...just like their stores, the site carries a great selection of high-quality items... you can't go wrong with Nordstrom—even online... quick shipping and easy site navigation... a little pricey, but great quality items... I've purchased a bunch of baby stuff from their website and have never had a problem... a great shoe selection for all ages... ❞

Furniture, Bedding & Decor .... ✓	✓ .... Gear & Equipment
Nursing & Feeding .... ✗	✓ .... Safety & Babycare
Clothing, Shoes & Accessories ...... ✓	✓ .... Books, Toys & Entertainment

oldnavy.com ★★★★☆

❝...shopping online with Old Navy makes it easy to find incredible bargains... site was easy to use and my products arrived quickly... site carries items that aren't necessarily available in their stores... an inexpensive way to get trendy baby clothes... you can return items directly to any store... check out the sale page of this web site for deep discounts on current season clothing... I signed up for the email savings and get free shipping several times a year... ❞

Furniture, Bedding & Decor .... ✗	✗ .... Gear & Equipment
Nursing & Feeding .... ✗	✗ .... Safety & Babycare
Clothing, Shoes & Accessories ...... ✓	✗ .... Books, Toys & Entertainment

oliebollen.com ★★★★☆

❝...perfect for the busy mom looking for a fun baby shower gift... this online-only store has all the best brands—Catamini and Tea Collection to name a couple... great for gifts and home stuff, too... lots of style... very easy to use... 30 days full refund, 60 days store credit... ❞

Furniture, Bedding & Decor .... ✓	✗ .... Gear & Equipment
Nursing & Feeding .... ✓	✗ .... Safety & Babycare
Clothing, Shoes & Accessories ...... ✓	✓ .... Books, Toys & Entertainment

onestepahead.com ★★★★☆

❝...one stop shopping site with everything parents are looking for... huge variety of items to choose from... I bought everything from a crib to a nursery bottle... high quality items, many of which are developmental in nature... great line of safety equipment... easy to order and fast delivery but you will pay for shipping... web site has helpful reviews... great site for hard to find items... ❞

Furniture, Bedding & Decor .... ✓	✓ .... Gear & Equipment
Nursing & Feeding .... ✓	✓ .... Safety & Babycare
Clothing, Shoes & Accessories ...... ✓	✓ .... Books, Toys & Entertainment

peapods.com

Furniture, Bedding & Decor .... ✓	✓ .... Gear & Equipment
Nursing & Feeding .... ✗	✓ .... Safety & Babycare
Clothing, Shoes & Accessories ...... ✓	✓ .... Books, Toys & Entertainment

pokkadots.com

Furniture, Bedding & Decor .... ✓	✓ .... Gear & Equipment
Nursing & Feeding .... ✓	✗ .... Safety & Babycare
Clothing, Shoes & Accessories ...... ✓	✓ .... Books, Toys & Entertainment

poshtots.com ★★★★☆

❝...incredible selection of whimsical and out-of-the-ordinary nursery decor... beautiful, unique designer room sets in multiple styles... they do boys and girls bedrooms... great for the baby that has everything—

participate in our survey at

including parents with an unlimited cash account... you can get great ideas about decor just from browsing the site, even if you don't buy... **"**

Furniture, Bedding & Decor .... ✓	✓ .... Gear & Equipment
Nursing & Feeding .... ✓	✗ .... Safety & Babycare
Clothing, Shoes & Accessories .... ✓	✓ .... Books, Toys & Entertainment

potterybarnkids.com ★★★★⯪

"...*beautiful high end furniture and bedding... they have a way with matching everything perfectly and I am always a sucker for that look... adorable merchandise of great quality... you will get what you pay for: high quality furniture at high prices... web site is easy to navigate... items like hooded towels and plush blankets make this place special... if I could afford it I would buy everything in the store...* **"**

Furniture, Bedding & Decor .... ✓	✓ .... Gear & Equipment
Nursing & Feeding .... ✗	✗ .... Safety & Babycare
Clothing, Shoes & Accessories .... ✗	✓ .... Books, Toys & Entertainment

preemie.com

Furniture, Bedding & Decor .... ✗	✓ .... Gear & Equipment
Nursing & Feeding .... ✓	✓ .... Safety & Babycare
Clothing, Shoes & Accessories .... ✓	✓ .... Books, Toys & Entertainment

rei.com

Furniture, Bedding & Decor .... ✗	✓ .... Gear & Equipment
Nursing & Feeding .... ✗	✗ .... Safety & Babycare
Clothing, Shoes & Accessories .... ✓	✓ .... Books, Toys & Entertainment

royalnursery.com ★★★⯪☆

"...*this used to be a store in San Diego and now it is only online... if you need a silver rattle, luxury baby blanket or shower gift—this is the place... a beautiful site with elegant baby clothes, jewelry, and gifts...love the hand print kits—they are my current favorite gift... high end baby wear and gear... be sure to check out the sale items...* **"**

Furniture, Bedding & Decor .... ✓	✗ .... Gear & Equipment
Nursing & Feeding .... ✗	✓ .... Safety & Babycare
Clothing, Shoes & Accessories .... ✓	✓ .... Books, Toys & Entertainment

showeryourbaby.com

Furniture, Bedding & Decor .... ✓	✓ .... Gear & Equipment
Nursing & Feeding .... ✓	✓ .... Safety & Babycare
Clothing, Shoes & Accessories .... ✓	✓ .... Books, Toys & Entertainment

snipsnsnails.com ★★★★⯪

"...*a great boys clothing store for infants to 14 years old... clothes for every occasion, from casual to special occasion... pajamas and swimsuits, too... pricey, but upscale and fun... items on the web site are not always in stock ...* **"**

Furniture, Bedding & Decor .... ✓	✗ .... Gear & Equipment
Nursing & Feeding .... ✗	✗ .... Safety & Babycare
Clothing, Shoes & Accessories .... ✓	✗ .... Books, Toys & Entertainment

strollerdepot.com

Furniture, Bedding & Decor .... ✗	✓ .... Gear & Equipment
Nursing & Feeding .... ✗	✗ .... Safety & Babycare
Clothing, Shoes & Accessories .... ✗	✓ .... Books, Toys & Entertainment

strollers4less.com ★★★⯪☆

"...*some of the best prices on strollers... I love this site... we purchased our stroller online for a lot less than it costs locally... online ordering went smoothly—from ordering through receiving... wide* *selection and some incredible deals... shipping is relatively fast... free shipping if you spend $100, which isn't hard to do...* **"**

Furniture, Bedding & Decor........... ✘	✔ ....Gear & Equipment	
Nursing & Feeding .... ✘	✘ ....Safety & Babycare	
Clothing, Shoes & Accessories .... ✘	✔ ....Books, Toys & Entertainment	

target.com ★★★★☆

"...*our favorite place to shop for kids stuff—good selection and very affordable... guilt free shopping—kids grow so fast so I don't want to pay high department store prices... everything from diapers and sippy cups to car seats and strollers... easy return policy... generally helpful staff, but you don't go for the service—you go for the prices... decent registry that won't freak your friends out with outrageous prices... easy, convenient shopping for well-priced items... all the big box brands available—Graco, Evenflo, Eddie Bauer, etc....* **"**

Furniture, Bedding & Decor........... ✔	✔ ....Gear & Equipment	
Nursing & Feeding .... ✔	✔ ....Safety & Babycare	
Clothing, Shoes & Accessories ...... ✔	✔ ....Books, Toys & Entertainment	

teddylux.com

Furniture, Bedding & Decor........... ✘	✘ ....Gear & Equipment	
Nursing & Feeding .... ✘	✘ ....Safety & Babycare	
Clothing, Shoes & Accessories .... ✘	✔ ....Books, Toys & Entertainment	

thebabyhammock.com ★★★★☆

"...*a family owned business selling parent-tested products from morning sickness relief products to baby carriers, natural skincare, gift sets and more... fast friendly service... natural products and waldorf influenced toys...* **"**

Furniture, Bedding & Decor........... ✔	✔ ....Gear & Equipment	
Nursing & Feeding .... ✔	✔ ....Safety & Babycare	
Clothing, Shoes & Accessories ...... ✔	✘ ....Books, Toys & Entertainment	

thebabyoutlet.com

Furniture, Bedding & Decor...........✘	✔ ....Gear & Equipment	
Nursing & Feeding .... ✔	✔ ....Safety & Babycare	
Clothing, Shoes & Accessories ....✘	✔ ....Books, Toys & Entertainment	

tinyride.com

Furniture, Bedding & Decor........... ✘	✔ ....Gear & Equipment	
Nursing & Feeding .... ✔	✘ ....Safety & Babycare	
Clothing, Shoes & Accessories .... ✘	✘ ....Books, Toys & Entertainment	

toadsandtulips.com

Furniture, Bedding & Decor........... ✔	✘ ....Gear & Equipment	
Nursing & Feeding .... ✘	✘ ....Safety & Babycare	
Clothing, Shoes & Accessories ...... ✔	✔ ....Books, Toys & Entertainment	

toysrus.com ★★★★☆

"...*makes shopping incredibly easy... well organized site with discount prices... makes registering for gifts super simple... even more products are online than in the actual stores... check out the outlet section and coupon codes for even more discounts... I did most of my Christmas shopping here, paid no shipping and had my gifts delivered in 3 days... web site includes helpful toy reviews... use this to send your wish lists to relatives...* **"**

Furniture, Bedding & Decor........... ✔	✔ ....Gear & Equipment	
Nursing & Feeding .... ✔	✔ ....Safety & Babycare	
Clothing, Shoes & Accessories ...... ✔	✔ ....Books, Toys & Entertainment	

tuttibella.com

"...well designed web site with beautiful, original clothing, toys, bedding and accessories... cute vintage stuff for babies and kids... stylish designer goods from here and abroad... your child will stand out among the Baby Gap-clothed masses... gorgeous fabrics... a great place to find that perfect gift for someone special and stylish..."

Furniture, Bedding & Decor	✓	✓ .... Gear & Equipment
Nursing & Feeding	✗	✗ .... Safety & Babycare
Clothing, Shoes & Accessories	✓	✗ .... Books, Toys & Entertainment

usillygoose.com

Furniture, Bedding & Decor	✓	✗ .... Gear & Equipment
Nursing & Feeding	✗	✗ .... Safety & Babycare
Clothing, Shoes & Accessories	✗	✓ .... Books, Toys & Entertainment

walmart.com

"...the site is packed with information, which can be a little difficult to navigate... anything and everything you need at a huge discount... good idea to browse the site and research prices before you visit a store... my order was delivered well before the estimated delivery date... I've found cheaper deals online than in the store..."

Furniture, Bedding & Decor	✓	✓ .... Gear & Equipment
Nursing & Feeding	✓	✓ .... Safety & Babycare
Clothing, Shoes & Accessories	✓	✓ .... Books, Toys & Entertainment

maternity clothing

South Dade & Downtown

★ ★ ★ ★ ★

"lila picks"

★ A Pea In The Pod

★ Meet Me In Miami

A Pea In The Pod ★★★★★

"...excellent if you are looking for stylish maternity clothes and don't mind paying for them... start here for special occasions and business wear... the decor is lovely and most of the clothes are beautiful... stylish fashion solutions, but expect to pay more than at department stores... keep your eyes open for the sale rack—the markdowns can be terrific... an upscale shop that carries everything from intimates to fancy dresses... stylish, fun and non-maternity-like..."

Casual wear	✓	$$$$	Prices
Business wear	✓	❹	Product availability
Intimate apparel	✓	❹	Customer service
Nursing wear	✓	❹	Decor

WWW.APEAINTHEPOD.COM

CORAL GABLES—350 SAN LORENZO AVE (AT S LE JEUNE RD); 305.648.1201; M-SA 10-9, SU 12-6

Baby Depot At Burlington Coat Factory ★★★☆☆

"...a surprisingly good selection of maternity clothes at great prices... staff can be hard to find so be prepared to dig... cute pants, skirts and sets... I wouldn't have thought that their selection would be as good as it is... not much other than casual items, but what they have is pretty good..."

Casual wear	✓	$$	Prices
Business wear	✗	❸	Product availability
Intimate apparel	✗	❸	Customer service
Nursing wear	✗	❸	Decor

WWW.BABYDEPOT.COM

MIAMI—11301 NW 12TH ST (AT 14TH ST); 305.594.7776; M-SA 10-9:30, SU 11-7; MALL PARKING

Gap Maternity ★★★★☆

"...the styles are very modern and attractive... the clothes are reasonably priced and wash well... comfy yet stylish basics... they have a great online resource and you can return online purchases at the store... average everyday prices, but catch a sale and you're golden... sizes run big so buy small... always a sale going on where you'll find hip items for a steal..."

Casual wear	✓	$$$	Prices
Business wear	✓	❸	Product availability
Intimate apparel	✓	❹	Customer service

Nursing wear .... ✓ ❸ .... Decor

WWW.GAP.COM

MIAMI—1455 NW 107TH AVE (AT MIAMI INTERNATIONAL MALL);
305.717.0985; M-SA 10-9, SU 11-7; MALL PARKING

JCPenney ★★★☆☆

66*...competitive prices and a surprisingly cute selection... they carry bigger sizes that are very hard to find at other stores... much cheaper than most maternity boutiques and they always seem to have some sort of sale going on... an especially large selection of maternity jeans for plus sizes... a more conservative collection than the smaller, hipper boutiques... good for casual basics, but not much for special occasions...* **99**

Casual wear	✓	$$	Prices
Business wear	✓	❸	Product availability
Intimate apparel	✓	❸	Customer service
Nursing wear	✗	❸	Decor

WWW.JCPENNEY.COM

MIAMI—1603 NW 107TH AVE (AT MIAMI INTERNATIONAL MALL);
305.477.1786; M-SA 10-9, SU 12-6; MALL PARKING

MIAMI—7201 N KENDALL DR (AT DADELAND MALL); 305.666.1911; M-SA,
10-9, SU 12-6; MALL PARKING

MIAMI—8881 SW 107TH AVE (AT N KENDALL DR); 305.412.0912; M-SA 10-9,
SU 12-6; MALL PARKING

M & M Maternity Shop ★★★★⯨

66*...it's definitely worth stopping here if you're still working and need some good-looking outfits... not cheap, but the quality is fantastic... not as expensive as A Pea In The Pod, but better quality than Motherhood Maternity... nice for basics that will last you through multiple pregnancies... perfect for work clothes, but pricey for the everyday stuff... good deals to be found on their sales racks... a good mix of high-end fancy clothes and items you can wear every day...* **99**

Casual wear	✓	$$$	Prices
Business wear	✓	❹	Product availability
Intimate apparel	✓	❹	Customer service
Nursing wear	✗	❸	Decor

CORAL GABLES—136 MIRACLE MILE (AT PONCE DE LEON BLVD);
305.448.7386; M-SA 9:30-5:30

Macy's ★★★⯨☆

66*...if your local Macy's has a maternity section, you're in luck... I bought my entire pregnancy work wardrobe at Macy's... the styles are all relatively recent and the brands are well known... you can generally find some attractive dresses at very reasonable prices on their sales rack... like other large department stores, you're bound to find something that works if you dig enough... very convenient because you can get your other shopping done at the same time... the selection isn't huge, but what they have is nice...* **99**

Casual wear	✓	$$$	Prices
Business wear	✓	❸	Product availability
Intimate apparel	✓	❸	Customer service
Nursing wear	✗	❸	Decor

WWW.MACYS.COM

MIAMI—13251 S DIXIE HWY (AT SW 132ND ST); 305.254.5700; M-SA 10-9,
SU 12-6; PARKING LOT

MIAMI—1405 NW 107TH AVE (AT MIAMI INTERNATIONAL MALL);
305.594.6300; M-SA 10-9:30, SU 12-8; MALL PARKING

MIAMI—22 E FLAGLER ST (AT N PERIMETER AVE); 305.577.1500; M-SA 10-6,
SU 11-5; PARKING LOT

MIAMI—7303 SW 88 ST (AT DADELAND MALL); 305.662.3400; M-SA 10-9:30, SU 12-6; MALL PARKING

MIAMI—7675 N KENDALL DR (AT DADELAND MALL); 305.662.3275; M-SA 10-9:30, SU 12-6; MALL PARKING

Meet Me In Miami

"*...best kept secret for high-end, funky maternity wear... it's a warehouse downtown where they do alterations on the spot... hard to get to, but worth it... the store is in the factory so they can be really creative... they will even help with maternity wedding dresses and custom outfits... inexpensive, easy to wash clothing...* **"**

Casual wear	✓	$$$	Prices
Business wear	✗	❺	Product availability
Intimate apparel	✗	❺	Customer service
Nursing wear	✗	❸	Decor

WWW.MEETMEINMIAMI.COM

MIAMI—5570 N E 4TH AVE (AT N MIAMI AVE); 305.759.4343; M-F 9-5

Mimi Maternity

"*...it's definitely worth stopping here if you're still working and need some good-looking outfits... not cheap, but the quality is fantastic... not as expensive as A Pea In The Pod, but better quality than Motherhood Maternity... nice for basics that will last you through multiple pregnancies... perfect for work clothes, but pricey for the everyday stuff... good deals to be found on their sales racks... a good mix of high-end fancy clothes and items you can wear every day...* **"**

Casual wear	✓	$$$	Prices
Business wear	✓	❹	Product availability
Intimate apparel	✓	❹	Customer service
Nursing wear	✓	❹	Decor

WWW.MIMIMATERNITY.COM

MIAMI—19575 BISCAYNE BLVD (AT AVENTURA MALL); 305.682.4940; M-SA 10-9:30, SU 12-8; MALL PARKING

MIAMI—7247 DADELAND MALL (AT DADELAND MALL); 305.665.0936; M-SA 10-9:30, SU 12-7; MALL PARKING

MIAMI—8888 SW 136TH ST (AT FALLS SHOPPING CTR); 305.969.9802; M-SA 10-9:30, SU 12-7

Mommy's Place

"*...cool selection of maternity wear... knowledgeable staff... limited selection of bras... lovely boutique with decent prices... trendy, good for special events... whatever you need—casual, office, sportswear or lingerie...* **"**

Casual wear	✓	$$$	Prices
Business wear	✓	❹	Product availability
Intimate apparel	✓	❹	Customer service
Nursing wear	✓	❸	Decor

WWW.MOMMYSPLACEMATERNITY.COM

SOUTH MIAMI—5845 SW 73RD ST (AT SW 58TH CT); 305.663.5636; M-SA 10-6

Motherhood Maternity

"*...a wide variety of styles, from business to weekend wear, all at a good price... affordable and cute... everything from bras and swimsuits to work outfits... highly recommended for those who don't want to spend a fortune on maternity clothes... less fancy and pricey than their sister stores—A Pea in the Pod and Mimi Maternity... they have frequent sales, so you just need to keep dropping in—you're bound to find something good...* **"**

Casual wear	✓	$$$	Prices

Business wear .... ✓ ❹ .... Product availability
Intimate apparel .... ✓ ❹ .... Customer service
Nursing wear .... ✓ ❸ .... Decor

WWW.MOTHERHOOD.COM

MIAMI—11401 NW 12TH ST (AT DOLPHIN MALL); 305.639.9622; M-SA 10-9:30, SU 11-7; MALL PARKING

MIAMI—19575 BISCAYNE BLVD (AT AVENTURA MALL); 305.937.1333; M-SA 10-9:30, SU 12-8; MALL PARKING

Ross Dress For Less ★★½☆☆

"...if you don't mind looking through a lot of clothes you can find some good pieces at great prices... they sometimes have larger sizes too... totally hit or miss depending on their most recent shipment... not the most fashionable clothing, but great for that everyday, casual T-shirt or stretchy pair of pants... **"**

Casual wear .... ✓ $$$ .... Prices
Business wear .... ✓ ❸ .... Product availability
Intimate apparel .... ✗ ❷ .... Customer service
Nursing wear .... ✗ ❷ .... Decor

WWW.ROSSSTORES.COM

CORAL GABLES—2 MIRACLE MILE (AT S DOUGLAS RD); 305.446.8440; M-SA 9:30-9:30, SU 11-7; PARKING LOT

MIAMI—100 S BISCAYNE BLVD (AT 1ST ST); 305.379.5339; M-SA 9:30-9:30, SU 11-7; PARKING LOT

MIAMI—11321 NW 12TH ST (AT NW 11TH AVE); 305.477.3188; M-SA 9:30-9:30, SU 11-7

MIAMI—7795 W FLAGLER ST (AT MALL OF THE AMERICAS); 305.264.1203; M-SA 9:30-9:30, SU 11-7

MIAMI—8505 MILLS DR (AT SHERRI LN); 305.598.5753; M-SA 9:30-9:30, SU 11-7

MIAMI—8549 SW 24TH ST (AT SW 84TH AVE); 305.267.5304; M-SA 9:30-9:30, SU 11-7; PARKING LOT

MIAMI—8605 S DIXIE HWY (AT SW 58TH CT); 305.669.1691; M-SA 9:30-9:30, SU 11-7; PARKING LOT

Sears ★★★☆☆

"...good place to get maternity clothes for a low price... the clearance rack always has good deals and their sales are quite frequent... not necessarily super high-quality, but if you just need them for nine months, who cares... good selection of nursing bras... I love the fact that they carry maternity wear in larger sizes—I got so tired of looking in those cutesy boutiques and then being disappointed because they didn't have my size... the only place I found maternity for plus-sized women... **"**

Casual wear .... ✓ $$ .... Prices
Business wear .... ✗ ❸ .... Product availability
Intimate apparel .... ✓ ❸ .... Customer service
Nursing wear .... ✓ ❸ .... Decor

WWW.SEARS.COM

MIAMI—1625 NW 107TH AVE (AT 19TH ST); 305.470.7800; M-F 10-5, SA 10-6, SU 11-5

MIAMI—20701 SW 112TH AVE (AT CUTLER RIDGE MALL); 305.378.5100; M-F 10-9, SA 8-9, SU 10-6

MIAMI—3655 CORAL WY (AT SW 22ND ST); 305.460.3400; M-SA 9:30-9, SU 11-6; PARKING LOT

MIAMI—8505 MILLS DR (OFF RT 94); 305.270.9200; M-F 10-9, SA 10-6, SU 11-5

Target

❝...*I was surprised at how fashionable their selection is—they carry Liz Lange and other really cute selections... the price is right—especially since you'll only be wearing these clothes for a few months... great for maternity basics—T-shirts, skirts, sweaters, even maternity bras... best of all, you can do some maternity shopping while you're shopping for other household basics... shirts for $10—you can't beat that... not the most exciting or romantic maternity shopping, but once you see the prices you'll get over it... as always, Target provides the perfectly priced solution...* **❞**

Casual wear	✓	$$	Prices
Business wear	✓	❸	Product availability
Intimate apparel	✓	❸	Customer service
Nursing wear	✓	❸	Decor

WWW.TARGET.COM

MIAMI—15005 SW 88TH ST (AT SW 151ST AVE); 305.386.1244; M-SA 8-10, SU 8-9; PARKING LOT

MIAMI—20500 SW 112TH AVE (AT CUTLER RIDGE MALL); 305.235.0839; M-SA 8-10, SU 8-9; PARKING LOT

MIAMI—7795 SW 40TH ST (AT SW 79TH AVE); 305.262.5767; M-SA 8-10, SU 8-9; PARKING LOT

MIAMI—8350 S DIXIE HWY (AT SW 70TH AVE); 305.668.0262; M-SA 8-10, SU 8-9; PARKING LOT

North Dade & Beaches

★★★★★

"lila picks"

★ Motherhood Maternity

A Pea In The Pod
★★★☆☆

"...excellent if you are looking for stylish maternity clothes and don't mind paying for them... start here for special occasions and business wear... the decor is lovely and most of the clothes are beautiful... stylish fashion solutions, but expect to pay more than at Motherhood Maternity—their sister store... keep your eyes open for the sale rack, the markdowns are terrific... a full scale shop that carries everything from intimates to fancy dresses... stylish, fun and non-maternity-like... **"**

Casual wear	✓	$$$$	Prices
Business wear	✓	❹	Product availability
Intimate apparel	✓	❹	Customer service
Nursing wear	✓	❹	Decor

WWW.APEAINTHEPOD.COM

BAL HARBOUR—9700 COLLINS AVE (AT BAL HARBOUR SHOPS); 305.866.7044; M-SA 10-9; FREE PARKING

Baby Depot At Burlington Coat Factory
★★★☆☆

"...a surprisingly good selection of maternity clothes at great prices... staff can be hard to find so be prepared to dig... cute pants, skirts and sets... I wouldn't have thought that their selection would be as good as it is... not much other than casual items, but what they have is pretty good... **"**

Casual wear	✓	$$	Prices
Business wear	✗	❸	Product availability
Intimate apparel	✗	❸	Customer service
Nursing wear	✗	❸	Decor

WWW.BABYDEPOT.COM

HIALEAH—590 W 49TH ST (AT W 6TH AVE); 305.820.9997; M-SA 10-9, SU 11-6; PARKING LOT

JCPenney
★★★☆☆

"...competitive prices and a surprisingly cute selection... they carry bigger sizes that are very hard to find at other stores... much cheaper than most maternity boutiques and they always seem to have some sort of sale going on... an especially large selection of maternity jeans for plus sizes... a more conservative collection than the smaller, hipper boutiques... good for casual basics, but not much for special occasions... **"**

Casual wear	✓	$$	Prices
Business wear	✓	❸	Product availability
Intimate apparel	✓	❸	Customer service

Nursing wear .... ✗ .... Decor

WWW.JCPENNEY.COM

AVENTURA—19252 BISCAYNE BLVD (AT AVENTURA MALL); 305.937.0022;
M-SA 10-9:30, SU 11-6; PARKING LOT

Macy's ★★★★⯪☆

"...if your local Macy's has a maternity section, you're in luck... I
bought my entire pregnancy work wardrobe at Macy's... the styles are
all relatively recent and the brands are well known... you can generally
find some attractive dresses at very reasonable prices on their sales
rack... like other large department stores, you're bound to find
something that works if you dig enough... very convenient because you
can get your other shopping done at the same time... the selection isn't
huge, but what they have is nice... **"**

Casual wear	✓	$$$	Prices
Business wear	✓	❸	Product availability
Intimate apparel	✓	❸	Customer service
Nursing wear	✗	❸	Decor

WWW.MACYS.COM

HIALEAH—1777 W 49TH ST (AT WESTLAND MALL); 305.825.7300; M-SA 10-9,
SU 12-6; MALL PARKING

MIAMI BEACH—1675 MERIDIAN AVE (AT LINCOLN LN N); 305.674.6300; M-
SA 10-9, SU 12-6; PARKING LOT

Motherhood Maternity ★★★★★

"...a wide variety of styles, from business to weekend wear, all at a
good price... affordable and cute... everything from bras and swimsuits
to work outfits... highly recommended for those who don't want to
spend a fortune on maternity clothes... less fancy and pricey than their
sister stores—A Pea in the Pod and Mimi Maternity... they have
frequent sales, so you just need to keep dropping in—you're bound to
find something good... **"**

Casual wear	✓	$$$	Prices
Business wear	✓	❹	Product availability
Intimate apparel	✓	❹	Customer service
Nursing wear	✓	❸	Decor

WWW.MOTHERHOOD.COM

AVENTURA—19575 BISCAYNE BLVD (AT AVENTURA MALL); 305.937.1333;
M-SA 10-9:30, SU 12-8 ; MALL PARKING

HIALEAH—1695 W 49TH ST (AT WESTLAND MALL); 305.558.6450; M-SA 10-9,
SU 11-6; MALL PARKING

Ross Dress For Less ★★⯪☆☆

"...if you don't mind looking through a lot of clothes you can find
some good pieces at great prices... they sometimes have larger sizes
too... totally hit or miss depending on their most recent shipment... not
the most fashionable clothing, but great for that everyday, casual T-
shirt or stretchy pair of pants... **"**

Casual wear	✓	$$$	Prices
Business wear	✓	❸	Product availability
Intimate apparel	✗	❷	Customer service
Nursing wear	✗	❷	Decor

WWW.ROSSSTORES.COM

HIALEAH—449 W 49TH ST (AT PALM SPRINGS MILE SHOPPING CTR);
305.512.8625; M-SA 9:30-9:30, SU 11-7

HIALEAH—5780 NW 183RD ST (AT MIAMI GARDENS SHOPPING CTR);
305.557.9933; M-SA 9:30-9:30, SU 11-7

NORTH MIAMI BEACH—12115 BISCAYNE BLVD (OFF NE 18TH AVE);
305.891.2412; M-SA 9:30-9:30, SU 11-7; PARKING IN FRONT OF BLDG

Sears ★★★☆☆

"...good place to get maternity clothes for a low price... the clearance rack always has good deals and their sales are quite frequent... not necessarily super high-quality, but if you just need them for nine months, who cares... good selection of nursing bras... I love the fact that they carry maternity wear in larger sizes—I got so tired of looking in those cutesy boutiques and then being disappointed because they didn't have my size... the only place I found maternity for plus-sized women..."

Casual wear	✓	$$	Prices
Business wear	✗	❸	Product availability
Intimate apparel	✓	❸	Customer service
Nursing wear	✓	❸	Decor

WWW.SEARS.COM

HIALEAH —1625 W 49TH ST (AT WESTLAND MALL); 305.364.3800; M-F 10-9, SA 10-6, SU 11-5

HIALEAH —5750 NW 183RD ST (AT RED RD); 305.907.2400; M-SA 8-10, SU 8-8

Target ★★★★☆

"...I was surprised at how fashionable their selection is—they carry Liz Lange and other really cute selections... the price is right—especially since you'll only be wearing these clothes for a few months... great for maternity basics—T-shirts, skirts, sweaters, even maternity bras... best of all, you can do some maternity shopping while you're shopping for other household basics... shirts for $10—you can't beat that... not the most exciting or romantic maternity shopping, but once you see the prices you'll get over it... as always, Target provides the perfectly priced solution..."

Casual wear	✓	$$	Prices
Business wear	✓	❸	Product availability
Intimate apparel	✓	❸	Customer service
Nursing wear	✓	❸	Decor

WWW.TARGET.COM

AVENTURA—21265 BISCAYNE BLVD (AT NE 213TH ST); 305.933.4616; M-SA 8-10, SU 8-9; PARKING IN FRONT OF BLDG

NORTH MIAMI—14075 BISCAYNE BLVD (AT NE 135TH ST); 305.944.5341; M-SA 8-10, SU 8-9; PARKING IN FRONT OF BLDG

Broward County

"lila picks"

★ Gap Maternity

★ Hollywood Mama Maternity

Baby Depot At Burlington Coat Factory

"...*a surprisingly good selection of maternity clothes at great prices... staff can be hard to find so be prepared to dig... cute pants, skirts and sets... I wouldn't have thought that their selection would be as good as it is... not much other than casual items, but what they have is pretty good...* **"**

Casual wear	✓	$$	Prices
Business wear	✗	❸	Product availability
Intimate apparel	✗	❸	Customer service
Nursing wear	✗	❸	Decor

WWW.BABYDEPOT.COM

CORAL SPRINGS—6251 W SAMPLE RD (AT NW 62ND AVE); 954.227.0274; M-SA 10-9, SU 11-6; PARKING LOT

SUNRISE—12801 W SUNRISE BLVD (AT SATIN LEAF WY); 954.846.7977; M-SA 10-9:30, SU 11-8; PARKING LOT

Gap Maternity

★★★★★

"...*the styles are very modern and attractive... the clothes are reasonably priced and wash well... comfy yet stylish basics... they have a great online resource and you can return online purchases at the store... average everyday prices, but catch a sale and you're golden... sizes run big so buy small... always a sale going on where you'll find hip items for a steal...* **"**

Casual wear	✓	$$$	Prices
Business wear	✓	❸	Product availability
Intimate apparel	✓	❹	Customer service
Nursing wear	✓	❸	Decor

WWW.GAP.COM

SUNRISE—12801 W SUNRISE BLVD (AT SATIN LEAF WY); 954.846.2115; M-SA 10-9:30, SU 11-8

Hollywood Mama Maternity

★★★★★

"...*it's possible to feel glamorous and sexy while being 6 months pregnant—they'll show you how... super cool, luxurious and pricey... over the top maternity that will blow your mind... the store is beautifully decorated and is fun just to stop in to check out... perfect for those special event dresses that you can't find elsewhere...* **"**

Casual wear	✓	$$$	Prices
Business wear	✓	❺	Product availability
Intimate apparel	✓	❺	Customer service

Nursing wear.............................. ✗ **❺** .... Decor

WWW.HOLLYWOODMAMA.COM

HOLLYWOOD—2037 TYLER ST (BTWN 20TH & 21ST AVES); 954.929.8886; T-SA 10-6

JCPenney
★★★☆☆

❝...competitive prices and a surprisingly cute selection... they carry bigger sizes that are very hard to find at other stores... much cheaper than most maternity boutiques and they always seem to have some sort of sale going on... an especially large selection of maternity jeans for plus sizes... a more conservative collection than the smaller, hipper boutiques... good for casual basics, but not much for special occasions...**❞**

Casual wear ....✓ $$ .... Prices
Business wear ....✓   **❸** .... Product availability
Intimate apparel ....✓   **❸** .... Customer service
Nursing wear..............................✗   **❸** .... Decor

WWW.JCPENNEY.COM

CORAL SPRINGS—9303 W ATLANTIC BLVD (AT CORAL SQUARE MALL); 954.752.8116; M-SA 10-9, SU 11-6; MALL PARKING

PEMBROKE PINES—11401 PINES BLVD (AT PEMBROKE LAKES MALL); 954.433.2445; M-SA 10-9, SU 12-6; MALL PARKING

PEMBROKE PINES—13650 PINES BLVD (AT NW 136TH AVE); 954.442.8171; M-SA 10-9, SU 12-7

PLANTATION—8000 W BROWARD BLVD (AT BROWARD MALL); 954.472.2500; M-SA 10-9, SU 11-6; MALL PARKING

Macy's
★★★⯪☆

❝...if your local Macy's has a maternity section, you're in luck... I bought my entire pregnancy work wardrobe at Macy's... the styles are all relatively recent and the brands are well known... you can generally find some attractive dresses at very reasonable prices on their sales rack... like other large department stores, you're bound to find something that works if you dig enough... very convenient because you can get your other shopping done at the same time... the selection isn't huge, but what they have is nice...**❞**

Casual wear ....✓ $$$ .... Prices
Business wear ....✓   **❸** .... Product availability
Intimate apparel ....✓   **❸** .... Customer service
Nursing wear..............................✗   **❸** .... Decor

WWW.MACYS.COM

CORAL SPRINGS—9129 W ATLANTIC BLVD (AT CORAL SQUARE MALL); 954.345.3300; M-SA 10-9, SU 12-6; MALL PARKING

FORT LAUDERDALE—2314 E SUNRISE BLVD (AT THE GALLERIA); 954.537.2300; M-SA 10-9, SU 12-6 ; PARKING LOT

FORT LAUDERDALE—4501 N FEDERAL HWY (AT FLORANANDA RD); 954.567.6500; M-SA 10-9, SU 12-6; PARKING LOT

POMPANO BEACH—1200 NE 23RD ST (AT POMPANO SQ); 954.786.6300; M-SA 10-9, SU 12-6; FREE PARKING

Motherhood Maternity
★★★★☆

❝...a wide variety of styles, from business to weekend wear, all at a good price... affordable and cute... everything from bras and swimsuits to work outfits... highly recommended for those who don't want to spend a fortune on maternity clothes... less fancy and pricey than their sister stores—A Pea in the Pod and Mimi Maternity... they have frequent sales, so you just need to keep dropping in—you're bound to find something good...**❞**

Casual wear ....✓ $$$ .... Prices

Business wear	✓	❹	Product availability
Intimate apparel	✓	❹	Customer service
Nursing wear	✓	❸	Décor

WWW.MOTHERHOOD.COM

CORAL SPRINGS—9469 W ATLANTIC BLVD (AT N UNIVERSITY DR);
954.755.3800; M-SA 10-9, SU 11-6

FORT LAUDERDALE—3200 N FEDERAL HWY (AT E OAKLAND PARK BLVD);
954.564.6984; M-SA 10-9, SU 11-6

HOLLYWOOD—3251 HOLLYWOOD BLVD (AT HOLLYWOOD MALL);
954.966.8812; M-SA 10-9, SU 11-6; MALL PARKING

PLANTATION—321 N UNIVERSITY DR (AT FASHION SQ MARKETPLACE);
954.382.1043; M-SA 8-9, SU 11-6

PLANTATION—8000 W BROWARD BLVD (AT BROWARD MALL); 954.476.2191;
M-SA 10-9, SU 10-6; MALL PARKING

SUNRISE—12801 W SUNRISE BLVD (AT NW 19TH ST); 954.846.2155; M-SA
10-9:30, SU 11-8

Sears ★★★☆☆

"...good place to get maternity clothes for a low price... the clearance rack always has good deals and their sales are quite frequent... not necessarily super high-quality, but if you just need them for nine months, who cares... good selection of nursing bras... I love the fact that they carry maternity wear in larger sizes—I got so tired of looking in those cutesy boutiques and then being disappointed because they didn't have my size... the only place I found maternity for plus-sized women...**"**

Casual wear	✓	$$	Prices
Business wear	✗	❸	Product availability
Intimate apparel	✓	❸	Customer service
Nursing wear	✓	❸	Decor

WWW.SEARS.COM

PEMBROKE PINES—12055 PINES BLVD (AT RTE 823); 954.438.3100; M-F 10-9, SA 10-6, SU 11-5

Target ★★★★☆

"...I was surprised at how fashionable their selection is—they carry Liz Lange and other really cute selections... the price is right—especially since you'll only be wearing these clothes for a few months... great for maternity basics—T-shirts, skirts, sweaters, even maternity bras... best of all, you can do some maternity shopping while you're shopping for other household basics... shirts for $10—you can't beat that... not the most exciting or romantic maternity shopping, but once you see the prices you'll get over it... as always, Target provides the perfectly priced solution...**"**

Casual wear	✓	$$	Prices
Business wear	✓	❸	Product availability
Intimate apparel	✓	❸	Customer service
Nursing wear	✓	❸	Decor

WWW.TARGET.COM

FORT LAUDERDALE—3200 N FEDERAL HWY (AT E OAKLAND PARK BLVD);
954.390.7992; M-SA 8-10, SU 8-9; PARKING IN FRONT OF BLDG

HOLLYWOOD—300 HOLLYWOOD MALL (AT N PARK RD); 954.963.1200; M-SA
8-10, SU 8-9; PARKING IN FRONT OF BLDG

MIRAMAR—16901 MIRAMAR PKWY (AT SW 172ND AVE); 954.435.2571; M-SA
8-10, SU 8-9; PARKING IN FRONT OF BLDG

PEMBROKE PINES—11253 PINES BLVD (AT N HIATUS RD); 954.435.3161; M-SA 8-10, SU 8-9; PARKING IN FRONT OF BLDG

PLANTATION—8201 FEDERATED W (AT W BROWARD BLVD); 954.377.0085;
M-SA 8-10, SU 8-9; PARKING IN FRONT OF BLDG

Palm Beach County

★ ★ ★ ★ ★

"lila picks"

★ Motherhood Maternity

A Pea In The Pod   ★★★★☆

"...*excellent if you are looking for stylish maternity clothes and don't mind paying for them... start here for special occasions and business wear... the decor is lovely and most of the clothes are beautiful... stylish fashion solutions, but expect to pay more than at department stores... keep your eyes open for the sale rack—the markdowns can be terrific... an upscale shop that carries everything from intimates to fancy dresses... stylish, fun and non-maternity-like...* **"**

Casual wear	✓	$$$$	Prices
Business wear	✓	❹	Product availability
Intimate apparel	✓	❹	Customer service
Nursing wear	✓	❹	Decor

WWW.APEAINTHEPOD.COM

BOCA RATON—6000 GLADES RD (AT ST ANDREWS BLVD); 561.955.1252; M-SA 10-9, SU 12-6

JCPenney   ★★★☆☆

"...*competitive prices and a surprisingly cute selection... they carry bigger sizes that are very hard to find at other stores... much cheaper than most maternity boutiques and they always seem to have some sort of sale going on... an especially large selection of maternity jeans for plus sizes... a more conservative collection than the smaller, hipper boutiques... good for casual basics, but not much for special occasions...* **"**

Casual wear	✓	$$	Prices
Business wear	✓	❸	Product availability
Intimate apparel	✓	❸	Customer service
Nursing wear	✗	❸	Decor

WWW.JCPENNEY.COM

WELLINGTON—10308 W FOREST HILL BLVD (AT WELLINGTON EDGE BLVD); 561.333.3399; M-SA 10-9, SU 12-6; PARKING LOT

WEST PALM BEACH—1801 PALM BEACH LAKES BLVD (NEAR PALM BEACH MALL); 561.683.5710; M-SA 10-9, SU 12-6; PARKING LOT

Macy's   ★★★½☆

"...*if your local Macy's has a maternity section, you're in luck... I bought my entire pregnancy work wardrobe at Macy's... the styles are all relatively recent and the brands are well known... you can generally find some attractive dresses at very reasonable prices on their sales rack... like other large department stores, you're bound to find something that works if you dig enough... very convenient because you can get your other shopping done at the same time... the selection isn't huge, but what they have is nice...* **"**

Casual wear............................ ✓	$$$..................................Prices	
Business wear........................ ✓	❸ ....Product availability	
Intimate apparel.................... ✓	❸ ....Customer service	
Nursing wear .... ✗	❸ .... Decor	

WWW.MACYS.COM

BOCA RATON—5700 W GLADES RD (AT ST ANDREWS BLVD); 561.393.4400;
  M-SA 10-9, SU 12-6; PARKING LOT

BOYNTON BEACH—801 N CONGRESS AVE (AT BOYTON BEACH MALL);
  561.738.4200; M-SA 10-9, SU 12-6; MALL PARKING

NORTH PALM BEACH—3101 PGA BLVD (AT KEW GARDEN AVE);
  561.625.2985; M-SA 10-9, SU 12-6; FREE PARKING

Motherhood Maternity

❝...*a wide variety of styles, from business to weekend wear, all at a
good price... affordable and cute... everything from bras and swimsuits
to work outfits... highly recommended for those who don't want to
spend a fortune on maternity clothes... less fancy and pricey than their
sister stores—A Pea in the Pod and Mimi Maternity... they have
frequent sales, so you just need to keep dropping in—you're bound to
find something good...* **❞**

Casual wear............................ ✓	$$$..................................Prices	
Business wear........................ ✓	❹ ....Product availability	
Intimate apparel.................... ✓	❹ ....Customer service	
Nursing wear .... ✓	❸ .... Decor	

WWW.MOTHERHOOD.COM

BOCA RATON—6000 GLADES RD (AT TOWN CTR MALL); 561.394.3185; M-SA
  10-9, SU 12-6; MALL PARKING

BOYNTON BEACH—801 N CONGRESS AVE (AT BOYNTON BEACH MALL);
  561.736.4878; M-SA 10-9, SU 12-6; MALL PARKING

PALM BEACH GARDENS—3107 PGA BLVD (AT KEW GARDENS AVE);
  561.691.4993; M-SA 10-9, SU 12-6

WELLINGTON—10300 W FOREST HILL BLVD (AT WELLINGTON EDGE BLVD);
  561.753.6318; M-SA 10-9, SU 11-6

WEST PALM BEACH—3101 PGA BLVD (AT GARDENS MALL); 561.626.4770;
  M-SA 10-9, SU 12-6

Online

★ ★ ★ ★ ★
"lila picks"

★ breastisbest.com ★ gap.com
★ maternitymall.com ★ naissance
maternity.com

babiesrus.com ★★★★☆
"...their online store is surprisingly plentiful for maternity wear in addition to all of the baby stuff... they carry everything from Mimi Maternity to Belly Basics... easy shopping and good return policy... the price is right and the selection is really good..."

Casual wear	✓	✓	Nursing wear
Business wear	✓	✓	Intimate apparel

babycenter.com ★★★★☆
"...it's babycenter.com—of course it's good... a small but well selected maternity section... I love being able to read other people's comments before purchasing... prices are reasonable and the convenience is priceless... great customer service and easy returns..."

Casual wear	✓	✓	Nursing wear
Business wear	✗	✗	Intimate apparel

babystyle.com ★★★★☆
"...beautiful selection of maternity clothes... very trendy, fashionable styles... take advantage of their free shipping offers to keep the cost down... items generally ship quickly... I found a formal maternity outfit for a benefit dinner, bought it on sale and received it on time... a nice variety of things and they ship in a timely manner..."

Casual wear	✓	✓	Nursing wear
Business wear	✓	✓	Intimate apparel

bellablumaternity.com

Casual wear	✓	✓	Nursing wear
Business wear	✓	✓	Intimate apparel

breakoutbras.com

Casual wear	✗	✓	Nursing wear
Business wear	✗	✓	Intimate apparel

breastisbest.com ★★★★★
"...by far the best resource for purchasing good quality nursing bras online... the site is easy to use and they have an extensive online fitting guide... returns are a breeze... since they are only online you may have to try a few before you get it exactly right..."

Casual wear	✓	✓	Nursing wear
Business wear	✗	✓	Intimate apparel

childishclothing.com

Casual wear	✓	✗	Nursing wear
Business wear	✗	✗	Intimate apparel

duematernity.com ★★★★☆

"...refreshing styles... fun and hip clothing... the site is easy to navigate and use... I've ordered a bunch of clothes from them and never had a problem... everything from casual wear to fun, funky items for special occasions... prices are reasonable..."

Casual wear	✓	✓	Nursing wear
Business wear	✓	✓	Intimate apparel

evalillian.com

Casual wear	✓	✓	Nursing wear
Business wear	✓	✓	Intimate apparel

expressiva.com ★★★★☆

"...the best site for nursing clothes... prices are good and their selection is terrific... lots of selection on dressy, casual, sleep, workout and even bathing suits... if you're going to shop for maternity online then be sure not to miss this cool site... good customer service—quite prompt in answering questions about my order..."

Casual wear	✓	✓	Nursing wear
Business wear	✗	✓	Intimate apparel

gap.com ★★★★★

"...stylish maternity clothes delivered right to your doorstep... always something worth buying... the best place for functional, comfortable and affordable maternity clothes... classic styles, not too trendy... more available online than in a store... no fancy dresses but lots of casual outfits that are cheap, look good and I don't mind parting with them after my baby is born... easy to use site and deliveries are generally prompt... you can return them to any Gap store..."

Casual wear	✓	✓	Nursing wear
Business wear	✓	✓	Intimate apparel

japaneseweekend.com ★★★★☆

"...pregnancy clothes that scream 'I am proud of my pregnant body'... a must for comfy, stylish stuff... they make the best maternity pants which cradle your belly as it grows... a little expensive but I lived in their pants my entire pregnancy—I definitely got my money's worth... really nice clothing that just doesn't look and feel like your traditional pregnancy wear—I still wear a couple of the outfits (my baby is now 6 months old)..."

Casual wear	✓	✓	Nursing wear
Business wear	✓	✓	Intimate apparel

jcpenney.com ★★★☆☆

"...competitive prices and a surprisingly cute selection... they carry bigger sizes that are very hard to find at other stores... much cheaper than most maternity boutiques and they always seem to have some sort of sale going on... an especially large selection of maternity jeans for plus sizes... a more conservative collection than the smaller, hipper boutiques... good for casual basics, but not much for special occasions..."

Casual wear	✓	✓	Nursing wear
Business wear	✓	✓	Intimate apparel

lizlange.com ★★★★☆

"...well-designed and cute... the real buys on this site are definitely in the sale section... cute, hip selection of jeans, skirts, blouses and

bathing suits... their evening and dressy clothes are the best with wonderful fabrics and designs... easy and convenient online shopping... practical but not frumpy styles—their web site made my maternity shopping so easy... **"**

Casual wear ....✓	✗..............................Nursing wear	
Business wear ....✓	✗...........................Intimate apparel	

maternitymall.com ★★★★★

"...I had great luck with maternitymall.com... a large selection of vendors in all price ranges... quick and easy without having to leave my house... found everything I needed... their merchandise tends to be true to size... site is a bit hard to navigate and cluttered with ads... sale and clearance prices are fantastic... **"**

Casual wear ....✓	✓..............................Nursing wear	
Business wear ....✓	✓...........................Intimate apparel	

mommygear.com

Casual wear ....✓	✓..............................Nursing wear	
Business wear ....✗	✓...........................Intimate apparel	

momsnightout.com

"...for that fashionable-not-frumpy fancy occasion dress... beautiful store with gorgeous selection of dresses from cocktail to bridal... one on one attention... expensive but worth it... **"**

Casual wear ....✗	✗..............................Nursing wear	
Business wear ....✓	✗...........................Intimate apparel	

motherhood.com ★★★★☆

"...a wide variety of styles, from business to weekend wear—all at a good price... affordable and cute... everything from bras and swimsuits to work outfits... highly recommended for those who don't want to spend a fortune on maternity clothes... less fancy and pricey than their sister stores—A Pea in the Pod and Mimi Maternity... they have frequent sales, so you just need to keep dropping in—you're bound to find something good... **"**

Casual wear ....✓	✓..............................Nursing wear	
Business wear ....✓	✓...........................Intimate apparel	

motherwear.com ★★★★⯪

"...excellent selection of cute and practical nursing clothes at reasonable prices... sign up for their e-mail newsletter for great offers, including free shipping... top quality clothes... decent selection of hard to find plus sizes... golden return policy, you can return any item (even used!) you aren't 100% happy with... they sell the only nursing tops I could actually wear outside the house... cute styles that aren't frumpy... so easy... pricey but worth it for the quality... top notch customer service... **"**

Casual wear ....✗	✓..............................Nursing wear	
Business wear ....✗	✓...........................Intimate apparel	

naissancematernity.com ★★★★★

"...the cutest maternity clothes around... hip and funky clothes for the artsy, well-dressed mom to be... their site is easy to navigate... if you can't make it down to the actual store in LA, just go online... clothes that make you look and feel sexy... it ain't cheap but you will look marvelous and the clothes will grow with you... web site is great and their phone order service was incredible... **"**

Casual wear ....✓	✗..............................Nursing wear	
Business wear ....✓	✗...........................Intimate apparel	

nordstrom.com ★★★☆☆

❝...now that they don't carry maternity in stores anymore, this is the only way to get any maternity from Nordstrom... overpriced but nice... makes returns harder, since you have to ship everything instead of just going back to a store... they carry Cadeau, Liz Lange, Belly Basics, etc... nice stuff, not so nice prices... **❞**

Casual wear .... ✓   ✓ .... Nursing wear
Business wear ...,,,,.   .... ✓   ✓ ....Intimate apparel

oldnavy.com ★★★★☆

❝...since not all Old Navy stores carry maternity clothes, this is the easiest way to go... just like their regular clothes, the maternity selection is great for casual wear... cheap, cheap, cheap... the quality is good and the price is definitely right... frequent sales make great prices even better... **❞**

Casual wear .... ✓   ✓ .... Nursing wear
Business wear .... ✗   ✗ ....Intimate apparel

onehotmama.com ★★★★½☆

❝...you'll find many things you must have... cool and very nice clothing... they carry everything from underwear and tights to formal dresses... you can find some real bargains online... super fast shipping... also, lots of choices for nursing and get-back-in-shape wear... **❞**

Casual wear .... ✓   ✓ .... Nursing wear
Business wear .... ✓   ✓ ....Intimate apparel

showeryourbaby.com

Casual wear .... ✓   ✓ .... Nursing wear
Business wear .... ✗   ✓ ....Intimate apparel

target.com ★★★★☆

❝...lots of Liz Lange at very fair prices... the selection is great and it's so easy to shop online—we bought most of our baby gear here and I managed to slip in a couple of orders for some maternity wear too... maternity shirts for $10—where else can you find deals like that... **❞**

Casual wear .... ✓   ✓ .... Nursing wear
Business wear .... ✓   ✓ ....Intimate apparel

activities & outings

South Dade & Downtown

★★★★★

"lila picks"

- ★ Miami Children's Museum
- ★ Miami Metro Zoo
- ★ Miami Seaquarium
- ★ Parrot Jungle & Gardens

Actors' Playhouse At The Miracle

❝...children entertaining children is extraordinary... never too young for the experience... kid friendly and wonderful theater... best for age 4 and up... you can even have birthday parties here... children's programs are great, but aimed at the elementary school-aged child... camps are geared to 7 years and up... ❞

Customer service..........................❹ $$$..Prices
Age range.....................4 yrs and up
WWW.ACTORSPLAYHOUSE.ORG

MIAMI—280 MIRACLE MILE (AT SALZEDO ST); 305.444.9293; CALL FOR SCHEDULE

Barnes & Noble

❝...wonderful weekly story times for all ages and frequent author visits for older kids... lovely selection of books and the story times are fun and very well done... they have evening story times—we put our kids in their pjs and come here as a treat before bedtime... they read a story, and then usually have a little craft or related coloring project... times vary by location so give them a call... ❞

Customer service..........................❹ $ ....Prices
Age range................. 6 mths to 6 yrs
WWW.BARNESANDNOBLE.COM

CORAL GABLES—152 MIRACLE MILE (AT GALIANO ST); 305.446.4152; CALL FOR SCHEDULE

MIAMI—12405 N KENDALL DR (AT SW 122ND AVE); 305.598.7727; CALL FOR SCHEDULE

MIAMI—7710 N KENDALL DR (AT SW 77TH AVE); 305.598.7292; CALL FOR SCHEDULE

Biscayne Nature Center

❝...it's fabulous with your own private beach there... great guided tours for kids and adults... great nature center for kids with aquariums teeming with aquatic wildlife, sea turtle demonstrations, archeological

participate in our survey at

finds and more... a great beach babies program... also a unique place for a birthday party... **"**

Customer service .... **❺** $.. Prices
Age range ....6 mths and up
WWW.BISCAYNENATURECENTER.ORG

KEY BISCAYNE—6767 CRANDON BLVD (AT KEY BISCAYNE); 305.361.6767;
CHECK SCHEDULE ONLINE; PARKING AVAILABLE

Borders Books ★★★★☆

"*...very popular weekly story time held in most branches (check the web site for locations and times)... call before you go since they are very popular and get extremely crowded... kids love the unique blend of songs, stories and dancing... Mr. Hatbox's appearances are a delight to everyone (unfortunately he doesn't make appearances at all locations)... large children's section is well categorized and well priced... they make it fun for young tots to browse through the board-book section by hanging toys around the shelves... the low-key cafe is a great place to have coffee with your baby and leaf through some magazines...* **"**

Customer service .... **❹** $.. Prices
Age range .... 6 mths to 6 yrs
WWW.BORDERSSTORES.COM

MIAMI—11401 NW 12TH ST (AT FLORIDA'S TPKE S); 305.597.8866; CALL
FOR SCHEDULE

MIAMI—8811 SW 107TH AVE (AT N KENDALL DR); 305.271.7457; CALL FOR
SCHEDULE

MIAMI—9205 S DIXIE HWY (AT DADELAND BLVD); 305.665.8800; CALL FOR
SCHEDULE

Chuck E Cheese's ★★★☆☆

"*...lots of games, rides, playrooms and very greasy food... the kids can play and eat and parents can unwind a little... a good rainy day activity... the kids love the food, but it's a bit greasy for adults... always crowded and crazy—but that's half the fun... can you ever go wrong with pizza, games and singing?.. although they do have a salad bar for adults, remember, you're not going for the food—you're going because your kids will love it... just about the easiest birthday party around—just pay money and show up...* **"**

Customer service .... **❸** $$... Prices
Age range .... 12 mths to 7 yrs
WWW.CHUCKECHEESE.COM

MIAMI—18575 S DIXIE HWY (AT QUAIL ROOST DR); 305.256.3886; SU-TH 9-
10, F-SA 9-11

MIAMI—8701 SW 124TH AVE (AT N KENDALL DR); 305.270.8716; SU-TH 9-
10, F-SA 9-11; FREE PARKING

Coral Gables Venetian Pool ★★★☆☆

"*...going to this pool is like stepping back in time... it was actually created from an old coral quarry and is filled with spring water... old school Miami... kids have to be at least 3 years old to come to this pool, but it is well worth the wait... sometimes a little dirty...* **"**

Customer service .... **❸** $$$....................................... Prices
WWW.VENETIANPOOL.COM

CORAL GABLES—2701 DE SOTO BLVD (AT GRANADA); 305.460.5306; CALL
FOR SCHEDULE; FREE PARKING

Coral Gables Youth Center ★★★★☆

"*...fun place to stimulate a young mind... a full scale recreational facility with a small theater, gymnasium, teaching kitchen, fitness center, playground, and outdoor athletic fields... lots of programming for kids of all ages to partake in ...* **"**

Customer service..........................❺ $$...Prices
Age range.................... 3 yrs to 8 yrs
WWW.CORALGABLES.COM

CORAL GABLES—405 UNIVERSITY DR (AT S LE JEUME RD); 305.460.5600; M-
   F 6-10, SA 7-7; FREE PARKING

Crandon Park Family Amusement Center   ★★⯪☆☆

"...a fun beach front mini amusement park... a cool old-school carousel that my son loves to ride on... the splash fountain is always good for a couple of hours—just make sure you lather your tots up with sun block... perfect for a birthday party—you can rent the pavilion for not too much... lots of people on weekends so you have to watch where your little one runs off to... **"**

Customer service..........................❸ $$$......................................Prices
Age range.................. 6 mths and up
WWW.CO.MIAMI-DADE.FL.US

KEY BISCAYNE—4000 CRANDON BLVD (AT GRAPETREE DR); 305.361.7385;
   DAILY 10-7; PARKING LOT

Dandy Bear   ★★★☆☆

"...a party and activity center... a show, video games and baby games you play with tokens... food's not great, but it is available... kind of like Chuck E. Cheese's ... **"**

Customer service..........................❷ $$...Prices
Age range.................... 3 yrs to 8 yrs
WWW.DANDYBEAR.COM

MIAMI—13700 SW 84TH ST (AT SW 137TH AVE); 305.557.0707; M-TH 10-10,
   F 10-11 SA 9-11, SU 9-10; FREE PARKING

Gameworks   ★★★☆☆

"...huge video arcade and high tech entertainment center... better for bigger kids, but does cater somewhat to the little ones... can rent for birthday parties... **"**

Customer service..........................❸ $$$......................................Prices
Age range.................. 6 mths and up
WWW.GAMEWORKS.COM

MIAMI—5701 SUNSET DR (AT SW 57TH AVE); 305.667.4263; M-TH 11-12, F-
   SA 11-2, SU 11-11

Gold Coast Railroad Museum   ★★★★☆

"...it's great fun... we love it here... my kids love trains and they have a real narrow gauge train that they can ride, and old cars that they can go inside of... great place for little train enthusiasts!.. lots of big old trains to walk through and hands on model train area with table top train sets to play with... train rides on the weekends are great for the whole family... **"**

Customer service..........................❹ $$...Prices
WWW.GOLDCOAST-RAILROAD.ORG

MIAMI—12450 SW 152ND ST (AT BURR RD); 305.253.0063; M-F 10-4, SA-SU
   11-4; FREE PARKING

Gymboree Play & Music   ★★★★⯪

"...we've done several rounds of classes with our kids and they absolutely love it... colorful, padded environment with tons of things to climb and play on... a good indoor place to meet other families and for kids to learn how to play with each other... the equipment and play areas are generally neat and clean... an easy birthday party spot... a guaranteed nap after class... costs vary, so call before showing up... **"**

Customer service .... **❹** $$$ .... Prices
Age range .... birth to 5 yrs
WWW.GYMBOREE.COM

MIAMI—10736 NW 58TH ST (AT NW 66TH ST); 305.594.3775; CHECK
  SCHEDULE ONLINE; MALL PARKING

MIAMI—11845 S DIXIE HWY (AT SW 120TH ST); 305.232.3399; CHECK
  SCHEDULE ONLINE; MALL PARKING

Jewish Community Center   ★★★★☆

❝...programs vary from facility to facility, but most JCCs have
outstanding early childhood programs... everything from mom and me
music classes to arts and crafts for older kids... a wonderful place to
meet other parents and make new friends... class fees are cheaper (if
not free) for members, but still quite a good deal for nonmembers... a
superb resource for new families looking for fun... ❞

Customer service .... **❹** $$$ .... Prices
Age range ....3 mths and up
WWW.ALPERJCC.ORG

MIAMI—11155 SW 112TH AVE (AT KILLIAN DR); 305.271.9000; CHECK
  SCHEDULE ONLINE

Kendall Ice Arena   ★★★½☆

❝...ice skating is always a blast, especially when it's hot and muggy...
lessons were at very convenient times... learn to skate in three classes
for $30... kids have a great time and the instructor has such patience...
rooms for birthday parties... game room, too... ❞

Customer service .... **❸** $$ .... Prices
Age range .... 3 yrs and up
WWW.KENDALLICEARENA.COM

MIAMI—10355 HAMMOCKS BLVD (AT SW 104TH ST); 305.386.8288; CALL
  FOR SCHEDULE

Miami Children's Museum   ★★★★★

❝...a must for all parents with toddlers... lots of hands on experiments
and fun... give yourself at least three to four hours... good for children
of all ages—there is a toddler section with age appropriate activities...
tons of interactive exhibits... I like that everything is bilingual and that
the focus is on cultural learning... a little loud and pricey for a larger
family, but a great addition to Miami... if you can overlook the
commercialism, you'll like it... ❞

Customer service .... **❹** $$$ .... Prices
Age range .... 12 mths to 12 yrs
WWW.MIAMICHILDRENSMUSEUM.ORG

MIAMI—980 MACARTHUR CSWY (AT PARROT JUNGLE TRL); 305.373.5437;
  DAILY 10-6; PARKING LOT

Miami Duck Tours

Age range ....6 mths and up
WWW.DUCKTOURSMIAMI.COM

MIAMI—1665 WASHINGTON AVE (AT LINCOLN AVE); 305.913.1365; CHECK
  SCHEDULE ONLINE

Miami Metro Zoo   ★★★★★

❝...animals in nice surroundings... educational and child-friendly... the
feeding times, shows and petting zoo allow for up close visits with the
animals... annual membership is the best deal... the misters help you
cool off from the heat... animals seem most active in the morning... the
playground is worth a visit... indoor hands-on activities... my kids love
the monorail that travels around the park... don't forget the stroller... ❞

Customer service .... **❹** $$$ .... Prices

Age range.................. 6 mths and up

WWW.ZSF.ORG

MIAMI—12400 SW 152ND ST (AT SW 124TH AVE); 305.251.0400; DAILY 9:30-5:30; PARKING LOT AT ZOO

Miami Museum Of Science & Planetarium

"...my daughter loves to go to the wildlife center... lots of hands on exhibits at the museum, but a little too advanced for my toddler... the planetarium is always amazing no matter how old you are... my toddler didn't 'get' much of it, but loved to play with all of the knobs and activities... **"**

Customer service.........................❹ $$$..Prices

Age range................ 12 mths and up

WWW.MIAMISCI.ORG

MIAMI—3280 S MIAMI AVE (AT SE 32ND RD); 305.646.4200; DAILY 10-6

Miami Seaquarium

★★★★★

"...awesome outdoor event for the whole family... . stroller accessibility is great... special summer water features, like a water park... incredible views of a huge killer whale... our kids love the dolphin shows... easy to get around... very kid friendly... gorgeous drive to get there... pricey so if you go a lot, get the annual pass... **"**

Customer service.........................❸ $$$..Prices

Age range................ 12 mths and up

WWW.MIAMISEAQUARIUM.COM

KEY BISCAYNE—4400 RICKENBACKER CSWY (AT ARTHUR LAMB JR RD); 305.361.5705; DAILY 9:30-6; PARKING LOT BY BLDG

Monkey Jungle

"...a bit out of the way, but a neat adventure for the kids... my kids loved being able to feed the monkeys in the tin cups... I went there as a kid and it's been great to see my kids enjoy it... cool monkey shows... worth a visit... **"**

Customer service.........................❹ $$...Prices

Age range................ 12 mths and up

WWW.MONKEYJUNGLE.COM

MIAMI—14805 SW 216TH ST (AT NARANJA RD); 305.235.1611; DAILY 9:30-5

Music Together

★★★★⯨

"...the best mom and baby classes out there... music, singing, dancing—even instruments for tots to play with... liberal make-up policy, great venues, take home books, CDs and tapes which are different each semester... it's a national franchise so instructors vary and have their own style... different age groups get mixed up which makes it a good learning experience for all involved... the highlight of our week—grandma always comes along... be prepared to have your tot sing the songs at home, in the car—everywhere... **"**

Customer service.........................❹ $$$..Prices

Age range.................. 2 mths to 5 yrs

WWW.MUSICTOGETHER.COM

CORAL GABLES—305.532.2253; CALL FOR SCHEDULE

MIAMI—305.532.2253; CALL FOR SCHEDULE

My Gym Children's Fitness Center

★★★★☆

"...a wonderful gym environment for parents with babies and older tots... classes range from tiny tots to school-aged children and the staff is great about making it fun for all ages... equipment and facilities are *really neat—ropes, pulleys, swings, you name it... the kind of place your kids hate to leave... the staff's enthusiasm is contagious... great for memorable birthday parties... although it's a franchise, each gym seems to have its own individual feeling... awesome for meeting playmates and other parents...* **"**

Customer service .... **4** $$$ .... Prices
Age range .... 3 mths to 9 yrs

WWW.MY-GYM.COM

MIAMI—12588 N KENDALL DR (AT SW 127TH AVE); 305.270.0230; CHECK
  SCHEDULE ONLINE

MIAMI—15801 S DIXIE HWY (AT SW 92ND AVE); 305.235.7922; CHECK
  SCHEDULE ONLINE

MIAMI—2531 CORAL WY (AT SW 25TH AVE); 305.285.9440; CHECK
  SCHEDULE ONLINE

MIAMI—7902 NW 36TH ST (AT DORAL RD); 305.500.9688; CHECK SCHEDULE
  ONLINE

Ocaquatics Swim School ★★★★☆

"*...swimming lessons for babies, kids and grown ups... professional instructors teach in a safe environment... it can be hard to reach the instructors, but once you do, it's worth it ...* **"**

Customer service .... **1** $$ .... Prices

WWW.OCAQUATICS.COM

CORAL GABLES—12595 SW 57TH AVE (AT CAMPAMENTO AVE);
  305.476.5255; M-F 1-7, SA 9-2

Parrot Jungle & Gardens ★★★★★

"*...every kind and color of bird plus wild cats and snakes... still fun, but not what it used to be... there are lots of shows daily, but my daughter was more interested in feeding the parrots... an annual pass is worth it if you go more than once... a beautiful place... the serpentarium show has moved to this beach location as well... it gets hot so don't forget your sunscreen...* **"**

Customer service .... **4** $$$ .... Prices

WWW.PARROTJUNGLE.COM

MIAMI—1111 PARROT JUNGLE TRL (AT NE 4TH ST); 305.258.6453; CALL
  FOR SCHEDULE; FREE PARKING

Perfect Party Place, The ★★★☆☆

"*...a party events place with different themed party suites... from tea parties, to toy building, you have a range of party themes... not as perfect as the name suggests, it's a little too cramped for a good party...* **"**

Customer service .... **3** $$$ .... Prices
Age range .... 6 mths to 12 yrs

WWW.THEPERFECTPARTYPLACE.COM

MIAMI—13063 SW 112TH ST (AT SW 132ND AVE); 305.387.7477; CALL FOR
  SCHEDULE

Play N Learn At Temple Samuel ★★★★★

"*...this has been such a warm and nurturing environment for my children... be assured your children will be well taken care of here... wonderful teachers and the staff make that extra effort to really know your child ...* **"**

Customer service .... **5** $$$ .... Prices
Age range .... 16 mths to 5 yrs

MIAMI—10680 SW 113TH PL (AT SW 107TH ST); 305.271.5756; M-F 7-6;
  PARKING LOT AT SCHOOL

South Florida Preschool PTA ★★★★★

"...a fantastic organization with playgroups, support groups and outings... an outstanding group of women... it was wonderful to have a place to meet other new moms after I had my first child... a nominal fee and you get so much for it ...**"**

Customer service..........................❺ $ ....Prices

WWW.MYSCHOOLONLINE.COM/FL/SFPPTA

MIAMI—14260 OLD CUTLER RD (AT SW 142ND TER); 305.238.2161; CHECK
  SCHEDULE ONLINE

Swim Gym ★★★★★

"...fabulous instructors and classes for all ages... instructors are warm and patient and have fun with the kids... some of the best teachers in town... they have a great 'mommy and me' swim program for the little ones... from 20 months and up...**"**

Customer service..........................❺ $$$.......................................Prices

Age range................ 12 mths and up

WWW.SWIMGYM.NET

MIAMI—11155 SW 112TH AVE (AT KILLIAN DR); 305.273.1129; CHECK
  SCHEDULE ONLINE

Tumblebees Gymnastics & Dance ★★★½☆

"...a great way for kids to exercise and have fun... so many different things for kids to try... the staff are always there and generally attentive to make sure they're safe...**"**

Customer service..........................❺ $$.......................................Prices

Age range................ 12 mths to yrs

WWW.TUMBLEBEESGYMNASTICS.COM

MIAMI—6950 SW 117TH AVE (AT SUNSET DR); 305.596.2337; CHECK
  SCHEDULE ONLINE; PARKING LOT

University of Miami (Music Time) ★★★★☆

"...excellent instructors make this a fun class... classes for babies and older children... a great way to enrich you baby's and children's lives with music, movement and listening skills... highly recommended...**"**

Customer service..........................❺ $$.......................................Prices

Age range.....................birth to 8 yrs

WWW.MUSIC.MIAMI.EDU/SPPROGS/MUSICTIME.HTML

MIAMI—VARIOUS LOCATIONS; 305.284.3176; CHECK SCHEDULE ONLINE

YMCA ★★★★☆

"...most of the Ys in the area have classes and activities for kids... swimming, gym classes, dance—even play groups for the really little ones... ... some facilities are nicer than others, but in general their programs are worth checking out... prices are more than reasonable for what is offered... the best bang for your buck... they have it all—great programs that meet the needs of a diverse range of families... check out their camps during the summer and school breaks...**"**

Customer service..........................❹ $$.......................................Prices

Age range................ 3 mths and up

WWW.YMCAMIAMI.ORG

HOMESTEAD—1034 NE 8TH ST (AT HARRIS FIELD); 305.248.5189; CHECK
  SCHEDULE ONLINE

MIAMI—16649 NE 19TH AVE (AT N GLADES DR); 305.944.1944; M-F 8-5

MIAMI—2370 NW 17TH AVE (AT ALLAPATTAH-COMSTOCK PARK);
  305.635.1813; CHECK SCHEDULE ONLINE

MIAMI—401 NW 71ST ST (AT NW 4TH AVE); 305.759.3317; M-F 6:30-8, SA 9-2

MIAMI—4300 SW 58TH AVE (AT SW 42ND TER); 305.665.3513; M-F 7-9, SA-SU 10-2

MIAMI—450 SW 16TH AVE (AT SW 5TH ST); 305.643.2626; M-F 7-6

MIAMI—9355 SW 134 ST (ACROSS FROM FALLS SHOPPING CTR); 305.254.0310; CHECK SCHEDULE ONLINE

activities & outings

North Dade & Beaches

★★★★★
"lila picks"

★ Barnes & Noble
★ My Gym Children's Fitness Center

Adventurers Cove (Aventura Mall)

❝...playground geared for younger children... my kids love climbing all over the pirate ship... even though the security guard really watches the kids, I still wouldn't leave my kids alone... an easy rainy day adventure... can be pretty crowded, especially during the holidays... not the cleanest place to play, but does the trick for a quick energy release during a shopping expedition... ❞

Customer service........................**❸** $ ....Prices
Age range.....................3 yrs and up
WWW.SHOPAVENTURAMALL.COM

AVENTURA—19501 BISCAYNE BLVD (AT AVENTURA MALL); 305.935.1110; M-SA 10-9:30, SU 12-8; MALL PARKING

Baby Stars

❝...a playgroup where babies' minds and bodies are exercised... multicultural educational experience... for kids 3- 10... super party spot... play groups with gym, puppets, games, songs, bubbles and parachute... classes in English and Spanish... ❞

Customer service........................**❹** $$$$ ....Prices
Age range................. 3 mths to 6 yrs
WWW.BABY-STARS.COM

AVENTURA—3565 NE 207TH ST (AT NE 34TH AVE); 305.466.1886; CALL FOR SCHEDULE; FREE PARKING

Barnes & Noble

❝...wonderful weekly story times for all ages and frequent author visits for older kids... lovely selection of books and the story times are fun and very well done... they have evening story times—we put our kids in their pjs and come here as a treat before bedtime... they read a story, and then usually have a little craft or related coloring project... times vary by location so give them a call... ❞

Customer service........................**❹** $ ....Prices
Age range................. 6 mths to 6 yrs
WWW.BARNESANDNOBLE.COM

AVENTURA—18711 BISCAYNE BLVD (AT 187TH ST); 305.935.9770; CALL FOR SCHEDULE; PARKING LOT

Borders Books

❝...very popular weekly story time held in most branches (check the web site for locations and times)... call before you go since they are

participate in our survey at

very popular and get extremely crowded... kids love the unique blend of songs, stories and dancing... Mr. Hatbox's appearances are a delight to everyone (unfortunately he doesn't make appearances at all locations)... large children's section is well categorized and well priced... they make it fun for young tots to browse through the board-book section by hanging toys around the shelves... the low-key cafe is a great place to have coffee with your baby and leaf through some magazines... 99

Customer service .... ❹ $... Prices
Age range .... 6 mths to 6 yrs
WWW.BORDERSSTORES.COM

AVENTURA—19925 BISCAYNE BLVD (AT AVENTURA BLVD); 305.935.0027; CALL FOR SCHEDULE

activities & outings

Chuck E Cheese's ★★★☆☆

66 *...lots of games, rides, playrooms and very greasy food... the kids can play and eat and parents can unwind a little... a good rainy day activity... the kids love the food, but it's a bit greasy for adults... always crowded and crazy—but that's half the fun... can you ever go wrong with pizza, games and singing?.. although they do have a salad bar for adults, remember, you're not going for the food—you're going because your kids will love it... just about the easiest birthday party around— just pay money and show up...* 99

Customer service .... ❸ $$... Prices
Age range .... 12 mths to 7 yrs
WWW.CHUCKECHEESE.COM

NORTH MIAMI—20335 BISCAYNE BLVD (AT NE 203RD ST); 305.936.0011; SU-TH 9-10, F-SA 9-11; FREE PARKING

Fontainebleau Hilton Octopus Pool ★★★★☆

66 *...great kiddie pool at a famous hotel... there is a day fee... kids love the octopus playland featuring 'Cookie' the octopus... also a wonderful lagoon style rock grotto pool with cascading waterfalls surrounded by lush tropical greenery...* 99

Customer service .... ❺ $$$....................................... Prices
Age range .... 6 mths and up
WWW.FONTAINEBLEAU.HILTON.COM

MIAMI BEACH—4441 COLLINS AVE (AT 43RD ST); 305.538.2000; CHECK SCHEDULE ONLINE

Gym Kidz ★★★⯪☆

66 *...movement classes for infants and up that stimulate and energize... great facility for gym lessons... also a nice spot for a birthday party...* 99

Customer service .... ❺ $$$....................................... Prices
Age range .... 12 mths and up
WWW.GYMKIDZMIAMI.COM

NORTH MIAMI BEACH—2038 NE 155TH ST (AT W DIXIE HWY); 305.944.4277; CHECK SCHEDULE ONLINE

Gymboree Play & Music ★★★★⯪

66 *...we've done several rounds of classes with our kids and they absolutely love it... colorful, padded environment with tons of things to climb and play on... a good indoor place to meet other families and for kids to learn how to play with each other... the equipment and play areas are generally neat and clean... an easy birthday party spot... a guaranteed nap after class... costs vary, so call before showing up...* 99

Customer service .... ❹ $$$....................................... Prices
Age range .... birth to 5 yrs
WWW.GYMBOREE.COM

NORTH MIAMI BEACH—3617 NE 163 ST (AT NE 35TH AVE); 305.919.9639;
  CHECK SCHEDULE ONLINE; MALL PARKING

Haulover Park

"...beautiful beach with picnic areas and bike path... take a walk on
the pier to check out the fishing boats... take the kids to the oceanfront
fire house here where the staff is so friendly and they always have time
for a tour Take the kids to an oceanfront fire house... the firemen and
women are so friendly and always have time for a tour of the facility...
no pole, but lots of other fun stuff.... **"**

Customer service..........................❺ $ ....Prices
Age range.................. 6 mths and up

WWW.MIAMIDADE.GOV/PARKS/PARKS/HAULOVER_PARK.ASP

MIAMI BEACH—10800 COLLINS AVE (OFF BAYVIEW DR); 305.944.3040;
  SUNRISE TO SUNSET

J Houston Gribble Pool

"...awesome for the whole family... baby pool and big kids pool,
slides, tunnel, water spouts etc... great place for a birthday party... you
can reserve the whole kiddie area to yourself Sunday mornings... nice
setting, but little supervision so stay VERY close to your little ones... **"**

Customer service..........................❹ $$...Prices
Age range.................. 2 yrs to 12 yrs

WWW.NORTHMIAMIFL.GOV

NORTH MIAMI—13150 NE 8TH AVE (AT NE 132ND ST); 305.891.7727; CALL
  FOR SCHEDULE; FREE PARKING

Jewish Community Center

"...programs vary from facility to facility, but most JCCs have
outstanding early childhood programs... everything from mom and me
music classes to arts and crafts for older kids... a wonderful place to
meet other parents and make new friends... class fees are cheaper (if
not free) for members, but still quite a good deal for nonmembers... a
superb resource for new families looking for fun... **"**

Customer service..........................❹ $$$......................................Prices
Age range.................. 3 mths and up

WWW.JEWISHMIAMI.ORG

MIAMI BEACH—4221 PINE TREE DR (AT W 42ND ST); 305.534.3206; M-TH
  8:30-5, F 8:30-4

NORTH MIAMI BEACH—18900 NE 25TH AVE (AT NE MIAMI GARDENS DR);
  305.534.3206; CALL FOR SCHEDULE

Miss Nava & Company (Mommy & Me)

"...a fun and educational 'mommy and me' program for babies and
toddlers... fun, energetic and captivating... classes are made up of free
play, circle time, story time, art time and a snack... a large space with
great equipment... each week has a theme... classes are about an
hour... small classes for extra attention... **"**

Customer service..........................❺ $$...Prices
Age range.................. 3 mths to 3 yrs

WWW.MISSNAVA.COM

MIAMI BEACH—7445 CARLYLE AVE (AT 74TH ST); 305.761.8205; CHECK
  SCHEDULE ONLINE

Miss Nava & Company (Swim Instruction)

"...Miss Nava taught my 3 year old daughter to swim through gentle and effective training... my child had fun and after 6 lessons she was swimming like a fish... classes in English and Spanish... **"**

Customer service .... ❺ $.. Prices

Age range .... 3 mths to 3 yrs

WWW.MISSNAVA.COM

AVENTURA—2790 NE 201 TERRACE (AT NE 27TH CT); 305.761.8205; CALL FOR APPT

Museum Of Contemporary Art (moca)

"...adult museum with programs for kids on some weekends... nice museum to stroll with your baby... kids programs include giant puppets and cultural music... **"**

Customer service .... ❹ $.. Prices

WWW.MOCA.COM

NORTH MIAMI—770 NE 125TH ST (AT NE 8TH AVE); 305.893.6211; T-SA 11-5; FREE PARKING

My Gym Children's Fitness Center

"...a wonderful gym environment for parents with babies and older tots... classes range from tiny tots to school-aged children and the staff is great about making it fun for all ages... equipment and facilities are really neat—ropes, pulleys, swings, you name it... the kind of place your kids hate to leave... the staff's enthusiasm is contagious... great for memorable birthday parties... although it's a franchise, each gym seems to have its own individual feeling... awesome for meeting playmates and other parents... **"**

Customer service .... ❹ $$$ .... Prices

Age range .... 3 mths to 9 yrs

WWW.MY-GYM.COM

AVENTURA—17881 BISCAYNE BLVD (AT POINT EAST DR); 305.933.0496; CHECK SCHEDULE ONLINE; FREE PARKING

Peaches School Of Dance

"...the best place for kid's dance lessons... from 5 up... easy drop off and pick up... aerobics, dance and drama... an all around after school place... **"**

Customer service .... ❹ $$ .... Prices

Age range .... 5 yrs and up

WWW.PEACHESSCHOOLOFDANCE.COM

NORTH MIAMI BEACH—16390 NE 26TH AVE (AT SUNNY ISLES BLVD); 305.940.3248; M-TH 3-9, F 3-8

Sans Souci Tennis Center

Age range .... 4 yrs and up

WWW.NORTHMIAMIFL.GOV

NORTH MIAMI—1795 SANS SOUCI BLVD (AT NE 18TH AVE); 305.893.7130; M-F 8-10, SA-SU 8-8

Temple Beth Sholom

Age range .... 20 mths to 5 yrs

WWW.TBSMB.ORG

MIAMI BEACH—4144 CHASE AVE (AT ARTHUR GODFREY RD); 305.538.7231; CHECK SCHEDULE ONLINE

YMCA

"...most of the Ys in the area have classes and activities for kids... swimming, gym classes, dance—even play groups for the really little ones... ... some facilities are nicer than others, but in general their programs are worth checking out... prices are more than reasonable for what is offered... the best bang for your buck... they have it all—great programs that meet the needs of a diverse range of families... check out their camps during the summer and school breaks... **"**

Customer service.........................❹ $$..Prices

Age range..................3 mths and up

WWW.YMCAMIAMI.ORG

HIALEAH—500 W 49TH ST (AT RED RD); 305.825.9622; CALL FOR SCHEDULE

participate in our survey at

Broward County

★★★★★
"lila picks"

★ Butterfly World
★ Mailman Segal Institute
★ Museum Of Discovery & Science
★ Young At Art Children's Museum

Amanda's Place

"...one of the best kept secrets in Broward County... each class has creative activities for children and moms—crafts, singing, dancing, free play and group discussion... terrific for newborns on up... also a great place to meet other moms whose kids are at the same stage as yours... you can't beat the price for meeting twice a week... **"**

Customer service .... **5** $ .... Prices
Age range .... 3 mths to 3 yrs
WWW.AMANDASPLACE.ORG

POMPANO BEACH—1400 NE 4TH ST (AT NE 13TH AVE); 954.786.7618; CALL FOR SCHEDULE

Barnes & Noble

"...wonderful weekly story times for all ages and frequent author visits for older kids... lovely selection of books and the story times are fun and very well done... they have evening story times—we put our kids in their pjs and come here as a treat before bedtime... they read a story, and then usually have a little craft or related coloring project... times vary by location so give them a call... **"**

Customer service .... **4** $ .... Prices
Age range .... 6 mths to 6 yrs
WWW.BARNESANDNOBLE.COM

CORAL SPRINGS—2790 UNIVERSITY DR (AT NW 28TH ST); 954.344.6291; CALL FOR SCHEDULE

FORT LAUDERDALE—2051 N FEDERAL HWY (AT NE 21ST ST); 954.561.3732; CALL FOR SCHEDULE

HOLLYWOOD—4170 OAKWOOD BLVD (AT OAKWOOD BLVD); 954.923.1738; CALL FOR SCHEDULE

PEMBROKE PINES—11820 PINES BLVD (AT PEMBROKE LAKES MALL); 954.441.0444; CALL FOR SCHEDULE

PLANTATION—591 S UNIVERSITY DR (AT SW 6TH ST); 954.723.0489; CALL FOR SCHEDULE

Batten's Strawberry Farm

"...a nice market with fresh produce and a 'pick-your-own strawberries' patch... kids love to look at and pet the friendly animals kept in clean pens... . a wonderful place... strawberries for an *unbeatable price... great strawberry shakes... no admission, just show up and pick... call to make sure they are open first ...* **"**

Customer service..................... ..**❹** $ .... Prices

DAVIE—5151 SW 64TH AVE (AT SW 49TH ST); 954.792.0068; DAILY 8-6

Borders Books ★★★★☆

"...*very popular weekly story time hold in most branches (check the web site for locations and times)... call before you go since they are very popular and get extremely crowded... kids love the unique blend of songs, stories and dancing... Mr. Hatbox's appearances are a delight to everyone (unfortunately he doesn't make appearances at all locations)... large children's section is well categorized and well priced... they make it fun for young tots to browse through the board-book section by hanging toys around the shelves... the low-key cafe is a great place to have coffee with your baby and leaf through some magazines...* **"**

Customer service........................**❹** $ .... Prices

Age range................. 6 mths to 6 yrs

WWW.BORDERSSTORES.COM

CORAL SPRINGS—700 UNIVERSITY DR (AT W ATLANTIC BLVD); 954.340.3307; CALL FOR SCHEDULE

FORT LAUDERDALE—2240 E SUNRISE BLVD (AT BAYVIEW DR); 954.566.6335; CALL FOR SCHEDULE

PLANTATION—12171 W SUNRISE BLVD (AT N FLAMINGO RD); 954.723.9595; CALL FOR SCHEDULE

British Swim School ★★★★☆

"...*swim lessons for infants, toddlers, kids and adults... heated and indoor pools make it nice for my baby and me... they can even teach 6-month-old's water survival skills... a necessary service and the instructors do a wonderful job at keeping it fun...* **"**

Customer service........................**❹** $$... Prices

Age range.................. 3 mths and up

WWW.BRITISHSWIMSCHOOL.COM

COCONUT CREEK—4500 W SAMPLE RD (AT LYONS RD); 954.747.7251; CALL FOR SCHEDULE

PEMBROKE PINES—6861 SW 196 AVE (AT SHERIDAN ST); 954.747.7251; CALL FOR SCHEDULE

SUNRISE—2084 N UNIVERSITY DR (AT W SUNRISE BLVD); 954.747.7251; CALL FOR SCHEDULE; FREE PARKING

Build-A-Bear Workshop ★★★⯪☆

"...*design and make your own bear—it's a dream come true... the most cherished toy my daughter owns... they even come with birth certificates... the staff is fun and knows how to play along with the kids' excitement... the basic stuffed animal is only about $15, but the extras add up quickly... great for field trips, birthdays and special occasions... how darling—my nephew is 8 years old now, and still sleeps with his favorite bear...* **"**

Customer service........................**❹** $$$... Prices

Age range.................... 3 yrs and up

WWW.BUILDABEAR.COM

CORAL SPRINGS—9581 W ATLANTIC BLVD (AT N UNIVERSITY DR); 954.575.0500; M-SA 10-9, SU 11-7

Butterfly World ★★★★★

"...*an excellent environment for all ages to relax, listen to music and watch thousands of flying beautiful butterflies... I love to sit with my baby and just watch nature unfold... pricey, but an annual pass pays for itself after 2 visits... the hummingbirds, lorikeets, goldfish ponds and*

exotic flowers are just as exciting as the butterflies... staff is extremely friendly and knowledgeable... it's nice that you can move around freely and stay as long as you like... **"**

Customer service .... ❹ $$$ .... Prices
Age range ....6 mths and up

WWW.BUTTERFLYWORLD.COM

COCONUT CREEK—3600 W SAMPLE RD (AT TRADEWINDS PARK); 954.977.4400; M-SA 9-5, SU 1-5; FREE PARKING

Castaway Island ★★★★☆

"*...great for cooling off during the summertime... small enough to keep your children under control... bring a cooler with some snacks and beverages... a wonderful place for kids of all ages... the best waterpark in Broward... great, fun, and easy on the wallet too!.. pools for the babies and the older kids...* **"**

Customer service .... ❹ $$ .... Prices
Age range ....6 mths and up

HOLLYWOOD—3300 N PARK RD (AT TOPEEKEEGEE YUGNEE PARK); 954.985.1980; CHECK SCHEDULE ONLINE

Champion Gymnastics ★★★⯨☆

"*...one of the best equipped facilities in town... . classes for walking toddlers and older... fun birthday party rental... lots of incredibly talented kids practicing—we love to just hang out and watch...* **"**

Customer service .... ❹ $ .... Prices
Age range ....18 mths and up

WWW.CHAMPIONGYMNASTICS.BIZ

CORAL SPRINGS—8030 W SAMPLE RD (AT RIVERSIDE DR); 954.341.3547; CALL FOR SCHEDULE

Chuck E Cheese's ★★★☆☆

"*...lots of games, rides, playrooms and very greasy food... the kids can play and eat and parents can unwind a little... a good rainy day activity... the kids love the food, but it's a bit greasy for adults... always crowded and crazy—but that's half the fun... can you ever go wrong with pizza, games and singing?.. although they do have a salad bar for adults, remember, you're not going for the food—you're going because your kids will love it... just about the easiest birthday party around— just pay money and show up...* **"**

Customer service .... ❸ $$ .... Prices
Age range .... 12 mths to 7 yrs

WWW.CHUCKECHEESE.COM

PEMBROKE PINES—8515 PINES BLVD (AT N DOUGLAS RD); 954.437.8178; SU-TH 9-10, F-SA 9-11; PARKING LOT

SUNRISE—8099 W OAKLAND PARK BLVD (AT N UNIVERSITY DR); 954.741.4099; SU-TH 9-10, F-SA 9-11; FREE PARKING

Flamingo Gardens ★★★★☆

"*...if you're looking for a fun outdoor adventure, then this is a fabulous outing for the entire family... a nice variety of animal for the kids to see... loaded with trees so it stays cool even in the summer... the setting is beautiful and very relaxing... my kids love the tram ride— just be sure to check the schedule before going... strolling under the spectacular champion trees is pleasant, no matter the season... great place to teach children about respecting nature...* **"**

Customer service .... ❹ $$$ .... Prices
Age range .... 12 mths and up

WWW.FLAMINGOGARDENS.ORG

DAVIE—3750 S FLAMINGO RD (AT SW 36TH CT); 954.473.2955; CHECK SCHEDULE ONLINE; PARKING LOT AT MAIN ENTRANCE

Gymboree Play & Music ★★★★⯪

"...we've done several rounds of classes with our kids and they absolutely love it... colorful, padded environment with tons of things to climb and play on... a good indoor place to meet other families and for kids to learn how to play with each other... the equipment and play areas are generally neat and clean... an easy birthday party spot... a guaranteed nap after class, costs vary, so call before showing up... **"**

Customer service.......................❹ $$$.......................................Prices
Age range.....................birth to 5 yrs
WWW.GYMBOREE.COM

COCONUT CREEK—4661 JOHNSON RD (AT LOYNS DR); 954.655.6987; CHECK SCHEDULE ONLINE

PEMBROKE PINES—11401 PINES BLVD (AT PEMBROKE LAKES MALL); 954.430.0180; CHECK SCHEDULE ONLINE; MALL PARKING

Holiday Park Activity Center ★★★☆☆

"...lots of different gymnastics programs for all ages—you're bound to find something that works for you... the open gym for toddlers is wonderful—they give you access to the entire gym for one hour out of the week... **"**

Customer service.......................❹ $$$.......................................Prices
Age range................ 18 mths and up
CI.FTLAUD.FL.US/CITYPARKS/HOLIDAY

FORT LAUDERDALE—800 N FEDERAL HWY (AT NE 8TH AVE); 954.761.5385; CALL FOR SCHEDULE

Infant & Young Child Survival Swimming

Age range.................. 3 mths and up
WWW.INFANTSURVIVALSWIMMING.COM

PLANTATION—9151 NW 2ND STR (AT CENTRAL PARK DR); 954.584.5884; CALL FOR SCHEDULE; FREE PARKING

Jack Nelson's Aquatots ★★★★⯪

"...my daughter started swimming here at 4 months and she loves the water... wonderful instruction... one of the best swim schools in the area... gentle and encouraging approach... **"**

Customer service.......................❺ $$$.......................................Prices
WWW.JNSS.NET

FORT LAUDERDALE—503 SEABREEZE BLVD (AT HALL OF FAME DR); 954.764.4822; CHECK SCHEDULE ONLINE; FREE PARKING

Jewish Community Center ★★★★☆

"...programs vary from facility to facility, but most JCCs have outstanding early childhood programs... everything from mom and me music classes to arts and crafts for older kids... a wonderful place to meet other parents and make new friends... class fees are cheaper (if not free) for members, but still quite a good deal for nonmembers... a superb resource for new families looking for fun... **"**

Customer service.......................❹ $$$.......................................Prices
Age range.................. 3 mths and up
WWW.SOREFJCC.ORG

CORAL SPRINGS—748 RIVERSIDE DR (AT RAMBLEWOOD DR); 954.344.6790; CALL FOR SCHEDULE

DAVIE—5850 S PINE ISLAND RD (AT STIRLING RD); 954.434.0499; CALL FOR SCHEDULE

PLANTATION—6501 W SUNRISE BLVD (AT 65TH AVE); 954.792.6700; CALL FOR SCHEDULE

Little Gym, The

"...a well thought-out program of gym and tumbling geared toward different age groups... a clean facility, excellent and knowledgeable staff... we love the small-sized gym equipment and their willingness to work with kids with special needs... activities are fun and personalized to match the kids' age... great place for birthday parties with a nice party room—they'll organize and do everything for you... **"**

Customer service .... ❹ $$$ .... Prices
Age range .... 4 mths to 12 yrs

WWW.THELITTLEGYM.COM

CORAL SPRINGS—10359 ROYAL PALM BLVD (AT CORAL SPRINGS DR); 954.344.9475; CALL FOR SCHEDULE; FREE PARKING

PLANTATION—1927 N PINE ISLAND RD (AT W SUNRISE BLVD); 954.916.9525; CALL FOR SCHEDULE

Mailman Segal Institute

"...amazing mommy and me classes along with a variety of music... huge selection of classes and a state of the art facility to boot... teachers are active and animated... you can start at 6 weeks... the new facility is beyond compare... lots of support and information for new parents... very creative and super stimulating for both parents and kids... **"**

Customer service .... ❹ $$$$ .... Prices
Age range .... 3 mths to 12 yrs

WWW.NOVA.EDU/MSI/PPLACE

FORT LAUDERDALE—3301 COLLEGE AVE (AT SW 30TH ST); 954.262.6900; CHECK SCHEDULE ONLINE

Museum Of Discovery & Science

"...learn about the Florida eco system, space exploration and wander through the changing exhibits... lots of special, engaging, hands-on exhibits... fun mixed with learning... highlights include space exhibits and the IMAX theater... very knowledgeable staff... a very stimulating place to be... birthday parties with cool themes... **"**

Customer service .... ❹ $$ .... Prices
Age range .... 2 yrs and up

WWW.MODS.ORG

FORT LAUDERDALE—401 SW 2ND ST (AT SW 4TH AVE); 954.467.6637; M-SA 10-5, SU 12-6 ; ARTS & ENTERTAINMENT PARKING GARAGE

Music Together

"...the best mom and baby classes out there... music, singing, dancing—even instruments for tots to play with... liberal make-up policy, great venues, take home books, CDs and tapes which are different each semester... it's a national franchise so instructors vary and have their own style... different age groups get mixed up which makes it a good learning experience for all involved... the highlight of our week—grandma always comes along... be prepared to have your tot sing the songs at home, in the car—everywhere... **"**

Customer service .... ❹ $$$ .... Prices
Age range .... 2 mths to 5 yrs

WWW.MUSICTOGETHER.COM

WESTON—954.217.6446; CALL FOR SCHEDULE

My Gym Children's Fitness Center

"...a wonderful gym environment for parents with babies and older tots... classes range from tiny tots to school-aged children and the staff *is great about making it fun for all ages... equipment and facilities are really neat—ropes, pulleys, swings, you name it... the kind of place your kids hate to leave... the staff's enthusiasm is contagious... great for memorable birthday parties... although it's a franchise, each gym seems to have its own individual feeling... awesome for meeting playmates and other parents...* **99**

Customer service.........................**4** $$$..................,,.   .... Prices
Age range................. 3 mths to 9 yrs
WWW.MY-GYM.COM

CORAL SPRINGS—4647 UNIVERSITY DR (AT WILES RD); 954.341.1853; CHECK SCHEDULE ONLINE

PEMBROKE PINES—954.441.6688; CHECK SCHEDULE ONLINE

PLANTATION—954.382.0222; CHECK SCHEDULE ONLINE; FREE PARKING

POMPANO BEACH—407 S FEDERAL HWY (AT POMPANO BEACH CEMETERY); 954.946.6838; CHECK SCHEDULE ONLINE

Park Avenue Gymnastics

"...a gymnastics gym with classes for children 24 months and up... they're flexible on the 24 months so if your child is close to that age, you may be able to join the mom and tot class anyway... a well-structured environment that will help your little one learn discipline and how to follow rules while still having fun... **99**

Customer service.........................**4** $$$$.....................................Prices
Age range.....................2 yrs and up
WWW.PARKAVENUEGYMNASTICS.COM

COOPER CITY—12239 SW 53RD ST (AT SW 122ND DR); 954.434.0099; CHECK SCHEDULE ONLINE; FREE PARKING

WESTON—2750 GLADES CIRCLE (AT ARVIDA PKWY); 954.659.8717; CHECK SCHEDULE ONLINE; FREE PARKING

Stella's Dancers' Studio

Age range.....................2 yrs and up
WWW.STELLASDANCERS.COM

COOPER CITY—9470 GRIFFIN RD (AT SW 100TH AVE); 954.434.8401; CHECK SCHEDULE ONLINE

Tag Gymnastics

"...we have attended several preschool sessions at this gym and my kids love it... the teachers are goodhearted... not a ton of structure more of a free flow class... the open gym is good for the little ones, but can get a little too crowded... **99**

Customer service.........................**3** $$$...Prices
Age range................ 18 mths and up
WWW.TAGGYMNASTICS.COM

WESTON—15851 SW 41ST ST (AT WESTON RD); 954.384.9393; CHECK SCHEDULE ONLINE

Ty Park

"...fun water park for kids of all ages... great park... a favorite in the area... a wonderful cool-off in the summer... the lagoon with the freshwater beach is a must for the babies... lots of activities here... **99**

Customer service.........................**4** $ ....,,.   .... Prices
Age range................. 6 mths and up
WWW.SOUTHFLORIDA.COM/ATTRACTIONS/18529,0,1439043.VENUE

HOLLYWOOD—3300 N PARK RD (AT N35TH AVE); 954.985.1980; PARK HRS: 6:30AM-6PM WINTER, 6:30AM-7:30PM SUMMER; OFC HRS: 8:30-6:30

participate in our survey at

Wannado City

"...a one-of-a-kind dress-up theme park... a bit expensive, but a really great experience for kids three and up... unbelievable how much there is to do, you could easily spend an entire day there without ever getting bored... don't go if you have young kids, they will not let you stay with your children... kids can 'be' whatever they want—a wonderful place for imaginative play... **"**

Customer service .... ❸ $$$$ .... Prices
Age range .... 2 yrs and up
WWW.WANNADOCITY.COM
SUNRISE—12801 W SUNRISE BLVD (AT SATIN LEAF WAY); 954.838.7100;
   CHECK SCHEDULE ONLINE

Way To Play

"...children's learning and activity center designed just for the little ones... classes from 6 months to 6 years... the equipment is nice and just the right size... a must stop 'mommy and me' activity in the Weston area... **"**

Customer service .... ❹ $$$ .... Prices
Age range .... 6 mths to 6 yrs
WWW.WAY2PLAY.NET
SUNRISE—1392 SW 160TH AVE (AT INDIAN TRACE CTR); 954.515.0161;
   DAILY 9-5

Young At Art Children's Museum

"...an absolute must for any family with kids from toddler age up to 10 years old... the weekly music classes are wonderful... a gem... everything is hands on, a wonderful staff, a toy store to die for, art classes for children, daily special activities free with admission... exhibits instill cultural and environmental awareness and teach values... only $5 to get in and you can stay all day... **"**

Customer service .... ❹ $$ .... Prices
Age range .... 2 yrs to 10 yrs
WWW.YOUNGATARTMUSEUM.ORG
DAVIE—11584 W STATE RD 84 (AT SW 119TH WAY); 954.424.0085; M-SA 10-
   5, SU 12-5

activities & outings

Palm Beach County

★★★★★
"lila picks"

★ Children's Museum

★ Palm Beach Zoo

★ Schoolhouse Children's Museum

Barnes & Noble   ★★★★⯪

"...wonderful weekly story times for all ages and frequent author visits for older kids... lovely selection of books and the story times are fun and very well done... they have evening story times—we put our kids in their pjs and come here as a treat before bedtime... they read a story, and then usually have a little craft or related coloring project... times vary by location so give them a call... **"**

Customer service........................ **4** $ .... Prices

Age range................. 6 mths to 6 yrs

WWW.BARNESANDNOBLE.COM

BOCA RATON—1400 GLADES RD (AT BROWARD AVE AT FLORIDA ATLANTIC UNIV); 561.750.2134; CALL FOR SCHEDULE

Boomer's Family Recreation
Center   ★★★★⯪

"...great for parties... fun outdoor activities... we love the mini golf, bumper boats and the laser tag... it does get a bit loud in the arcade... amazing arcade with go-carts, roller coaster, batting cages, bumper cars etc. better for the older kids... **"**

Customer service........................ **3** $$.. Prices

Age range................. 6 mths and up

WWW.BOOMERSPARKS.COM

BOCA RATON—3100 AIRPORT RD (AT BOCA RATON AIRPORT); 561.347.1888; CHECK SCHEDULE ONLINE; FREE PARKING

Borders Books   ★★★★☆

"...very popular weekly story time held in most branches (check the web site for locations and times)... call before you go since they are very popular and get extremely crowded... kids love the unique blend of songs, stories and dancing... Mr. Hatbox's appearances are a delight to everyone (unfortunately he doesn't make appearances at all locations)... large children's section is well categorized and well priced... they make it fun for young tots to browse through the board-book section by hanging toys around the shelves... the low-key cafe is a great place to have coffee with your baby and leaf through some magazines... **"**

Customer service........................ **4** $ .... Prices

Age range................. 6 mths to 6 yrs

WWW.BORDERSSTORES.COM

BOCA RATON—9887 GLADES RD (AT HWY 7 & CAROUSEL CIR); 561.883.5854; CALL FOR SCHEDULE

BOYNTON BEACH—525 N CONGRESS AVE (AT OLD BOYNTON RD); 561.734.2021; CALL FOR SCHEDULE

WEST PALM BEACH—1801 PALM BEACH LAKES BLVD (AT W EXECUTIVE CTR DR); 561.689.4112; CALL FOR SCHEDULE

British Swim School

"...swim lessons for infants, toddlers, kids and adults... heated and indoor pools make it nice for my baby and me... they can even teach 6-month-old's water survival skills... a necessary service and the instructors do a wonderful job at keeping it fun... **"**

Customer service .... ❹ $$ .... Prices
Age range ....3 mths and up
WWW.BRITISHSWIMSCHOOL.COM

WELLINGTON—3141 FORTUNE WAY; 954.747.7251; CALL FOR SCHEDULE

Build-A-Bear Workshop

"...design and make your own bear—it's a dream come true... the most cherished toy my daughter owns... they even come with birth certificates... the staff is fun and knows how to play along with the kids' excitement... the basic stuffed animal is only about $15, but the extras add up quickly... great for field trips, birthdays and special occasions... how darling—my nephew is 8 years old now, and still sleeps with his favorite bear... **"**

Customer service .... ❹ $$$ .... Prices
Age range .... 3 yrs and up
WWW.BUILDABEAR.COM

PALM BEACH GARDENS—3101 PGA BLVD (AT GARDENS OF THE PALM BEACHES); 561.630.7734; M-SA 10-9, SU 12-6

Calypso Bay Water Park

"...a great inexpensive way to spend a hot, summer day... pools and water park complete with water slides and play area... swim lessons for the kids... a great place to rent for birthday parties... picnic tables and a concession stand make it a perfect day out... **"**

Customer service .... ❺ $ .... Prices
Age range ....3 mths and up
WWW.PBCGOV.COM/PARKS/WATERPARKS/CALYPSO.HTM

ROYAL PALM BEACH—151 LAMSTEIN LN (AT SEMINOLE PALMS PARK); 561.790.6160

Children's Museum

"...great little museum... we enjoyed that the kids could play in the general store room and multicultural room... real hands-on place for exploring science, culture, art & history... great historic home setting... intimate surroundings... lovely place... **"**

Customer service .... ❹ $$ .... Prices
Age range .... 2 yrs and up
WWW.CMBOCA.ORG

BOCA RATON—498 CRAWFORD BLVD (AT 4TH DIAGONAL); 561.368.6875; T-SA 12-4; FREE PARKING

Chuck E Cheese's

"...lots of games, rides, playrooms and very greasy food... the kids can play and eat and parents can unwind a little... a good rainy day activity... the kids love the food, but it's a bit greasy for adults... always crowded and crazy—but that's half the fun... can you ever go wrong with pizza, games and singing?.. although they do have a salad bar for adults, remember, you're not going for the food—you're going because *your kids will love it... just about the easiest birthday party around— just pay money and show up...* **"**

Customer service........................**❸** $$........................... Prices
Age range................12 mths to 7 yrs

WWW.CHUCKECHEESE.COM

BOCA RATON—21697-A STATE RD 7 (AT W PALMETTO PARK RD); 561.487.7645; SU-TH 9-10, F-SA 9-11; FREE PARKING

WEST PALM BEACH—4646 OKEECHOBEE BLVD (AT N MILITARY TRL); 561.478.9372; SU-TH 9-10, F-SA 9-11

Cityplace   ★★★☆☆

"...*a great place to take kids on a warm day to stroll around... they can cool off with some gelato or go to Barnes and Noble and play with their trains and read books... the fountains located in the center are always mesmerizing to babies and toddlers, and there is usually live music in the plaza on the weekends...* **"**

Customer service........................**❸** $$$........................ Prices
Age range.................. 3 mths and up

WWW.CITYPLACE.COM

WEST PALM BEACH—700 S ROSEMARY AVE (AT HIBISCUS ST); 561.366.1000

Coconut Cove Waterpark   ★★★⯪☆

"...*my children love this water park, especially the younger ones... a little pricey for what is there, but still makes for a fun family event... better for small children... big water slide for the bigger kids, lazy river with tires and a water playground... food court is available with reasonable prices... infants free... sometimes long lines...* **"**

Customer service........................**❸** $$$........................ Prices
Age range.................. 3 mths and up

WWW.PBCGOV.COM/PARKS/WATERPARKS/COCONUT.HTM

BOCA RATON—11200 PARK ACCESS RD (AT CAIN BLVD); 561.274.1140; CALL FOR SCHEDULE; FREE PARKING

Gymboree Play & Music   ★★★★⯪

"...*we've done several rounds of classes with our kids and they absolutely love it... colorful, padded environment with tons of things to climb and play on... a good indoor place to meet other families and for kids to learn how to play with each other... the equipment and play areas are generally neat and clean... an easy birthday party spot... a guaranteed nap after class... costs vary, so call before showing up...* **"**

Customer service........................**❹** $$$........................ Prices
Age range.....................birth to 5 yrs

WWW.GYMBOREE.COM

BOCA RATON—2104 N FEDERAL HWY (AT NE 20TH ST); 561.392.6658; CHECK SCHEDULE ONLINE

GREENACRES—6611 FOREST HILL BLVD (AT JOG RD); 561.966.5805; CHECK SCHEDULE ONLINE

Jewish Community Center   ★★★★☆

"...*programs vary from facility to facility, but most JCCs have outstanding early childhood programs... everything from mom and me music classes to arts and crafts for older kids... a wonderful place to meet other parents and make new friends... class fees are cheaper (if not free) for members, but still quite a good deal for nonmembers... a superb resource for new families looking for fun...* **"**

Customer service........................**❹** $$$........................ Prices
Age range.................. 3 mths and up

WWW.LEVISJCC.ORG

participate in our survey at

BOCA RATON—9801 DONNA KLEIN BLVD (BY W BOCA MEDICAL CTR);
561.852.3200; CALL FOR SCHEDULE

BOYNTON BEACH—8500 JOG RD (OFF GATEWAY BLVD); 561.740.9000; CALL
FOR SCHEDULE

WEST PALM BEACH—3151 N MILITARY TRL (OFF COMMUNITY DR);
561.689.7700; CALL FOR SCHEDULE

Lake Lytal Pool

"...*lap pool and children's swimming pool... water playground and water slides for the older kids... a break from the summer heat that is nicely maintained... a good family day...* **"**

Customer service .... ❸ $$$ .... Prices
Age range ....6 mths and up

WWW.CO.PALM-BEACH.FL.US/PARKS/LOCATIONS/NORTH/LAKELYTAL.HTM

WEST PALM BEACH—3645 GUN CLUB RD (AT LANDES DR); 561.233.1426;
CHECK SCHEDULE ONLINE

Lion Country Safari

"...*a drive-through cageless zoo where your babies will very well see their first lion, tiger or bear... even the infants will love the petting zoo with Pygmy goats, sheep, and pot-bellied pigs... I went there as a child and now I take my own kids... play areas, a carousel, mini golf, the train and boat ride make it a family day adventure...* **"**

Customer service .... ❸ $$$ .... Prices
Age range .... 2 yrs and up

WWW.LIONCOUNTRYSAFARI.COM

LOXAHATCHEE—2003 LION COUNTRY SAFARI RD (AT DEER RUN BLVD);
561.793.1084; CHECK SCHEDULE ONLINE; PARKING AVAILABLE

Little Gym, The

"...*a well thought-out program of gymnastics and tumbling geared toward different age groups... a clean facility, excellent and knowledgeable staff... we love the small-sized gym equipment and their willingness to work with kids with special needs... activities are fun and personalized to match the kids' age... great place for birthday parties with a nice party room—they'll organize and do everything for you...* **"**

Customer service .... ❹ $$$ .... Prices
Age range .... 4 mths to 12 yrs

WWW.THELITTLEGYM.COM

WELLINGTON—13889 WELLINGTON TRACE (AT GREENVIEW SHORES BLVD);
561.784.9998; CALL FOR SCHEDULE

Little Ladies Victorian Tea
Parties

"...*our girls really enjoyed the dress up and pictures... best for girls 7 and under... your little girls will feel like little ladies drinking from real china here...* **"**

Customer service .... ❹ $$$ .... Prices
Age range .... 3 yrs to 7 yrs

WWW.SOUTHFLORIDA.COM/SFPARENTING/SFE-SFP-
PARTYGUIDE2004TEA,0,4947726.STORY

BOCA RATON—364 E PALMETTO PARK RD (AT SE 4TH AVE); 561.391.5177;
CALL FOR SCHEDULE

Little Palm Family Theatre

"...*live theater for the whole family to enjoy... very fun for the kids... kids love the classes and summer camp... highly recommended... the building is not much to look at, but the staff is very kind and fun...* **"**

Customer service .... ❺ $$ .... Prices

activities & outings

Age range....................2 yrs and up

WWW.LITTLEPALM.ORG

BOCA RATON—154 NW 16TH ST (AT NW BOCA RATON BLVD); 561.394.0206;
 CHECK SCHEDULE ONLINE

Music Together ★★★★½

"...the best mom and baby classes out there... music, singing,
dancing—even instruments for tots to play with... liberal make-up
policy, great venues, take home books, CDs and tapes which are
different each semester... it's a national franchise so instructors vary
and have their own style... different age groups get mixed up which
makes it a good learning experience for all involved... the highlight of
our week—grandma always comes along... be prepared to have your
tot sing the songs at home, in the car—everywhere... **"**

Customer service.........................❹ $$$.......................................Prices

Age range................. 2 mths to 5 yrs

WWW.MUSICTOGETHER.COM

BOCA RATON—561.740.2735; CALL FOR SCHEDULE

PALM BEACH GARDENS—561.315.7974; CALL FOR SCHEDULE

My Gym Children's Fitness
Center ★★★★☆

"...a wonderful gym environment for parents with babies and older
tots... classes range from tiny tots to school-aged children and the staff
is great about making it fun for all ages... equipment and facilities are
really neat—ropes, pulleys, swings, you name it... the kind of place your
kids hate to leave... the staff's enthusiasm is contagious... great for
memorable birthday parties... although it's a franchise, each gym seems
to have its own individual feeling... awesome for meeting playmates
and other parents... **"**

Customer service.........................❹ $$$.......................................Prices

Age range................. 3 mths to 9 yrs

WWW.MY-GYM.COM

BOCA RATON—21753 STATE RD 7 (AT CENTRAL PARK BLVD); 925.487.1842;
 CHECK SCHEDULE ONLINE

JUPITER—3755 MILITARY TRL (155TH LN N); 561.575.2434; CHECK
 SCHEDULE ONLINE

ROYAL PALM BEACH—518 N STATE RD (SOUTHERN BLVD); 561.798.5656;
 CHECK SCHEDULE ONLINE; FREE PARKING

Palm Beach Zoo ★★★★★

"...one of our favorite places to go and spend time together as a
family... great animals, including bears and kangaroos and a carousel to
boot... a great place to go with young children, especially toddlers... be
sure to bring a bathing suit and towel so your little one can run
through the water fountains ... **"**

Customer service.........................❹ $$.......................................Prices

WWW.PALMBEACHZOO.ORG

WEST PALM BEACH—1301 SUMMIT BLVD (AT DREHER TRL N);
 561.547.9453; DAILY 9-5

Playmobil Fun Park ★★★★☆

"...a great destination for your kid's imagination, there is a fantasy
dollhouse, a medieval village, a western town, and other 'places'... a
favorite destination for our children... our children can stay for hours
playing with the toys and at $1 the admission is worth it.... make sure
to bring a change of clothes for the water play area ... **"**

Customer service.........................❹ $$.......................................Prices

Age range................. 6 mths and up

WWW.PLAYMOBIL.COM

WEST PALM BEACH—8031 N MILITARY TRL (AT LILLIAN AVE); 561.691.9880;
   M-SA 10-6, SU 12-5

Puppetry Arts Center

Age range .... 2 yrs and up

WWW.PUPPETCENTER.ORG

WEST PALM BEACH—1200 S CONGRESS AVE (AT PALMARITA RD);
   561.967.3231; CALL FOR SCHEDULE

Schoolhouse Children's
Museum

*"...we LOVE this museum... everything is hands on with nothing that
can break under little hands... there is a huge playground out back that
is a destination in itself... the family membership pays for itself... worth
the trip... a terrific museum... a great place for little minds to explore
and learn, even the babies ... "*

Customer service .... **❺** $$ .... Prices
Age range .... 2 yrs and up

WWW.SCHOOLHOUSEMUSEUM.ORG

BOYNTON BEACH—129 E OCEAN AVE (AT S SEACREST BLVD); 561.742.6780;
   T-SA 10-5; PARKING LOT ON EAST SIDE

South Florida Science Museum

*"...interactive hands on science fun and exhibits... mini-golf is a hit
with the kids... even babies love the planetarium and aquarium... live
music events and family nights are wonderful... "*

Customer service .... **❸** $$$ .... Prices

WWW.SFSM.ORG

WEST PALM BEACH—4801 DREHER TRL N (AT DREHER PARK);
   561.832.1988; M-F 10-5, SA 10-6 (10PM IN SUMMER), SU 12-6; FREE
   PARKING AVAIL

The Keys

Caribbean Watersports

Age range............................ 5 yrs to

WWW.CARIBBEANWATERSPORTS.COM/

KEY LARGO—97000 OVERSEAS HWY US 1 (AT POISONWOOD RD);
 305.852.4707; CHECK SCHEDULE ONLINE; FREE PARKING

Conch Tour Train ★★★☆☆

❝...take a tour through historic Key West... relaxing and fun for
babies, kids and grown ups... a neat way to see the area... **❞**

Customer service......................... ❸ $$$...Prices

Age range.................. 6 mths and up

WWW.CONCHTOURTRAIN.COM

KEY WEST—501 FRONT ST (AT DUVAL ST); 305.294.5161; DAILY 9-4:30

Dolphin Cove Research & Education Center ★★★☆☆

❝...dolphin, ecology, crocodile tours and other charters make this an
interesting place... while baby won't understand what's going on, it's a
good relaxing outing... even a sunset cruise in a comfortable boat... **❞**

Customer service......................... ❸ $$$...Prices

WWW.DOLPHINSCOVE.COM

KEY LARGO—101900 OVERSEAS HWY (AT GUMBO LIMBO DR); 305.451.4060;
 CHECK SCHEDULE ONLINE; FREE PARKING

Dolphins Plus

Age range.................... 4 yrs and up

WWW.DOLPHINSPLUS.COM

KEY LARGO—31 CORRINE PL (AT S OCEAN BAY DR); 305.451.1993; CALL
 FOR APPT; FREE PARKING

Harry Harris Park ★★★☆☆

❝...park and beach with beautiful views... lots of playgrounds and
space to run around... nice place to spend the day with the family...
check signs to make sure beach isn't closed due to bacteria ... **❞**

Customer service......................... ❸ $ ....Prices

Age range.................. 6 mths and up

WWW.THEFLORIDAKEYS.COM/PARKS/HARRIS.HTM

TAVERNIER—MILE MARKER 935; 305.852.7161; DAILY 8-SUNSET

Jacobs Aquatic Center ★★★★½

❝...a huge swimming facility, but we always go to the 'kiddie' area
which has a shallow wading pool, lots of climbing, water play
equipment... kids can't get enough of the pirate ship area... swim
lessons too... a great summer outing... **❞**

Customer service......................... ❺ $ ....Prices

Age range.................. 6 mths and up

WWW.JACOBSAQUATICCENTER.ORG

KEY LARGO—320 LAGUNA AVE (AT CARRIBEAN DR); 305.453.7946; CHECK
 SCHEDULE ONLINE

John Pennekamp Coral Reef State Park

Age range.................. 6 mths and up

WWW.PENNEKAMPPARK.COM

KEY LARGO—MILE MARKER 1025, OVERSEAS HWY (OFF HWY 1); 305.451.1202; DAILY 8-SUNSET

Key Largo Princess Glass Bottom Boat

Age range ....6 mths and up

WWW.ICHOTELSGROUP.COM/H/D/6C/1/EN/HD/KYLFL

KEY LARGO—HOLIDAY INN DOCKS, MILE MARKER 100, OCEANSIDE (AT OVERSEAS HWY); 305.451.4655; DEPARTS DAILY AT 10, 1 AND 4

Key West Aquarium

"...a unique and beautiful aquarium... kids love the daily shark and turtle feedings... a hands-on underwater sea experience... a special time for the family, even the babes... **"**

Customer service .... ❸ $$$ .... Prices

Age range ....6 mths and up

WWW.KEYWESTAQUARIUM.COM

KEY WEST—1 WHITEHEAD ST (AT WALL ST); 305.296.2051; DAILY 10-6

Key West Butterfly & Nature Conservatory

WWW.KEYWESTBUTTERFLY.COM

KEY WEST—1316 DUVAL ST (AT UNITED ST); 305.296.2988; DAILY 9-4; FREE PARKING

Key West Lighthouse Museum

"...88 steps to the top observation deck with views to die for... may not be for the babies, but older kids and grown ups will enjoy this visit... recreated and restored historic home is fun... **"**

Customer service .... ❸ $$$ .... Prices

WWW.KWAHS.COM/LIGHTHOUSE.HTM

KEY WEST—938 WHITEHEAD ST (AT TRUMAN AVE); 305.294.0012; CHECK SCHEDULE ONLINE; FREE PARKING

Mel Fisher Maritime Heritage Society & Museum

Age range ....6 mths and up

WWW.MELFISHER.ORG

KEY WEST—200 GREENE ST (AT FRONT ST); 305.294.2633; DAILY 9:30-5:30

Theater Of The Sea

"...educational and fun marine animal park... dolphin, sea lion and parrot shows give kids an up close look at these creatures... older kids and grown ups can swim with the dolphins... a fun activity in the Keys... not the cleanest place and lots of stray cats... **"**

Customer service .... ❸ $$$ .... Prices

Age range ....6 mths and up

WWW.THEATEROFTHESEA.COM

ISLAMORADA—84721 OVERSEAS HWY (AT WINDLEY KEY); 305.664.2431; DAILY 9:30-5:30

Tropical Crane Point Hammock

Age range ....6 mths and up

WWW.CRANEPOINT.ORG

MARATHON—5550 OVERSEAS HWY (AT SOMBRERO BEACH DR); 305.743.9100; M-SA 9-5, SU 12-5

activities & outings

parks & playgrounds

South Dade & Downtown

"lila picks"

★ Coral Reef Park   ★ Dante Fascell Park
★ Crandon Park Beach   ★ Tropical Park

AD 'Doug' Barnes Park

"...a large park with a lot of variety... one of the few parks around that has a place to swim... the pool is nice and warm and also has a floor that can move up and down to make it safer for the kids... the picnic shelters provide good shade... not as crowded as the more popular parks... the nature center next door is always worth a visit with curious tots... the paths are all smooth and good for regular strollers..."

Equipment/play structures............⑤   ⑤ ....Maintenance
WWW.CO.MIAMI-DADE.FL.US
MIAMI—3401 SW 72ND AVE (AT N WATERWAY DR); 305.662.4124

Alice Wainwright Park

"...a beautiful park overlooking Biscayne Bay... a sand bottom play area is great for the kids... a nice spot for picnicking and playing catch... a path leads down to the water... gorgeous setting..."

Equipment/play structures............⑤   ⑤ ....Maintenance
MIAMI—2845 BRICKELL AVE (AT BRICKELL CT); 305.856.6794

Belle Meade Mini Park

"...a shaded, small tot park in a family friendly neighborhood... toddler sized equipment makes it a joy... worth the trip... nice trees..."

Equipment/play structures............⑤   ⑤ ....Maintenance
WWW.CI.MIAMI.FL.US
MIAMI—NE 8TH AVE (AT 77TH ST)

Bill Baggs Cape Florida State Park

"...a gorgeous family friendly park at the tip of Key Biscayne... lots and lots of beach here... you can see Stiltsville out on the water from here... no playground per se, but many picnic areas and open areas to run around on... great bird watching... seafood restaurant on the premises..."

Equipment/play structures............⑤   ⑤ ....Maintenance
WWW.FLORIDASTATEPARKS.ORG/CAPEFLORIDA
KEY BISCAYNE—1200 S CRANDON BLVD (AT GRAPETREE DR); 305.361.5811

Bill Sadowski Park

"...an amazing destination for the family... a small playground with pretty standard equipment... a nice picnicking spot in the midst of

beautiful tall trees... restrooms nearby make this a convenient park for me and my two boys... **"**

Equipment/play structures .... ❸   ❸ .... Maintenance

WWW.CO.MIAMI-DADE.FL.US

MIAMI—17555 SW 79TH AVE (AT SW 175TH ST); 305.255.4767

Biscayne National Park ★★★★☆

"...we love this beach/park because its close and safe and has Crocodile Warning signs all over... so much fun... beautiful place to take the family for a swim and picnic...** "**

Equipment/play structures .... ❹   ❸ .... Maintenance

WWW.NPS.GOV/BISC

HOMESTEAD—9700 SW 328TH ST (AT BISCAYNE NATIONAL PARK); 305.230.7275

Blanche Park ★★★★★

"...a perfect park for toddlers—small and enclosed so there is no worry of a child running off... the equipment is small enough for little ones to play on safely... picnic tables and a water fountain make a nice lunch spot... my kids love to watch the dogs play at the dog park next to it ...** "**

Equipment/play structures .... ❺   ❺ .... Maintenance

WWW.CI.MIAMI.FL.US

COCONUT GROVE—SHIPPING AVE (AT VIRGINA ST); 305.416.1318

Castellow Hammock Preserve
& Nature Center ★★★½☆

"...a great nature park to see birds and picnic... a nice butterfly garden... the park is staffed by well known local wildlife author Roger Hammer... a good part day outing to see a hammock setting... beware that the path is not stroller friendly, so be prepared to carry younger children... experienced and kid friendly guides ...** "**

Equipment/play structures .... ❹   ❺ .... Maintenance

WWW.METRO-DADE.COM/PARKS/PARKS/CASTELLO_HAMMOCK.ASP

MIAMI—22301 SW 162ND AVE; 305.242.7688

Coral Reef Park ★★★★★

"...our favorite south Dade park, so much to do in such a big space... nice for a walk with your little one... a large, pretty park with relatively new playground equipment for tots... lots of fields for baseball and soccer—a good place to practice walking when they aren't being used... lots of local families playing here all day long...** "**

Equipment/play structures .... ❹   ❺ .... Maintenance

WWW.METRO-DADE.COM/PARK

MIAMI—7895 SW 152ND ST (AT SW 79TH AVE); 305.235.1593

Crandon Park Beach ★★★★★

"...fabulous beach for kids... waves are small and beach is shallow... during the week it's almost like you have your own private beach... they have hands-on activities both in the water and indoors... water fountains available for playing on those hot summer days... carousels are open on weekdays... don't forget the bug repellent as there are lots of mosquitoes...** "**

Equipment/play structures .... ❹   ❹ .... Maintenance

WWW.CO.MIAMI-DADE.FL.US

KEY BISCAYNE—4000 CRANDON BLVD (AT GRAPETREE DR); 305.361.5421; SUNRISE TO SUNSET; PARKING LOT

parks & playgrounds

Dante Fascell Park

"...playground equipment for older children and three baby swings, a little slide area, some rocking horses and a seesaw for the babies... my favorite thing as a kid and now with my kid is the huge sculpture of a woman that my kids love to play on... big field with a covered patio—perfect for birthday parties... borders on very busy Red Road, so be prepared to keep an eye on your toddler... **"**

Equipment/play structures............**4**   **4**................................Maintenance

WWW.CITYOFSOUTHMIAMI.NET

MIAMI—8700 SW 57TH AVE (AT SW 87TH ST); 305.666.8680

Everglades National Park

"...an amazing place for the entire family to see wildlife, especially during February's dry season!... the annual pass is worth the small price to get into any national park... so much to do—visit their web site—plan ahead... **"**

Equipment/play structures............**4**   **4**................................Maintenance

WWW.NPS.GOV/EVER

HOMESTEAD—4000L STATE RD 9336; 305.242.7700

Fairchild Tropical Botanic Garden

"...wonderful place to spend the day with your family or play group... a first rate botanical garden—good with either a baby or older kids... no playground equipment, but the plants are quite amazing to look at... I love coming here to push my baby in the stroller and take in the beautiful plants and birds... **"**

Equipment/play structures............**4**   **5**................................Maintenance

WWW.CO.MIAMI-DADE.FL.US

MIAMI—10901 OLD CUTLER RD (AT SNAPPER CREEK RD); 305.667.1651

Greynolds Park

"...a tot lot devoted to small kids is great... nice rental pavilions for birthday parties... huge oasis in the middle on North Miami Beach... a coral rock castle structure is fun for the older kids to play on ... **"**

Equipment/play structures............**3**   **3**................................Maintenance

WWW.CO.MIAMI-DADE.FL.US

MIAMI—17530 W DIXIE HWY; 305.945.3425

Kendale Lakes Park

"...great tot lot for the little ones... a grassy hill area provides a nice relaxation and picnic spot for you and baby... **"**

Equipment/play structures............**5**   **5**................................Maintenance

WWW.CO.MIAMI-DADE.FL.US

MIAMI—7850 SW 142ND AVE (AT SW 78TH AVE); 305.385.4750

Kennedy Park

"...a great place to bring the dogs and walk around with your baby... a good place to meet up with other moms and their babies... you can get a lot of walking in... spend the day under a tree relaxing with a book and picnicking with your family... a beautiful setting... while we kick back on the picnic blanket, my husband usually goes for a run on the vita course... **"**

Equipment/play structures............**4**   **5**................................Maintenance

WWW.CI.MIAMI.FL.US

MIAMI—2200 S BAYSHORE DR (AT 22ND AVE); 305.575.5256

participate in our survey at

Matheson Hammock Park

❝...what a kid friendly place... great to take the little ones for some beach time—no waves and natural palm tree shade... the clean restrooms are a plus... bring your own snacks because there is no concession stand... great to go with little kids... great lagoon for wading and swimming... **❞**

Equipment/play structures .... **4**   **4** .... Maintenance

WWW.METRO-DADE.COM/PARKS

MIAMI—9610 OLD CUTLER RD (AT CAMPANA AVE); 305.665.5475

Peacock Park

❝...a convenient park, right on the bay and right near the shops of Cocowalk... my 7 month old loves watching the skaters in the skate park... the playground is probably better for kids over two... not always the cleanest place ... **❞**

Equipment/play structures .... **3**   **3** .... Maintenance

WWW.MIAMIGOV.COM

MIAMI—2820 MCFARLANE RD (AT S BAYSHORE DR); 305.442.0375

Pinecrest Gardens

❝...the settings and gardens are lovely and well-kept... one of the most beautiful parks I've been to and the kids just love it... my kids love the splash park, huge jungle gym, and petting zoo and I love that it's free!... quite fun to feed the giant koi and turtles with the kids... be forewarned the petting zoos aren't always opened when they should be... a wonderful spot, I can't say enough good things about it... **❞**

Equipment/play structures .... **4**   **4** .... Maintenance

WWW.PINECREST-FL.GOV

PINECREST—11000 RED RD (AT 57ᵀᴴ AVE); 305.669.6942

Pinecrest Park

❝...small, but fun... no messy sand, which is a godsend... the new play set under the shade awning makes for a much cooler and more pleasant park experience... lots of neighborhood kids and parents... right across from Gardner's market for a snack... **❞**

Equipment/play structures .... **4**   **4** .... Maintenance

WWW.PINECREST-FL.GOV/PARKFACILITIES.HTM

MIAMI—8200 SW 124TH ST (AT S DIXIE HWY); 305.234.2110

Suniland Park

❝...one of the best parks for kids under 5—most of their equipment is low to ground and it is all shaded from the sun... **❞**

Equipment/play structures .... **4**   **4** .... Maintenance

WWW.PINECREST-FL.GOV

PINECREST—12855 S DIXIE HWY (AT SW 128TH); 305.234.2120

Tropical Park

❝...this park has a little bit of everything for everyone... loads of playground facilities, some even with lots of shade... nice sidewalks for strolling, rollerblading or biking with baby... my kids love to climb the hill... lots to do here... you can reserve a hut for a fun birthday party... really an average park that's plenty large, but not quite an oasis due to the highway running down one side ... **❞**

Equipment/play structures .... **4**   **4** .... Maintenance

WWW.METRO-DADE.COM/PARKS

MIAMI—7900 SW 40TH ST (AT SW 79TH AVE); 305.226.8315

parks & playgrounds

Village Green, The

"...perfect for little Key babies... very nice equipment and a special area for toddlers... a large grassy area and splash fountain make it a favorite community spot... age appropriate slides and tunnels are fun... "

Equipment/play structures............❹   ❹................................Maintenance

WWW.KEYBISCAYNE.FL.GOV

KEY BISCAYNE—CRANDON BLVD (AT W MESHTA DR); 305.365.8901

participate in our survey at

North Dade & Beaches

★★★★★

"lila picks"

★ Oleta River State Park
★ Bay Harbor Park Tot Lot

Amelia Earhart Park ★★★★☆

"...beautiful area with several playgrounds that are safe and fun for the kids... a perfect spot for a birthday party—you rent a pavilion and watch the kids run around... bring along bread to feed the ducks... the Bill Graham Village Farm is a stone's throw away and is a guaranteed hit with curious little minds... a petting zoo with sheep, pigs and horses... there's a concession stand with ice cream and snacks..."

Equipment/play structures .... ❹ ❹ .... Maintenance

WWW.GMCVB.COM

HIALEAH—401 E 65TH ST (AT E 4TH AVE); 305.685.8389

Bay Harbor Park Tot Lot ★★★★★

"...a great neighborhood park on the water... swings, slides, grass and plenty of shade... the park is clean and fun and a nice place to meet friends... it does get a bit crowded at times, but I find that most kids are well supervised and play well together... a perfect play spot for the five and under crowd..."

Equipment/play structures .... ❹ ❺ .... Maintenance

WWW.CO.MIAMI-DADE.FL.US

BAY HARBOR ISLANDS—96TH ST (AT BROADVIEW); 305.866.6241

Enchanted Forest Elaine Gordon Park ★★★★☆

"...lovely place with lots of space to run around... lots of shade means you can spend the whole day having fun... a couple of playgrounds that are nicely kept... my kids really love going over to be with the ponies—they can't wait to be bigger to ride them... lots of nature walks and activities..."

Equipment/play structures .... ❹ ❹ .... Maintenance

WWW.NORTHMIAMIFL.GOV

NORTH MIAMI—1725 NE 135TH ST (AT NE 15TH CT); 305.895.1119

Fisher Park ★★★★☆

"...a great park for toddlers... large jungle gyms and always plenty of children to play with... good equipment—sandbox and swings... big open field is fun for running around (but not fenced in)... clean, well-maintained and fenced in... plenty of shade, park benches and tables for eating... not a beautiful place, but a great safe neighborhood park..."

Equipment/play structures .... ❺ ❺ .... Maintenance

WWW.CI.MIAMI-BEACH.FL.US

MIAMI BEACH—50TH ST (AT ALTON RD); 305.604.2489

Flamingo Park ★★★★☆

"...a large variety of activities for all ages... the new water park is a hit with the kids, but make sure to make reservations... tot lot and open space is great in the middle of Miami Beach... **"**

Equipment/play structures............ ❹ ❹ ....Maintenance

WWW.CI.MIAMI-BEACH.FL.US

MIAMI BEACH—11TH ST (AT JEFFERSON AVE); 305.673.7730

Founders Park ★★★☆☆

"...a great playground for the little ones and paved path which is wonderful for strolling the baby while getting exercise... lots of open space for running around, baseball, soccer or other things... the bay walk overlooking the waterway is beautiful ... **"**

Equipment/play structures............ ❸ ❸ ....Maintenance

WWW.ISLAMORADA.FL.US

AVENTURA—3105 NE 190TH ST (AT W COUNTRY CLUB DR); 305.664.2345

Haulover Park ★★★★★

"...great public beach... kids can also visit the kite park and watch kite flying or buy one of their own... also a waterfront fire station is on the premises and worth a visit.... **"**

Equipment/play structures............ ❹ ❹ ....Maintenance

WWW.MIAMIDADE.GOV/PARKS/PARKS/HAULOVER_PARK.ASP

MIAMI BEACH—10800 COLLINS AVE (OFF BAYVIEW DR); 305.944.3040;
  SUNRISE TO SUNSET

Muse Park ★★★☆☆

"...nice playground and tot lot in a large area... good option for a birthday party... a convenient neighborhood park that has a pavilion for shade... **"**

Equipment/play structures............ ❸ ❸ ....Maintenance

WWW.CI.MIAMI-BEACH.FL.US

MIAMI BEACH—4400 CHASE AVE (AT W 44TH ST); 305.673.7730

North Shore Open Space Park ★★★★☆

"...this brand new Miami Beach facility is open to residents and non-residents and has so much to offer... better for older kids—sports programs, tennis courts, plus lots more... can be rented for a great birthday party... **"**

Equipment/play structures............ ❺ ❹ ....Maintenance

WWW.MIAMIBEACHPARKS.COM

MIAMI BEACH—7929 ATLANTIC WY (AT 79TH ST); 305.993.2032

Oleta River State Park ★★★★★

"...huge state park with a great beach for babies and toddlers... clean and beautiful setting... gorgeous beach, bike trails, playground, kayak rentals and more... my baby and I relax at the beach while daddy gets to go mountain biking on the trails... the water is shallow and the picnic facilities are nice too... **"**

Equipment/play structures............ ❹ ❺ ....Maintenance

WWW.FLORIDASTATEPARKS.ORG/OLETARIVER/DEFAULT.CFM

NORTH MIAMI—3400 NE 163RD ST (AT NE 35TH AVE); 305.919.1846

Surfside Park ★★★★☆

"...small, friendly neighborhood park with lots of shade... good equipment, but kids get bored by the time they are three years old...

participate in our survey at

sand area, swings, slides, a jungle gym and picnic tables with benches...
bug repellent is a must... no bathroom... **"**

Equipment/play structures .... **4**   **4** .... Maintenance

WWW.TOWN.SURFSIDE.FL.US

SURFSIDE—9572 BAY DR (AT 96TH ST); 305.993.1371

Westland Gardens Park ★★★☆☆

"*...they have it all... a complete playground, swimming pool and*
tennis courts... an excellent place to throw a birthday party—you can
rent the facilities for a reasonable rate... **"**

Equipment/play structures .... **5**   **5** .... Maintenance

WWW.CITYOFHIALEAHGARDENS.ORG

HIALEAH—13501 NW 107TH AVE (AT NW 134TH ST); 305.558.2331; M-SA 9-
9, SU 10-7; PARKING LOT AT 13501 NW 107 AVE

parks & playgrounds

Broward County

"lila picks"

- ★ CB Smith Park (Paradise Cove)
- ★ Markham Park
- ★ Topeekeegee Yugnee Park
- ★ Tradewinds Park

Betti Stradling Park ★★☆☆☆

"...big park that caters to the whole family... baby swings and other tot appropriate equipment... could use a little updating and some more shade..."

Equipment/play structures............ ❹ ❷ ....Maintenance

WWW.CORALSPRINGS.ORG

CORAL SPRINGS—10301 WILES RD (AT CORAL SPRINGS DR); 954.344.1000

Brian Piccolo Park ★★★★☆

"...a huge sports complex with some ball fields attached... basically a big open space to run around or bring tricycles along... fun for the whole family—my husband plays basketball while the kids and I play at the playground... the bike race track is also fun to watch..."

Equipment/play structures............ ❹ ❹ ....Maintenance

WWW.CO.BROWARD.FL.US/PARKS

HOLLYWOOD—9501 SHERIDAN STR (AT NW 24TH PL); 954.437.2600

CB Smith Park (Paradise Cove) ★★★★★

"...a nice playground, but the real attractions are the water slides... a huge activity complex with something for the whole family... the waterpark is great for kids of all ages but you will need one adult for each child because it's big... perfect for picnicking and spending the day... I like walking near the lake with the stroller while my husband and son romp around elsewhere..."

Equipment/play structures............ ❹ ❹ ....Maintenance

WWW.CO.BROWARD.FL.US/PARKS

HOLLYWOOD—900 N FLAMINGO RD (AT NW 124 AVE, PEMBROKE MALL); 954.437.2650; MALL PARKING

Colohatchee Park ★★★☆☆

"...a pretty waterfront park with a boardwalk overlooking the river... pavilions and picnic tables make this ideal for an afternoon outing... a playground, basketball and sand volleyball court too... good nature watching..."

Equipment/play structures............ ❸ ❸ ....Maintenance

WWW.WILTONMANORS.COM

participate in our survey at

WILTON MANORS—1975 NE 15TH AVE (AT COLOHATCHEE PARK);
954.328.5231

Cypress Park

WWW.CO.BROWARD.FL.US/PARKS

POMPANO BEACH—1301 CORAL SPRINGS DR (OFF ATLANTIC BLVD);
954.345.2109

Deicke Park

"...a nice park with a small children's play area... the large tot lot may be better for older children... nice passive park with restrooms ... "

Equipment/play structures .... ❸　　❸............................... Maintenance

WWW.PLANTATION.ORG/PARKS/CITYPARKS/DEICKE-PARK.HTML

PLANTATION—1200 NW 106TH AVE

Everglades Holiday Park

"...this recently renovated park has a great playground for kids... for the little ones tons of slides and swings and a great seesaw too... nature park lets you get a close up view of the everglades and its many wonders—older kids will probably get more out of it... a treat... "

Equipment/play structures .... ❺　　❺............................... Maintenance

WWW.EVERGLADESHOLIDAYPARK.COM

FORT LAUDERDALE—21940 GRIFFIN RD (AT HIGHWAY 818); 954.434.8111

Firefighters Park

"...a medium sized park with a playground for toddlers and older children... great place if your kids like to play in the sand... nice equipment for the little ones... my friends and I strollercise with our babies around the walking trail... the play area has a combination of rubber flooring and clean white sand... plenty of open areas to play ball and practice walking... "

Equipment/play structures .... ❹　　❹............................... Maintenance

WWW.MARGATEFL.COM

MARGATE—2500 ROCK ISLAND RD (AT HOLIDAY SPRINGS BLVD);
954.972.6458

Floyd Hull Stadium Park

"...this park is adjacent to a baseball field and has a great jungle gym for kids and picnic area under old oak trees... complete with a very large bbq area that can handle a large crowd for a party... "

Equipment/play structures .... ❸　　❸............................... Maintenance

WWW.CI.FTLAUD.FL.US/CITYPARKS/FLOYD_HULL/INDEX.HTM

FORT LAUDERDALE—800 SW 28TH ST; 800.227.8669

Hugh Taylor Birch State Recreation Area

"...fantastic for picnics and day trips with the family... convenient beach access... the park itself is beautiful and full of wildlife... "

Equipment/play structures .... ❸　　❹............................... Maintenance

WWW.ABFLA.COM/PARKS/HUGHTAYLORBIRCH/HUGHTAYLORBIRCH.HTML

FORT LAUDERDALE—3109 E SUNRISE BLVD (AT NE 9TH ST); 954.564.4521

Island City Park Preserve

"...a playground within a pretty preserve... a boardwalk with a beautiful view of the river... lots of amenities for the whole family including courts, kayaks and a playground ... "

Equipment/play structures .... ❸　　❸............................... Maintenance

WWW.WILTONMANORS.COM

WILTON MANORS—823 NE 28TH ST (AT NE 8TH ST); 954.390.2180

Joe DiMaggio Park

"...a fantastic covered playground... a large lake and lots of grassy areas to relax at... a two mile track to exercise on with your baby... it's located inside an exclusive development, but it is a public City of Hollywood park... **"**

Equipment/play structures............**4** **3**................................Maintenance

WWW.SOUTHFLORIDA.COM

HOLLYWOOD—1016 WASHINGTON ST (AT S 10TH AVE)

John U. Lloyd Beach State Park

"...a nice outing for a beach day and picnic... scenic beach with swimming and snorkeling... lots of activities like kayaking for the older kids ... **"**

Equipment/play structures............**5** **4**................................Maintenance

WWW.FLORIDASTATEPARKS.ORG

DANIA—6503 N OCEAN DR; 954.923.2833

Markham Park

"...so much to do at this park so be sure to plan to stay awhile... wonderful playground for the little ones, but bring the sunblock because there isn't a lot of shade... a little difficult to find the swing sets, but a beautiful place to be... real nice and quiet during the week... lakes, a pool, a model airplane field are all hits with my kids... great park for the whole family... convenient with so many activities... a new dog park is opening soon... **"**

Equipment/play structures............**4** **5**................................Maintenance

WWW.CO.BROWARD.FL.US/PARKS

FORT LAUDERDALE—16001 W STATE RD 84 (AT WESTON RD); 954.389.2000

Mullins Park

"...a great playground for toddlers and up... it's hard to locate behind the ball fields, but worth the effort... the entire playground has the rubberized flooring... each play areas is covered shaded with a canopy keeping the kids cool... the small gated playground is great, you can actually feel comfortable letting your little ones run and play... **"**

Equipment/play structures............**4** **4**................................Maintenance

WWW.CORALSPRINGS.ORG

CORAL SPRINGS—10000 NW 29TH ST (AT CORAL SPRINGS DR);
  954.345.2200; DAILY 8-DUSK; PLAYGROUND HAS A PARKING LOT

Plantation Heritage Park

"...a nice stroll with baby on the path around the duck pond... this park is always shady which is nice... not a designer play clothes kind of playground, the surface is made of shredded tires and the kids will get dirty... lots of squirrels that will come up close to the kids... **"**

Equipment/play structures............**4** **4**................................Maintenance

WWW.BROWARD.ORG/PARKS

PLANTATION—1100 S FIG TREE LN; 954.791.1025

Quiet Waters Park ★★★☆☆

"...the highlight of this park is the large water playground Splash Adventure... my kids love the water park with the interactive activities... the water depth accommodates babies and kids of all ages... check out the baby friendly beach too... **"**

Equipment/play structures............**3** **3**................................Maintenance

WWW.CO.BROWARD.FL.US/PARKS

DEERFIELD BEACH—401 S POWERLINE RD (AT SW 4TH AVE); 954.360.1315

Topeekeegee Yugnee Park ★★★★★

"...a fabulous park that is huge and shady... great jungle gym area... we go to 'Castaway Island', a water play area, every chance we get... the covered playground is a respite in the summer... lots of open space, basketball, tennis and camping... rangers are super nice and admission is free on weekdays... **"**

Equipment/play structures .... ❹   ❹ .... Maintenance

WWW.FTLAUDERDALEWWW.COM/AREAGUIDE/PARKS/PARKS.HTML

HOLLYWOOD—3300 N PARK RD (AT N 34TH AVE); 954.985.1980

Tradewinds Park ★★★★★

"...great park with wonderful farm tours and a steam train to ride... fun for all ages... my son loves to ride the ponies and see the farm animals on the weekends... the playground equipment is older... nice trail around the lake... it's nice that Butterfly World is right there—my kids think it's the neatest thing in the world... **"**

Equipment/play structures .... ❹   ❹ .... Maintenance

WWW.BROWARD.ORG/PARKS

COCONUT CREEK—3600 W SAMPLE RD (AT FLORIDA'S TPKE S); 954.968.3880

Tree Tops Park ★★★★☆

"...this is a great park... the kids always have a good time here, they love the playground and the butterfly garden... the playground is clean, updated and very peaceful... amazing woods for the kids to play in... great for the older kids too with an observation tower, trails and fishing and horseback riding... **"**

Equipment/play structures .... ❹   ❺ .... Maintenance

WWW.DAVIE-FL.GOV

DAVIE—3900 SW 100TH AVE (AT WHISPERING PINES RD); 954.370.3750

Volunteer Park ★★★★☆

"...this park has six different educational play structures for children of all ages... the park is brand new and very clean, but bring the sun block because it has very little shade... may be a little difficult for one adult and two different age children since it is very large, but it is fenced in. .. we enjoy the quiet, peaceful nature trails... **"**

Equipment/play structures .... ❺   ❺ .... Maintenance

PLANTATION—12050 W SUNRISE BLVD

Welleby Park ★★★★★

"...the best maintained and cleanest park in the area, not to mention it's free!.. the park has ample pavilions for having a picnic with your family... my kids really enjoy the extensive play area and I enjoy the rubber safety surface underneath... a great walking path for strolling the baby... **"**

Equipment/play structures .... ❺   ❺ .... Maintenance

WWW.SUNRISEFL.GOV/2PARK_WELLEBY.HTML

SUNRISE—11100 NW 44TH ST (AT WELLEBY PARK)

West Lake Park ★★★★☆

"...an awesome place for a party—just make sure you book well in advance... there is a great splash fountain that runs through a safe and fun playground... my kids love this park... the paved path is perfect for strolling with my baby and for my four year old to bike on... hands on eco center is great for the older kids... the park is so so... **"**

Equipment/play structures .... ❸   ❹ .... Maintenance

WWW.CO.BROWARD.FL.US/PARKS

parks & playgrounds

Weston Regional Park

"...this park has two great tot lots one is sand and one is mulch and they are both completely covered... my kids love the sand tot lot and I love that it is fenced in... the sand park is probably a little bit better for the little ones... this is a huge park with something for the whole family from soccer, basketball, baseball, tot lots and even a skate park... the walking path is a great way to get exercise with the baby... "

Equipment/play structures............❺   ❺ ....Maintenance

WESTON—20200 SADDLE CLUB RD (AT S POST RD)

participate in our survey at

Palm Beach County

"lila picks"

★ Patch Reef Park

★ Sugar Sand Park Playground

parks & playgrounds

John D. Macarthur Beach State Park And Nature Center ★★★½☆

"...large park with lots to do for the entire family... nice beach day... all ages can play and have fun..."

Equipment/play structures .... ❹   ❹ .... Maintenance

WWW.MACARTHURBEACH.ORG

NORTH PALM BEACH—10900 STATE RD 703; 561.624.6952

Loxahatchee National Wildlife Refuge ★★★☆☆

"...walking and bike trails are fun for the family... babies enjoy the butterfly garden too... beautiful natural environment in the Everglades..."

Equipment/play structures .... ❸   ❸ .... Maintenance

WWW.LOXAHATCHEE.FWS.GOV

BOYNTON BEACH—10216 LEE RD (AT HWY 441); 561.735.6030

Mirasol Park ★★★☆☆

"...this large neighborhood park is a definite destination with our small children... the running loop is a good place to strollercize with your babe... check out the playground... lots of other activities for older kids and grown ups..."

Equipment/play structures .... ❸   ❸ .... Maintenance

WWW.PBGFL.COM/RESIDENT/PARKS/PARKFACILITIES.ASP

PALM BEACH GARDENS—12385 JOG RD (AT PGA BLVD)

Patch Reef Park ★★★★★

"...great for all ages—we go here with our infant and my 12-year-old... it has one of the best playgrounds around... a huge playground with lots of equipment... bike trails, basketball courts, play fields—the works... always a fun time given how many new friends we can meet..."

Equipment/play structures .... ❺   ❺ .... Maintenance

WWW.CI.BOCA-RATON.FL.US/PARKS/PATCHREEF.CFM

BOCA RATON—2000 NW 51ST ST (AT YAMATO RD); 561.997.0791

Sugar Sand Park Playground ★★★★★

"...an amazing park with so much to do... well designed and never boring... hands down my kids' favorite park... play in the water area and then walk to the cool interactive science museum for free and for

all ages... my kids love the 3 story high tree house with slides, activities, a space station and play areas for all ages... the trails and picnic area are nice too... clean facility... convenient and lots of parking... a great facility for mommy-and-me classes... **"**

Equipment/play structures............**❺**   **❺** ....Maintenance

WWW.CI.BOCA-RATON.FL.US

BOCA RATON—300 S MILITARY TRL (AT PARK PALMETTO PARK RD); 954.347.3906

Tiger Shark Cove   ★★★☆☆

"...*the playground and pavilion make this a good outing with the kids... lots of sports related activities for the older children...* **"**

Equipment/play structures............**❸**   **❸** ....Maintenance

WWW.CI.WELLINGTON.FL.US

WELLINGTON—13800 GREENBRIAR BLVD (AT GREENVIEW SHORES BLVD); 561.791.4000

Veterans Park   ★★★★☆

"...*we really enjoy this park with one playground for the babies and one for the older kids... because it's right on the intercoastal, there is always a beautiful breeze coming through... a park with plenty of shade and a nice picnic areas—what a treat... lots of art festivals on Saturdays... conveniently located near downtown Delray and the green market* ... **"**

Equipment/play structures............**❹**   **❹** ....Maintenance

WWW.MYDELRAYBEACH.COM

DELRAY BEACH—802 NE 1ST ST (AT VETERANS PARK); 561.243.7350

The Keys

Bahia Honda State Park ★★★★☆

"...we love to visit this park... an enjoyable day of beach combing for washed up 'treasures' and snorkeling with the older kids... beautiful... excellent bird watching, a treat for babies..."

Equipment/play structures .... ❸   ❸ .... Maintenance

WWW.FLORIDASTATEPARKS.ORG

BIG PINE—36850 OVERSEAS HWY; 305.872-2353

Blue Hole ★★★☆☆

"...a sinkhole from the old railroad days is now a beautiful wildlife attraction... a place to see alligators, turtles and freshwater fish, safely..."

Equipment/play structures .... ❸   ❸ .... Maintenance

WWW.FLORIDAKEYS.COM/LOWERKEYS/ATTRACTIONS.HTM

BIG PINE—KEY DEER BLVD; 305.872.0074

Harry Harris Park ★★★☆☆

"...great view, playground and lots of room to run... beach is sometimes closed due to bacterial contamination, but that happens occasionally at most Keys parks—check postings near the beaches..."

Equipment/play structures .... ❸   ❸ .... Maintenance

WWW.THEFLORIDAKEYS.COM/PARKS/HARRIS.HTM

TAVERNIER—MILE MARKER 935; 305.852.7161; DAILY 8-SUNSET

Jack Watson's Nature Trail ★★★☆☆

"...a nice nature walk for you and baby, you may want a baby jogger or other off-road type stroller..."

Equipment/play structures .... ❸   ❸ .... Maintenance

WWW.FLORIDAKEYSBEST.COM/FAMILIES/FLORIDA_KEYS_NATURE_TRAILS.HTM

BIG PINE—KEY DEER BLVD MM 305; 305.872.2239

John Pennekamp Coral Reef State Park ★★★⯪☆

"...sun, swim, picnic, camp or fish at this wonderful state park... glass bottom boat tours and other activities are family friendly and fun... visitor's center hosts a huge aquarium the kids love to see... the snorkeling is great for older kids who are confident swimmers..."

Equipment/play structures .... ❹   ❹ .... Maintenance

WWW.PENNEKAMPPARK.COM

KEY LARGO—MILE MARKER 1025, OVERSEAS HWY (OFF HWY 1);
   305.451.1202; DAILY 8-SUNSET

Lignumvitae Key Botanical State Park ★★★⯪☆

"...nothing else like it, but bring the mosquito spray!... it's wonderful but you must plan ahead because it is only accessible by charter or private boat... a bird watcher's paradise..."

Equipment/play structures .... ❹   ❹ .... Maintenance

WWW.FLORIDASTATEPARKS.ORG/LIGNUMVITAEKEY/DEFAULT.CFM

ISLAMORADA—US 1 MILE MARKER 785; 305.664.2540

Long Key State Park

"...no playground here, but a beautiful natural setting with tons for you and your baby to observe... pack the baby on your back and get out to nature here... "

Equipment/play structures............❹   ❹ ....Maintenance

WWW.FLORIDASTATEPARKS.ORG

LONG KEY—67400 OVERSEAS HWY MM 676, 305.664.4015

Sombrero Beach

"...a nice sized beach that was recently renovated is a good stop with your children... the landscaping is interesting and their is a gentle roped off swimming area for the babies and kids to wade in... the playground, walkways and picnic areas make for a good whole day outing... "

Equipment/play structures............❸   ❸ ....Maintenance

HTTP://THEFLORIDAKEYS.COM/PARKS/SOMBRERO.HTM

KEY LARGO—OVERSEAS HWY MM 50

Windley Key Fossil Reef
Geological State Park

"...more for grown up tourists... "

Equipment/play structures............❸   ❸ ....Maintenance

WWW.FLORIDASTATEPARKS.ORG/WINDLEYKEY/DEFAULT.CFM

ISLAMORADA—OVERSEAS HWY MM 855; 305.664.2540

restaurants

South Dade & Downtown

★ ★ ★ ★ ★

"lila picks"

- ★ Benihana
- ★ Dogma Grill
- ★ Flanigan's Seafood Bar & Grill
- ★ Johnny Rockets
- ★ Red Lobster Restaurant
- ★ Shorty's BBQ
- ★ Whip-N-Dip

Andiamo ★ ★ ★ ★ ★

"...great outdoor pizza place and traditonal itlian pizza and salads... get your car washed while you eat... great for multitasking moms... **"**

Children's menu	✗	$$	Prices
Changing station	✗	❺	Customer service
Highchairs/boosters	✓	❺	Stroller access

WWW.ANDIAMOPIZZA.COM

MIAMI—5600 BISCAYNE BLVD (AT 56TH ST); 305.762.5751; SU-TH 11-11, F-SA 11-12

Archie's Pizza ★ ★ ★ ⯪ ☆

"...my son's favorite pizza place... great Italian restaurant sells regular pizza, spaghetti, salad and has great price... filled with families on Sundays... kids seem to love it there... **"**

Children's menu	✓	$$$	Prices
Changing station	✗	❹	Customer service
Highchairs/boosters	✓	❸	Stroller access

WWW.ARCHIESPIZZA.COM

MIAMI—9769 NW 41ST ST (AT 97TH AVE); 305.499.9757; DAILY 11-10

Benihana ★ ★ ★ ★ ★

"...stir-fry meals are always prepared in front of you—it keeps everyone entertained, parents and kids alike... chefs often perform especially for the little ones... tables sit about 10 people, so it encourages talking with other diners... tend to be pretty loud so it's pretty family friendly... delicious for adults and fun for kids... **"**

Children's menu	✗	$$$	Prices
Changing station	✓	❹	Customer service
Highchairs/boosters	✓	❸	Stroller access

WWW.BENIHANA.COM

MIAMI—8717 SW 136TH ST (AT S DIXIE HWY); 305.238.2131; M-TH 12-2:30, 5:30-10:30, F12-2:30, 5:30-11, SA 12-11:30, SU 12-9:30

Big Cheese Pizza

"...fab pizza... they have booth, table and patio seating... can be very busy especially on weekends... kids are usually treated with a ball of raw pizza dough to keep them entertained... pizza maker is always in view... prices are low and food is great..."

Children's menu ....✓ $... Prices
Changing station........................✗   ❹ .... Customer service
Highchairs/boosters ....✓   ❹ ....Stroller access

WWW.BIGCHEESEMIAMI.COM

MIAMI—8080 SW 67TH AVE (AT LUDLAM AVE); 305.662.6855; M-TH 11-11, F 11-12, SA 12-12, SU 4-10

Cafe Tu Tu Tango

"...little plates from around the world... nice way to try lots of different dishes... tight for strollers, but we love the decor and the food... pizzas, soups, salads and a wide variety of appetizers... local artists display their pictures on the walls which adds to the ambiance... interesting music... an artist is often painting right by your table..."

Children's menu ....✓ $$$ .... Prices
Changing station........................✗   ❹ .... Customer service
Highchairs/boosters ....✓   ❸ ....Stroller access

WWW.CAFETUTUTANGO.COM

MIAMI—3015 GRAND AVE (AT MCFARLANE RD); 305.529.2222; SU-W 11:30-12AM, TH 11:30-1AM, F-SA 11:30-2AM

Canton Chinese Restaurant

"...helpful and friendly staff... totally mellow when my baby started to cry and even helped me with the blanket when it was time for his feeding... solid chinese food, the chicken soup is a big winner in our family... we must have spilled 20 times one night and the waiter didn't even blink an eye..."

Children's menu ....✓ $$ .... Prices
Changing station........................✗   ❺ .... Customer service
Highchairs/boosters ....✓   ❹ ....Stroller access

WWW.CANTONRESTAURANTS.COM

MIAMI—14487 S DIXIE HWY (AT SW 144TH ST); 305.233.6224; M-TH 11-11, F-SA 11-12, SU 12-11

Cheesecake Factory, The

"...although their cheesecake is good, we come here for the kid-friendly atmosphere and selection of good food... eclectic menu has something for everyone... they will bring your tot a plate of yogurt, cheese, bananas and bread free of charge... we love how flexible they are—they'll make whatever my kids want... lots of mommies here... always fun and always crazy... no real kids menu, but the pizza is great to share... waits can be really long..."

Children's menu ....✗ $$$ .... Prices
Changing station........................✓   ❹ .... Customer service
Highchairs/boosters ....✓   ❸ ....Stroller access

WWW.THECHEESECAKEFACTORY.COM

MIAMI—3015 GRAND AVE (AT MAYFAIR SHOPS); 305.447.9898; M-TH 11:30-11:30, F-SA 11:30-12:30, SU 10-11; PARKING AVAILABLE

MIAMI—DADELAND MALL (AT DADELAND BLVD); 305.665.5400; M-TH 11:30-11:30, F-SA 11:30-12:30, SU 10-11; MALL PARKING

Chevys Fresh Mex

"...a nice combo of good food for adults and a nice kid's menu... always a sure bet with tots in tow... tasty Mexican food with a simple kids menu (especially the quesedillas)... the tortilla making machine is

sure to grab your toddler's attention until the food arrives... an occasional balloon making man... party-like atmosphere with colorful decorations... huge Margaritas for mom and dad... service generally excellent and fast, but you may have to wait for a table at peak hours... long tables can accommodate the multifamily get-together... **"**

Children's menu	✓	$$	Prices
Changing station	✓	❹	Customer service
Highchairs/boosters	✓	❹	Stroller access

WWW.CHEVYS.COM

MIAMI—8191 NW 12TH ST (AT NW 82ND AVE); 305.392.2883; M-TH 11-11, F 11-12, SA 12-12, SU 12-10; PARKING AT 8191 NW 12TH ST

Chicken Kitchen

"...*easy, fresh, convenient... in and out... many locations to choose from...* **"**

Children's menu	✗	$$	Prices
Changing station	✗	❹	Customer service
Highchairs/boosters	✗	❸	Stroller access

WWW.CHICKENKITCHEN.COM

MIAMI—9741 NW 41ST ST (AT DORAL BLVD); 305.599.1811; M-SA 11-10, SU 11-9

Dave & Buster's

"...*lively bar and dining room paired with an adult style arcade... games and television throughout the restaurant give you plenty to keep your eyes on... decent food... can get a little loud and smoky for your average tot... most games are geared for adults... keep your eyes on your kids—it gets crowded...* **"**

Children's menu	✓	$$$	Prices
Changing station	✓	❹	Customer service
Highchairs/boosters	✓	❹	Stroller access

WWW.DAVEANDBUSTERS.COM

MIAMI—11481 NW 12TH ST (AT NW 11TH AVE); 305.468.1555; SU-W 11:30-12AM, TH 11:30-1AM, F-SU 1:30-2AM

Denny's

"...*inexpensive, coloring books, crayons and a good kids menu... you can customize your order to accommodate your tots needs... the layout is roomy so strollers can be parked right next to your table... booths provide plenty of cover if you need to breastfeed... nothing fancy, but very convenient if you need to quickly find a place to rest up with your babes...* **"**

Children's menu	✓	$$	Prices
Changing station	✓	❹	Customer service
Highchairs/boosters	✓	❹	Stroller access

WWW.DENNYS.COM

MIAMI—12000 SW 88TH ST (AT SW 124TH AVE); 305.598.0307; OPEN 24 HOURS

Dogma Grill

"...*great outdoor hotdog stand where you can get delicious hot dogs and 'not' dogs, fries, homemade potato chips, etc... always fun and bustling with families... a convenient stop for an 'out-of-the-ordinary' snack—my kids love it... service is fast and generally friendly...* **"**

Children's menu	✗	$	Prices
Changing station	✗	❺	Customer service
Highchairs/boosters	✓	❺	Stroller access

WWW.DOGMAGRILL.COM

MIAMI—7030 BISCAYNE BLVD (AT 70TH ST); 305.759.3433; DAILY 10-11

participate in our survey at

Flanigan's Seafood Bar & Grill ★★★★★

"...easy family dining—kids love the seafood decor... ribs, seafood, chicken—all tasty... three cheers for the goody bags with crayons, coloring books and an animal mask... entertaining decor varies from location to location with fish tanks and play houses... basically greasy bar food, but you can get the BBQ chicken without the sauce for a healthy alternative... they love the fish pictures on the walls, the video games and the kids menu..."

Children's menu .... ✓ $$ .... Prices
Changing station........................ ✗   .... Customer service
Highchairs/boosters .... ✓   ❸ ....Stroller access

WWW.FLANIGANS.NET

MIAMI—12790 SW 88TH ST (AT SW 127TH AVE); 305.380.0521; DAILY 11-1AM

Fuddruckers ★★★★☆

"...a super burger chain with fresh and tasty food... colorful and noisy with lots of distraction until the food arrives... loads of fresh toppings so that you can make your perfectly cooked burger even better... great kids deals that come with a free treat... noise not a problem in this super casual atmosphere... some locations have video games in the back which will buy you an extra half hour if you need it... low-key and very family friendly..."

Children's menu .... ✓ $$ .... Prices
Changing station........................ ✓   .... Customer service
Highchairs/boosters .... ✓   ❹ ....Stroller access

WWW.FUDDRUCKERS.COM

MIAMI—10680 NW 19TH ST (AT NW 107TH ST); 305.591.4050; SU-TH 11-10, F-SA 11-11; FREE PARKING

MIAMI—7800 SW 104TH ST (AT S DIXIE HWY); 305.274.1228; SU-TH 11-11, F-SA 11-12

Gordon Biersch ★★★★☆

"...a fantastic brewery that serves delicious food... awesome beer that is brewed onsite... fun atmosphere that works well for kids... high-end bar food... staff seems to adore babies... server was very doting and attentive to my family's needs... best to go early before the after work scene gets going... the big vats and pipes provide for a fun walk-around with my tot..."

Children's menu .... ✓ $$$ .... Prices
Changing station........................ ✓   ❹ .... Customer service
Highchairs/boosters .... ✓   ❹ ....Stroller access

WWW.GORDONBIERSCH.COM

MIAMI—1201 BRICKELL AVE (AT 12TH ST); 786.425.1130; SU-W 11:30-10, F-SA 11:30-11

Green Street Cafe ★★★☆☆

"...fun sidewalk eating in the heart of the Grove... they have all the basics—burgers, chicken, pasta... delicious... good people watching... friendly service... reasonable prices..."

Children's menu .... ✓ $$ .... Prices
Changing station........................ ✗   .... Customer service
Highchairs/boosters .... ✓   ❶ ....Stroller access

WWW.GREENSTREETCAFE.NET

COCONUT GROVE—3110 COMMODORE PLAZA (AT MAIN HWY); 305.567.0662; SU-TH 7-11, F-SA 7-3AM

restaurants

Greenstreet Cafe

"*...nothing better than a delicious breakfast in the grove... stroller access is a tight squeeze, but the food is worth it... huge portions for reasonable prices... outside covered dining area...* **"**

Children's menu	✓	$$$	Prices
Changing station	✗	❹	Customer service
Highchairs/boosters	✓	❸	Stroller access

WWW.GREENSTREETCAFE.NET

MIAMI—3468 MAIN HWY (AT ST COMMODORE PL); 305.444.0244; SU-TH 7:30-10:45, F-SA 7:30-11:45

Hard Rock Cafe

"*...fun and tasty if you can get in... the lines can be horrendous so be sure to check in with them first... a good spot if you have tots in tow—food tastes good and the staff is clearly used to messy eaters... hectic and loud... fun for adults as well as kids...* **"**

Children's menu	✓	$$$	Prices
Changing station	✓	❹	Customer service
Highchairs/boosters	✓	❸	Stroller access

WWW.HARDROCK.COM

MIAMI—401 BISCAYNE BLVD (AT NE 4TH ST); 305.377.3110; M-TH 11-11, F-SU 11-12

Johnny Rockets

"*...burgers, fries and a shake served up in a 50's style diner... we love the singing waiters—they're always good for a giggle... my daughter is enthralled with the juke box and straw dispenser... sit at the counter and watch the cooks prepare the food... simple, satisfying and always a hit with the little ones...* **"**

Children's menu	✓	$$	Prices
Changing station	✗	❹	Customer service
Highchairs/boosters	✓	❸	Stroller access

WWW.JOHNNYROCKETS.COM

COCONUT GROVE—3040 GRAND AVE (AT MAYFAIR SHOPS); 305.444.1000; SU-W 11-12, TH-SA 11-3; FREE PARKING

MIAMI—1025 LINCOLN RD (AT LINCOLN RD); 305.531.6585; M-TH 11-10:30, F-SA 11-12, SU 11-11; FREE PARKING

MIAMI—11401 NW 12TH ST (AT DOLPHIN MALL); 305.500.9923; M-TH 9-10, F-SA 9-11, SU 9-9; MALL PARKING

MIAMI—3036 GRAND AVE (AT MCFARLANE RD); 305.444.1000; M-TH 11-12, F-SA 11-2AM, SU 11-12

MIAMI—728 OCEAN DR (AT SOUTH BEACH); 305.538.2115; M-TH 9-12, F-SA 9-3, SU 9-1; FREE PARKING

MIAMI—7439 N KENDALL DR (AT DADELAND MALL); 305.663.8864; SU-TH 11-9, F-SA 9-9, SU 11-6; FREE PARKING

MIAMI—7501 SW 88TH ST (AT DADELAND MALL); 305.663.8864; M-TH 11-9, F-SA 8-9, SU 12-6; FREE PARKING

MIAMI—8888 SW 136TH ST (AT SW 88TH PL); 305.252.8181; M-TH 9-10, F-SA 9-11, SU 9-9

SOUTH MIAMI—5701 SUNSET DR (AT SW 57TH AVE); 305.663.1004; M-TH 11-10, F-SA 11-12, SU 11-10

Main Street Cafe

"*...cool little hippie style cafe with great soups!.. they hold regular performances on the weekends, mostly folk, blues, and classic rock, but it varies a lot... we have even watched belly dancing there!.. it's not a kids place, but kids are always welcome, and well treated...* **"**

Children's menu	✗	$$	Prices

participate in our survey at

| Changing station | ✗ | ❹ | Customer service |
| Highchairs/boosters | ✓ | ❸ | Stroller access |

WWW.MAINSTREETCAFE.NET

HOMESTEAD—134 N KROME AV (AT NW 1ST ST); 305.245.7575; T 11-3:30, W-SA 11-12

Moe's Southwest Grill ★★★⯪☆

"...fresh Mex food—burritos, quesedillas and tacos... there always are a ton of babies and kids there... if you want a drink other than juice or soda, bring your own sippy cup... tasty, good quality, cheap chow that satisfies both young and old... kids' meals for less than $3 and free on Monday nights... they only serve sodas and fruit punch for the kids... **"**

Children's menu	✓	$$	Prices
Changing station	✓	❹	Customer service
Highchairs/boosters	✓	❹	Stroller access

WWW.MOES.COM

PINECREST—11421 S DIXIE HWY (AT KILLIAN DR); 305.969.5898; M-SA 11-10, SU 10-9

Monty's ★★★★★

"...great outdoor dining on the water and easy to tote the kid along... music on the weekends and a kid's menu to boot... **"**

Children's menu	✓	$$$	Prices
Changing station	✗	❺	Customer service
Highchairs/boosters	✓	❺	Stroller access

WWW.MONTYSSTONECRAB.COM

MIAMI—2550 S BAYSHORE DR (AT AVIATION AVE); 305.858.1431; SU-TH 11:30-12, F-SA 11:30-2

MIAMI—300 ALTON RD (OFF 5TH ST); 305.673.8168; SU-TH 5:30-11, F-SA 5:30-12

Mr Moe's ★★★★☆

"...fun for a change of pace... Montana style decor... sports on TV, so noise from kids not an issue... big booth seating inside and out... lots to look at during dinner walkabouts... **"**

Children's menu	✓	$$	Prices
Changing station	✓	❹	Customer service
Highchairs/boosters	✓	❹	Stroller access

MIAMI—3131 COMMODORE PLZ (AT MAIN HWY); 305.442.1114; DAILY 11:30-5AM

Olive Garden ★★★★☆

"...finally a place that is both kid and adult friendly... tasty Italian chain with lot's of convenient locations... the staff consistently attends to the details of dining with babies and toddlers—minimizing wait time, highchairs offered spontaneously, bread sticks brought immediately... food is served as quickly as possible... happy to create special orders... our waitress even acted as our family photographer... **"**

Children's menu	✓	$$	Prices
Changing station	✓	❹	Customer service
Highchairs/boosters	✓	❹	Stroller access

WWW.OLIVEGARDEN.COM

MIAMI—8201 W FLAGLER (AT SW 82ND AVE); 305.266.5000; SU-TH 11-10, F-SA 11-11

Original Pancake House ★★★★⯪

"...consistently the best breakfast around... great flapjacks and appropriately-sized kids meals... food comes quickly... the most amazing apple pancakes ever... service is always friendly, but sometimes it can take a while to actually get the food... the highlight *for my daughter is the free balloon when we leave... always a lot of families here with small children on the weekends, so you don't have to worry about being the only one...* **"**

Children's menu	✓	$$	Prices
Changing station	✓	❹	Customer service
Highchairs/boosters	✓	❸	Stroller access

WWW.ORIGINALPANCAKEHOUSE.COM

MIAMI—11510 SW 72ND ST (AT 117TH AVE); 305.274.9215

MIAMI—9901 NW 41ST (AT EDMUND BENSON BLVD); 786.507.0564

Red Lobster Restaurants ★★★★★

"*...better than I expected from the TV commercials... food was enjoyable, especially the garlic-cheese biscuits... sea-themed decor is popular with kids... friendly staff was terrific with our kids—they must all be parents... servers even offered to heat up the baby food we brought along from home... not the cheapest prices around... kids menu offers lots of appealing choices... a comfortable place to bring kids...* **"**

Children's menu	✓	$$$	Prices
Changing station	✓	❹	Customer service
Highchairs/boosters	✓	❹	Stroller access

WWW.REDLOBSTER.COM

MIAMI—11550 SW 88TH ST (AT SW 17TH AVE); 305.595.2849; SU-TH 11-10, F-SA 11-11

MIAMI—1695 NW 87TH AV (AT NW 17TH ST); 305.392.5552; SU-TH 11-10, F-SA 11-11

MIAMI—8705 SW 136TH ST (AT FALLS SHOPPING CTR); 305.233.8994; SU-TH 11-10, F-SA 11-11; PARKING LOT AT CENTER

Roadhouse Grill ★★★★☆

"*...delicious grilled steak, chicken and shrimp... pasta too... my kids love that you can throw peanut shells on the floor... nice, simple childrens' menu... they also give your child a balloon when you walk in... reasonable prices and nice atmosphere—an easy choice for when you want to take a break from cooking...* **"**

Children's menu	✓	$$	Prices
Changing station	✓	❹	Customer service
Highchairs/boosters	✓	❹	Stroller access

WWW.ROADHOUSEGRILL.COM

MIAMI—1400 NW 87TH AVE (OFF RT 836); 305.599.1413; SU-TH 11-10, F-SA 11-11

MIAMI—7199 SW 117TH AVE (AT 72ND ST); 305.274.4696; SU-TH 11-10, F-SA 11-11

Romano's Macaroni Grill ★★★★☆

"*...family oriented and tasty... noisy so nobody cares if your kids make noise... the staff goes out of their way to make families feel welcome... they even provide slings by the table for infant carriers... the noise level is pretty constant so it's not too loud, but loud enough so that crying babies don't disturb the other patrons... good kids' menu with somewhat healthy items... crayons for kids to color on the paper tablecloths...* **"**

Children's menu	✓	$$$	Prices
Changing station	✓	❹	Customer service
Highchairs/boosters	✓	❹	Stroller access

WWW.MACARONIGRILL.COM

MIAMI—8700 NW 18TH TER (AT NW 87TH AVE); 305.477.6676; M-TH 11-10:30, F-SA 11-11:30

participate in our survey at

Ruby Tuesday

"...nice variety of healthy choices on the kids' menu—turkey, spaghetti, chicken tenders... you can definitely find something healthy here... prices are on the high side, but at least everyone can find something they like... service is fast and efficient... my daughter makes a mess and they never let me clean it up... your typical chain, but it works—you'll be happy to see ample aisle space, storage for your stroller, and attentive staff... **"**

Children's menu	✓	$$	Prices
Changing station	✓	❹	Customer service
Highchairs/boosters	✓	❸	Stroller access

WWW.RUBYTUESDAY.COM

HOMESTEAD—801 NORTHEAST 8TH ST (OFF S DIXIE HWY); 305.245.2292; M-TH 11-11, F-SA 11-12, SU 11-10

MIAMI—12075 S 152ND ST (AT 121ST AVE); 305.238.6036; SU-TH 11-11, F-SA 11-12

MIAMI—18801-B BISCAYNE BLVD (AT LOEHMANN'S FASHION ISL); 305.933.9585; SU-TH 11-11, F-SA 11-12

Samurai Japanese Steak & Seafood

"...evening entertainment and dinner all wrapped into one... Japanese food prepared and cooked in the middle of the table... flying shrimp always elicits squeals of joy from my infant... fried rice is a favorite... plenty to share... **"**

Children's menu	✓	$$$	Prices
Changing station	✗	❺	Customer service
Highchairs/boosters	✓	❺	Stroller access

WWW.BENIHANA.COM

MIAMI—8717 SW 136TH ST (AT FALLS SHOPPING CTR); 305.238.2131; M-F 12-2:30 5:30-10:30, SA 12-11,30, SU 12-9:30

Scotty's Landing

"...delicious seafood... you can even pull up here on a boat... we love this for a casual, Miami Sunday... **"**

Children's menu	✗	$$	Prices
Changing station	✗	❹	Customer service
Highchairs/boosters	✓	❺	Stroller access

COCONUT GROVE—3381 PAN AMERICAN DR (OFF S BAYSHORE DR); 305.854.2626; SU-TH 11-10, F-SA 11-11

Shorty's BBQ

"...incredible BBQ that's not too spicy for toddlers... beef sandwiches. and delicious sauces... we always end up well fed and happy... you can get as dirty as you want and nobody minds... totally casual and I love that my kids can eat with their hands—it makes it so much more fun for them... **"**

Children's menu	✓	$$$	Prices
Changing station	✓	❸	Customer service
Highchairs/boosters	✓	❸	Stroller access

WWW.SHORTYS.COM

MIAMI—11575 SW 40TH ST (AT SW 117TH AVE); 305.227.3196; M-TH 11-10, F-SU 11-11

MIAMI—2255 NW 87TH AVE (AT NW 25TH ST); 305.471.5554; M-TH 11-10, F-SU 11-11

MIAMI—9200 S DIXIE HWY (AT DADELAND BLVD); 305.670.7732; M-TH 11-10, F-SU 11-11

restaurants

Sushi Maki

"...nice and roomy... ample room for strollers... nice banquette area in back for families and outdoor Japanese garden... friendly and accommodating staff..."

Children's menu........................... ✓ $$$...Prices
Changing station .... ✓   ❹ ....Customer service
Highchairs/boosters........,,,,   ✓   ❺ .... Stroller access

WWW.SUSHIMAKIRESTAURANTS.COM

MIAMI—14491 S DIXIE HWY (AT SW 144TH ST); 305.232.6636; SU-TH 11-10:30, F-SA 11:30-12

TGI Friday's

"...good old American bar food with a reasonable selection for the healthier set as well... I love that the kids meal includes salad... my daughter requests the potato skins on a regular basis (which is good because they are also my favorite)... moderately priced... cheerful servers are used to the mess my kids leave behind... relaxed scene... I'd steer clear on a Friday night unless you don't mind waiting and watching the singles scene..."

Children's menu........................... ✓ $$...Prices
Changing station .... ✓   ❹ ....Customer service
Highchairs/boosters..................... ✓   ❸ .... Stroller access

WWW.TGIFRIDAYS.COM

CORAL GABLES—1200 S DIXIE HWY (AT MARIPOSA CT); 305.668.7808; M-TH 11-1, F-SA 11-2, SU 11-12

MIAMI—11401 NW 12TH ST (AT 111TH AVE); 305.470.9885; SU-TH 11-12, F-SA 11-2; PARKING LOT

MIAMI—8888 HOWARD DR (OFF SW 136TH ST); 305.255.1480; SU-TH 11-12, F-SA 11-1; PARKING LOT

Tony Roma's

"...ribs, ribs, ribs... mmmm... ribs are great finger foods... a kid package keeps your children entertained while waiting for your food... plenty of highchairs... low key, quick service..."

Children's menu........................... ✓ $$$...Prices
Changing station .... ✓   ❺ ....Customer service
Highchairs/boosters..................... ✓   ❹ .... Stroller access

WWW.TONYROMAS.COM

MIAMI—9525 N KENDALL DR (AT SW 94TH AVE); 305.595.7427; M-TH 11-11, F-SA 11-12, SU 12-11

Whip-n-dip

"...mom-and-pop ice-cream parlor that serves up some of the best homemade ice cream and gelatos in town... everyone there was very friendly, we loved it... satisfies every crunchy, nutty, or sweet craving kids and adults might have..."

Children's menu...........................✗ $$...Prices
Changing station ....✗   ❹ ....Customer service
Highchairs/boosters.....................✗   ❹ .... Stroller access

MIAMI—1407 SUNSET DR (AT SW 53RD PL); 305.665.2565; M-TH 11-10:30, F-SA 11-11:30, SU 12-10:30

North Dade & Beaches

"lila picks"

- ★ Arnie And Richies
- ★ Benihana
- ★ Dogma Grill
- ★ Flanigan's Seafood Bar & Grill
- ★ Johnny Rockets
- ★ Mario The Baker
- ★ Red Lobster Restaurant

restaurants

Arnie and Richie's ★★★★★

"...an awesome deli with the best food for little and big people... always packed with kids and smiling families... casual and very friendly... nobody cares if your tot makes a mess... they have some good classics like chopped liver and corned beef, but plenty for picky eaters too... you can't beat the atmosphere—always fun..."

Children's menu .... ✓
Changing station.......................... ✗
Highchairs/boosters .... ✓

$$$ .... Prices
❸ .... Customer service
❸ .... Stroller access

MIAMI BEACH—525 41ST ST (AT ROYAL PALM AVE); 305.531.7691; DAILY 7-4

Benihana ★★★★★

"...stir-fry meals are always prepared in front of you—it keeps everyone entertained, parents and kids alike... chefs often perform especially for the little ones... tables sit about 10 people, so it encourages talking with other diners... tend to be pretty loud so it's pretty family friendly... delicious for adults and fun for kids..."

Children's menu .... ✗
Changing station.......................... ✓
Highchairs/boosters .... ✓

$$$ .... Prices
❹ .... Customer service
❸ .... Stroller access

WWW.BENIHANA.COM

MIAMI BEACH—1100 LINCOLN RD (AT LENOX AVE); 305.695.8383; M-TH 12-3:30, 5-12, F 12-3:30, 5-1, SA 3-1, SU 2-11

MIAMI BEACH—1665 NE 79 ST CAUSEWAY (AT NORTHBAY VILLAGE); 305.866.2768; M-TH 12-2 5:30-11, F-SA 12-2, 5:30-11:30, SU 1-10

Big Pink ★★★☆☆

"...American comfort food with a gourmet twist... fun atmosphere geared to the kid in everyone... easy stroller access... all fresh ingredients and everything is made from scratch..."

Children's menu .... ✓
Changing station.......................... ✓
Highchairs/boosters .... ✓

$$$ .... Prices
❹ .... Customer service
❸ .... Stroller access

MIAMI BEACH—157 COLLINS AVE (AT 2ND ST); 305.532.4700; SU-TH 9-1AM, F-SA 9-2AM

Captain Jim's

"...great restaurant with fresh fish daily... all paper products and very kid-friendly... reasonably priced... take-out fish too..."

Children's menu	✓	$$	Prices
Changing station	✗	❺	Customer service
Highchairs/boosters	✓	❹	Stroller access

NORTH MIAMI—12950 W DIXIE HWY (AT 129TH ST); 305.002.2812; M-SA 10-9

Cheesecake Factory, The

"...although their cheesecake is good, we come here for the kid-friendly atmosphere and selection of good food... eclectic menu has something for everyone... they will bring your tot a plate of yogurt, cheese, bananas and bread free of charge... we love how flexible they are—they'll make whatever my kids want... lots of mommies here... always fun and always crazy... no real kids menu, but the pizza is great to share... waits can be really long..."

Children's menu	✗	$$$	Prices
Changing station	✓	❹	Customer service
Highchairs/boosters	✓	❸	Stroller access

WWW.THECHEESECAKEFACTORY.COM

AVENTURA—19501 BISCAYNE BLVD (AT WILLIAM LEHMAN CSWY); 305.792.9696; M-TH 11:30-1130, F-SA 11:30-12:30, SU 10-11

Dogma Grill

"...great outdoor hotdog stand where you can get delicious hot dogs and 'not' dogs, fries, homemade potato chips, etc... always fun and bustling with families... a convenient stop for an 'out-of-the-ordinary' snack—my kids love it... service is fast and generally friendly..."

Children's menu	✗	$	Prices
Changing station	✗	❺	Customer service
Highchairs/boosters	✓	❺	Stroller access

MIAMI BEACH—1500 WASHINGTON AVE (AT 15TH ST); 305.759.3433; DAILY 10-11

Flanigan's Seafood Bar & Grill ★★★★★

"...easy family dining—kids love the seafood decor... ribs, seafood, chicken—all tasty... three cheers for the goody bags with crayons, coloring books and an animal mask... entertaining decor varies from location to location with fish tanks and play houses... basically greasy bar food, but you can get the BBQ chicken without the sauce for a healthy alternative... they love the fish pictures on the walls, the video games and the kids menu..."

Children's menu	✓	$$	Prices
Changing station	✗	❹	Customer service
Highchairs/boosters	✓	❸	Stroller access

WWW.FLANIGANS.NET

HIALEAH—1550 W 84TH ST (AT W 16TH AVE); 305.821.0993; M 11-1:30AM, T-W SU 11-2AM, TH-SA 11-2AM

NORTH MIAMI—13205 BISCAYNE BLVD (AT NE 135TH ST); 305.893.0506; M 11-1:30AM, T-W SU 11-2AM, TH-SA 11-2AM

SURFSIDE—9516 HARDING AV (AT 95TH ST); 305.867.0099; SU-TH 11-1AM, F-SA 11-2AM

Front Porch Cafe

"...the best place for a sunday brunch and great seating on the sidewalk... sometimes a line to be seated, but it goes quick... great food!.."

Children's menu	✓	$$$	Prices

Changing station	✗	**❸**	Customer service
Highchairs/boosters	✓	**❺**	Stroller access

MIAMI BEACH—1418 OCEAN DR (AT 14TH ST); 305.531.8300; M-TH 8-10:30, F-SU 8-10:30

Fuddruckers

"...a super burger chain with fresh and tasty food... colorful and noisy with lots of distraction until the food arrives... loads of fresh toppings so that you can make your perfectly cooked burger even better... great kids deals that come with a free treat... noise not a problem in this super casual atmosphere... some locations have video games in the back which will buy you an extra half hour if you need it... low-key and very family friendly..."

Children's menu	✓	$$	Prices
Changing station	✓	**❹**	Customer service
Highchairs/boosters	✓	**❹**	Stroller access

WWW.FUDDRUCKERS.COM

AVENTURA—17985 BISCAYNE BLVD (OFF W DIXIE HWY); 305.933.3572; SU-TH 11-11, F-SA 11-12

MIAMI BEACH—1555 WASHINGTON AV (AT NE 13TH ST); 305.538.4330; DAILY 11-9; FREE PARKING

Fuji Hana Japanese Restaurant

"...the best Sushi and Thai around... very accommodating to kids... friendly and great service..."

Children's menu	✓	$$	Prices
Changing station	✗	**❺**	Customer service
Highchairs/boosters	✓	**❺**	Stroller access

AVENTURA—18757 BISCAYNE BLVD (AT LOEHMANN'S FASHION ISL); 305.932.8080; M-TH 12-11, F-SA 12-11:30, SU 12-10:30

Ghirardelli Chocolate Shop ★★★★★

"...great ice cream... fun for the kids... delicious, fun treats to choose from..."

Children's menu	✗	$$	Prices
Changing station	✗	**❺**	Customer service
Highchairs/boosters	✗	**❹**	Stroller access

WWW.GHIRARDELLI.COM

MIAMI BEACH—801 LINCOLN RD (AT MERIDIAN AVE); 305.532.2538; SU-TH10-12, F-SA 10-1:30

Here Comes The Sun

"...delicious health food and very child-friendly... soy cheese pizzas are delicious as is all of the entrees... great daily soup specials... to go is just as good as in... healthy good food for the entire family... family run and friendly service... booths and tables..."

Children's menu	✓	$$$	Prices
Changing station	✓	**❹**	Customer service
Highchairs/boosters	✓	**❹**	Stroller access

NORTH MIAMI—2188 NE 123RD ST (AT SANS SOUCI BLVD); 305.893.5711; M-SA 10-8:30

Johnny Rockets ★★★★★

"...burgers, fries and a shake served up in a 50's style diner... we love the singing waiters—they're always good for a giggle... my daughter is enthralled with the juke box and straw dispenser... sit at the counter and watch the cooks prepare the food... simple, satisfying and always a hit with the little ones..."

Children's menu	✓	$$	Prices
Changing station	✗	**❹**	Customer service

restaurants

Highchairs/boosters .... ✓ ❸ .... Stroller access

WWW.JOHNNYROCKETS.COM

AVENTURA—19501 BISCAYNE BLVD (AT AVENTURA MALL); 305.682.7979; M-TH 9-10, F-SA 9-11, SU 9-9; MALL PARKING

HIALEAH—6769 MAIN ST (AT NEW BARN RD); 305.827.0055; SU-TH 11-9, F-SA 11-12

Mario The Baker ★★★★★

❝...this place isn't fancy, but they've got the best garlic rolls around... place hasn't changed since I was a kid and the food is still awesome... pizza is the best around... quick service and prices are unbeatable... ❞

Children's menu .... ✗ $$ .... Prices
Changing station .... ✗ ❹ .... Customer service
Highchairs/boosters .... ✗ ❹ .... Stroller access

NORTH MIAMI—13695 W DIXIE HWY (AT NE11TH AVE); 305.891.7641; SU-TH 11-10, F-SA 11-11

Nexxt Cafe ★★★★☆

❝...this is our favorite place to eat on the Beach... Lincoln road is so much easier with kids than Ocean, but you still get the outdoor experience and great people watching... large portions, wide selection, good service... ❞

Children's menu .... ✓ $$ .... Prices
Changing station .... ✓ ❸ .... Customer service
Highchairs/boosters .... ✓ ❸ .... Stroller access

MIAMI BEACH—700 LINCOLN RD (AT EUCLID AVE); 305.532.6643; M-TH 11:30-11, F-SA 11:30-12, SU 11-11; STREET PARKING

North Miami Ale House ★★★⯪☆

❝...great family restaurant, good prices, good food... ❞

Children's menu .... ✓ $$ .... Prices
Changing station .... ✓ ❹ .... Customer service
Highchairs/boosters .... ✓ ❹ .... Stroller access

WWW.ALEHOUSEINC.COM

NORTH MIAMI BEACH—3227 NE 163RD ST (AT INTERAMA BLVD); 305.945.6878; M-SA 11-2, SU 11-12

Olive Garden ★★★★☆

❝...finally a place that is both kid and adult friendly... tasty Italian chain with lot's of convenient locations... the staff consistently attends to the details of dining with babies and toddlers—minimizing wait time, highchairs offered spontaneously, bread sticks brought immediately... food is served as quickly as possible... happy to create special orders... our waitress even acted as our family photographer... ❞

Children's menu .... ✓ $$ .... Prices
Changing station .... ✓ ❹ .... Customer service
Highchairs/boosters .... ✓ ❹ .... Stroller access

WWW.OLIVEGARDEN.COM

AVENTURA—18101 BISCAYNE BLVD (AT NE180TH ST); 305.935.5742; SU-TH 11-10, F-SA 11-11

Original Pancake House ★★★★⯪

❝...consistently the best breakfast around... great flapjacks and appropriately-sized kids meals... food comes quickly... the most amazing apple pancakes ever... service is always friendly, but sometimes it can take a while to actually get the food... the highlight for my daughter is the free balloon when we leave... always a lot of families here with small children on the weekends, so you don't have to worry about being the only one... ❞

Children's menu .... ✓ $$ .... Prices

Changing station..........................✓ ❹........................Customer service
Highchairs/boosters ....✓ ❸.............................Stroller access

WWW.ORIGINALPANCAKEHOUSE.COM

AVENTURA—21215 BISCAYNE BLVD (AT NE 213TH ST); 305.933.1966; DAILY 7-9

Outback Steakhouse ★★★★☆

❝...Aussie style eatery with big steaks and shrimp on the barbie... don't miss the bloomin' onion, but be prepared to share—it's huge... very understanding of our screaming infant and gave us a booth a little out of the way... gave us extra whipped cream for dessert and on occasion free ice cream... the wait for a table can get long so go early to avoid the masses... nice wide aisles makes maneuvering around with strollers easy... tables toys in the waiting area... **❞**

Children's menu ....✓ $$$ .... Prices
Changing station..........................✓ ❹........................Customer service
Highchairs/boosters ....✓ ❸.............................Stroller access

WWW.OUTBACKSTEAKHOUSE.COM

MIAMI BEACH—2201 COLLINS AVE (AT 22ND ST); 305.531.1338; M-TH 5-11, F-SA 4-11:30, SU 4-10:30

Pizza Roma ★★★☆☆

❝...amazing pizza plus other Italian dishes and salads... they have an ice cream cooler for the kids to pick specialty ice cream from... a personal favorite, they sing when the pizza is arriving... **❞**

Children's menu ....✓ $.. Prices
Changing station..........................✗ ❺........................Customer service
Highchairs/boosters ....✓ ❺.............................Stroller access

AVENTURA—19090 NE 29TH AV (AT CONCORDE CTR DR); 305.937.4884; SU-TH 11-10, F-SA 11-11

Rascal House ★★★★☆

❝...loud and always busy... awesome food that's guaranteed to please everyone, but the 'scene' can be overwhelming... you can make a mess and have your baby screaming and nobody will notice... the staff is always friendly to us and 'gets' kids... a local institution that's definitely worth checking out... **❞**

Children's menu ....✓ $$$ .... Prices
Changing station..........................✗ ❸........................Customer service
Highchairs/boosters ....✓ ❸.............................Stroller access

SUNNY ISLES BEACH—17190 COLLINS AVE (AT 172ND ST); 305.947.4581; 24 HOURS

Red Lobster Restaurants ★★★★★

❝...better than I expected from the TV commercials... food was enjoyable, especially the garlic-cheese biscuits... sea-themed decor is popular with kids... friendly staff was terrific with our kids—they must all be parents... servers even offered to heat up the baby food we brought along from home... not the cheapest prices around... kids menu offers lots of appealing choices... a comfortable place to bring kids... **❞**

Children's menu ....✓ $$$ .... Prices
Changing station..........................✓ ❹........................Customer service
Highchairs/boosters ....✓ ❹.............................Stroller access

WWW.REDLOBSTER.COM

HIALEAH—1760 W 49TH ST (AT WESTLAND MALL); 305.557.3088; SU-TH 11-10, F-SA 11-11; MALL PARKING

NORTH MIAMI—13300 BISCAYNE BLVD (AT NE 130TH ST AND IXOTA LN); 305.895.6095; SU-TH 11-10, F-SA 11-11

Roadhouse Grill ★★★★☆

"...delicious grilled steak, chicken and shrimp... pasta too... my kids love that you can throw peanut shells on the floor... nice, simple childrens' menu... they also give your child a balloon when you walk in... reasonable prices and nice atmosphere—an easy choice for when you want to take a break from cooking..."

Children's menu	✓	$$...	Prices
Changing station	✓	❹	Customer service
Highchairs/boosters	✓	❹	Stroller access

WWW.ROADHOUSEGRILL.COM

NORTH MIAMI—12599 BISCAYNE BLVD (AT KEYSTONE BLVD); 305.893.7433; SU-TH 11-10, F-SA 11-11

NORTH MIAMI—12599 BISCAYNE BLVD (OFF 123RD ST); 305.893.7433; SU-TH 10-10, F-SA 10-11

Romano's Macaroni Grill ★★★★☆

"...family oriented and tasty... noisy so nobody cares if your kids make noise... the staff goes out of their way to make families feel welcome... they even provide slings by the table for infant carriers... the noise level is pretty constant so it's not too loud, but loud enough so that crying babies don't disturb the other patrons... good kids' menu with somewhat healthy items... crayons for kids to color on the paper tablecloths..."

Children's menu	✓	$$$	Prices
Changing station	✓	❹	Customer service
Highchairs/boosters	✓	❹	Stroller access

WWW.MACARONIGRILL.COM

AVENTURA—16395 BISCAYNE BLVD (AT NE 23RD BLVD); 305.945.7990; SU-TH 11-10, F-SA 11-11

Sara's Kosher Restaurant ★★★★☆

"...Kosher family restaurant with a wide variety... pizza and other items for the kids... yogurt shakes... service is okay, but the choice of food is great..."

Children's menu	✓	$$	Prices
Changing station	✗	❸	Customer service
Highchairs/boosters	✓	❸	Stroller access

NORTH MIAMI—2214 NE 123RD ST (AT N BAYSHORE DR); 305.891.3312; SU-TH 7-10PM, F 7-3PM, SA 9PM-1AM; PLENTY

Steve's Pizza ★★★⯪☆

"...no highchairs, not much room to sit down or wait in line... umbrellas strollers do fit, but not at peak times... great food, so suggest calling in for carryout or delivery..."

Children's menu	✗	$$$	Prices
Changing station	✗	❸	Customer service
Highchairs/boosters	✗	❸	Stroller access

NORTH MIAMI—12101 BISCAYNE BLVD (AT NE 123RD ST); 305.891.0202; M-TH 11-3AM, F-SA 11-4AM, SU 11-2AM

Tamarind Thai Restaurant ★★★★☆

"...we have been bringing our baby here since he was first born... they always make room for the stroller and are happy to have us there... the food is very good Thai—we had our son's baptism lunch there and they prepared a special menu including dessert for a very reasonable price..."

Children's menu	✗	$$	Prices
Changing station	✗	❹	Customer service
Highchairs/boosters	✓	❹	Stroller access

WWW.TAMARINDTHAI.US

MIAMI BEACH—946 NORMANDY DR (AT 71ST ST); 305.861.6222; T-SU 12-3,
  5:30-10, F-SA 12-11

TGI Friday's   ★★★★☆

"...*good old American bar food with a reasonable selection for the
healthier set as well... I love that the kids meal includes salad... my
daughter requests the potato skins on a regular basis (which is good
because they are also my favorite)... moderately priced... cheerful
servers are used to the mess my kids leave behind... relaxed scene... I'd
steer clear on a Friday night unless you don't mind waiting and
watching the singles scene...* **"**

Children's menu .... ✓ $$ .... Prices
Changing station.......................... ✓   ❹ .... Customer service
Highchairs/boosters .... ✓   ❸ ....Stroller access

WWW.TGIFRIDAYS.COM

MIAMI BEACH—500 OCEAN DR (AT 5TH ST); 305.673.8443; SU-TH 11-2, F-
  SA 11-3

restaurants

Broward County

★★★★★
"lila picks"

- ★ Benihana
- ★ Flanigan's Seafood Bar & Grill
- ★ Johnny Rockets
- ★ Red Lobster Restaurant
- ★ Shorty's BBQ

Antonio's Pizzeria   ★★★★★

❝...*this is a mom and pop pizza joint that welcomes children of all ages... the food is delicious and very inexpensive... every service person is patient and truly attentive to your little one...* **❞**

Children's menu	✗	$	Prices
Changing station	✗	❺	Customer service
Highchairs/boosters	✓	❺	Stroller access

MIRAMAR—6890 MIRAMAR PKY (OFF FLORIDA TPKE); 954.966.3332; M-TH 11-10, F-SA 11-11, SU 2-10

Benihana   ★★★★★

❝...*stir-fry meals are always prepared in front of you—it keeps everyone entertained, parents and kids alike... chefs often perform especially for the little ones... tables sit about 10 people, so it encourages talking with other diners... tend to be pretty loud so it's pretty family friendly... delicious for adults and fun for kids...* **❞**

Children's menu	✗	$$$	Prices
Changing station	✓	❹	Customer service
Highchairs/boosters	✓	❸	Stroller access

WWW.BENIHANA.COM

FORT LAUDERDALE—276 E COMMERCIAL BLVD (AT N ANDREWS AVE); 954.776.0111; M-F 12-2 5-11, SA 1-3, 5-11, SU 1-10

California Pizza Kitchen   ★★★★⯨

❝...*you can't go wrong with their fabulous pizza... always clean... the food's great, the kids drinks all come with a lid... the staff is super friendly to kids... crayons and coloring books keep little minds busy... most locations have a place for strollers at the front... no funny looks or attitude when breastfeeding... open atmosphere with friendly service... tables are well spaced so you don't feel like your kid is annoying the diners nearby (it's usually full of kids anyway)...* **❞**

Children's menu	✓	$$	Prices
Changing station	✓	❹	Customer service
Highchairs/boosters	✓	❹	Stroller access

WWW.CPK.COM

participate in our survey at

PEMBROKE PINES—11401 PINE BLVD (AT PEMBROKE LAKES MALL); 954.432.1498; M-TH 11-10, F-SA 11-11, SU 11-10; MALL PARKING

Cheeburger Cheeburger ★★★½☆

"...old time feel... classic 50's and 60's rock and roll on the radio... big, big burgers—salads too... you can choose whatever topping you want for your burgers and salads... great shakes... don't miss the clown on Friday nights—free face painting and my kids love it... good food and a very relaxed environment..."

Children's menu	✓	$$ .... Prices
Changing station	✓	❹ .... Customer service
Highchairs/boosters	✓	❸ .... Stroller access

WWW.CHEEBURGER.COM

CORAL SPRINGS—1853 UNIVERSITY DR (AT NW 19TH ST); 954.346.6666; M-TH 11-9, F-SA 11-10, SU 12-9; FREE PARKING

FORT LAUDERDALE—17 S FT LAUDERDALE BEACH BLVD (AT VALENCIA ST); 954.769.9953; M-TH 11-9, F-SA 11-12, SU 12-9

FORT LAUDERDALE—900 S FEDERAL HWY (AT SE 9TH ST); 954.462.7255; M-TH 11-9, F-SA 11-10, SU 12-9; FREE PARKING

FORT LAUDERDALE—SOUTHWEST TERMINAL #1 (AT INT'L AIRPORT); FREE PARKING

LAUDERHILL—5409 N UNIVERSITY DR (AT W COMMERCIAL BLVD); 954.749.4666; M-TH 11-9, F-SA 11-11, SU 12-9

PEMBROKE PINES—2010 N FLAMINGO RD (AT SHERIDAN ST); 954.441.9799; M-TH 11-9, F-SA 11-10, SU 12-9; FREE PARKING

SUNRISE—2602 SAWGRASS MILLS CIR (AT SAMGRASS MILLS); 954.838.7555; M-TH 11-9, F-SA 11-11, SU 12-9

WESTON—1793 BELL TOWER LN (AT TOWN CTR CIR); 954.659.1115; M-TH 11-9, F-SA 11-11, SU 12-9

Cheesecake Factory, The ★★★★☆

"...although their cheesecake is good, we come here for the kid-friendly atmosphere and selection of good food... eclectic menu has something for everyone... they will bring your tot a plate of yogurt, cheese, bananas and bread free of charge... we love how flexible they are—they'll make whatever my kids want... lots of mommies here... always fun and always crazy... no real kids menu, but the pizza is great to share... waits can be really long..."

Children's menu	✗	$$$ .... Prices
Changing station	✓	❹ .... Customer service
Highchairs/boosters	✓	❸ .... Stroller access

WWW.THECHEESECAKEFACTORY.COM

FORT LAUDERDALE—620 E LAS OLAS BLVD (AT SE 4TH ST); 954.463.1999; M-TH 11:30-11:30, F-SA 11:30-12:30, SU 10-11

SUNRISE—2612 SAWGRASS MILLS CIR (AT SAWGRASS MALL); 954.835.0966; M-TH 11:30-11:30, F-SA 11:30-12:30, SU 10-11; MALL PARKING

Dave & Buster's ★★★☆☆

"...lively bar and dining room paired with an adult style arcade... games and television throughout the restaurant give you plenty to keep your eyes on... decent food... can get a little loud and smoky for your average tot... most games are geared for adults... keep your eyes on your kids—it gets crowded..."

Children's menu	✓	$$$ .... Prices
Changing station	✓	❹ .... Customer service
Highchairs/boosters	✓	❹ .... Stroller access

WWW.DAVEANDBUSTERS.COM

HOLLYWOOD—3000 OAKWOOD BLVD (OFF SHERIDAN ST); 954.923.5505; SU-W 11:30-12, TH 11:30-1, F-SA 11:30-2

restaurants

Del Vechio Pizza ★★★★★

" *...the best pizza around... yummm!...* **"**

Children's menu	✓	$$		Prices
Changing station	✗	❹		Customer service
Highchairs/boosters	✓	❹		Stroller access

WESTON—1795 BELL TOWER LANE (AT TOWN CTR CIR); 954.888.9494; M-TH 11-10, F-SA 11-11, SU 12-10

Flanigan's Seafood Bar & Grill ★★★★★

" *...easy family dining—kids love the seafood decor... ribs, seafood, chicken—all tasty... three cheers for the goody bags with crayons, coloring books and an animal mask... entertaining decor varies from location to location with fish tanks and play houses... basically greasy bar food, but you can get the BBQ chicken without the sauce for a healthy alternative... they love the fish pictures on the walls, the video games and the kids menu...* **"**

Children's menu	✓	$$		Prices
Changing station	✗	❹		Customer service
Highchairs/boosters	✓	❸		Stroller access

WWW.FLANIGANS.NET

FORT LAUDERDALE—2505 N UNIVERSITY DR (AT SUNSET STRIP); 954.964.3793; SU-TH 11-12, F-SA 11-1; FREE PARKING

FORT LAUDERDALE—2600 DAVIE BLVD (OFF FLORIDA'S TPKE); 954.791.3942; SU-TH 11-12, F-SA 11-1

FORT LAUDERDALE—5450 N STATE RD 7 (AT SW 54TH CT); 954.733.0514; SU-TH 11-12, F-SA 11-1; FREE PARKING

HALLANDALE—4 N FEDERAL HWY (AT SE 5TH AVE); 954.458.2566; SU-TH 11-12, F-SA 11-1; FREE PARKING

WESTON—2460 WESTON RD (AT EXECUTIVE PARK DR); 954.385.8080; SU-TH 11-1, F-SA 11-2

Fuddruckers ★★★★☆

" *...a super burger chain with fresh and tasty food... colorful and noisy with lots of distraction until the food arrives... loads of fresh toppings so that you can make your perfectly cooked burger even better... great kids deals that come with a free treat... noise not a problem in this super casual atmosphere... some locations have video games in the back which will buy you an extra half hour if you need it... low-key and very family friendly...* **"**

Children's menu	✓	$$		Prices
Changing station	✓	❹		Customer service
Highchairs/boosters	✓	❹		Stroller access

WWW.FUDDRUCKERS.COM

PLANTATION—1801 N UNIVERSITY DR (AT NW 17TH CT); 954.476.8111; SU-TH 11-11, F-SA 11-12

Hard Rock Cafe ★★★½☆

" *...fun and tasty if you can get in... the lines can be horrendous so be sure to check in with them first... a good spot if you have tots in tow—food tastes good and the staff is clearly used to messy eaters... hectic and loud... fun for adults as well as kids...* **"**

Children's menu	✓	$$$		Prices
Changing station	✓	❹		Customer service
Highchairs/boosters	✓	❸		Stroller access

WWW.HARDROCK.COM

HOLLYWOOD—1 SEMINOLE WY (OFF OSCEOLA DR); 954.315.9112; SU-TH 11-11, F-SA 11-2

participate in our survey at

Japan Inn

"...fun, Japanese food where they cook on your table... this is dinner and entertainment at the same time... my son loves the rice here... we love the sushi..."

Children's menu ✓	$$$ ...... Prices
Changing station ✗	❹ ...... Customer service
Highchairs/boosters ✓	❸ ...... Stroller access

WESTON—1798 MARKET ST (AT TWN CTR CIR); 954.659.7847; DAILY 11:30-3, 4:30-11

Johnny Rockets

"...burgers, fries and a shake served up in a 50's style diner... we love the singing waiters—they're always good for a giggle... my daughter is enthralled with the juke box and straw dispenser... sit at the counter and watch the cooks prepare the food... simple, satisfying and always a hit with the little ones..."

Children's menu ✓	$$ ...... Prices
Changing station ✗	❹ ...... Customer service
Highchairs/boosters ✓	❸ ...... Stroller access

WWW.JOHNNYROCKETS.COM

FORT LAUDERDALE—300 SW 1ST AV (AT BRICKELL AVE); 954.522.8181; SU-TH 11-9, F-SA 11-12

Legal Sea Foods

"...wonderful choices... great selection of food and very friendly service..."

Children's menu ✓	$$$$ ...... Prices
Changing station ✗	❺ ...... Customer service
Highchairs/boosters ✓	❹ ...... Stroller access

WWW.LEGALSEAFOODS.COM

SUNRISE—2602 SAWGRASS MILLS CIR (AT PINK FLAMINGO LN); 954.846.9011; M-TH 11:30-10, F-SA 11:30-11, SU 12-9

Lucille's American Cafe

"...great place for kids because you can sit outside and eat... the kid's meals are huge portions and the adult food is good..."

Children's menu ✓	$$ ...... Prices
Changing station ✓	❺ ...... Customer service
Highchairs/boosters ✓	❹ ...... Stroller access

WWW.LUCILLESCAFE.COM

WESTON—2250 WESTON RD (AT N COMMERCE PKY); 954.384.9007; SU-TH 11-10, F-SA 11-11

Mr Latin Grill

"...the food is excellent and the dining area is very open, so there is very easy access with the stroller..."

Children's menu ✓	$$ ...... Prices
Changing station ✗	❺ ...... Customer service
Highchairs/boosters ✓	❺ ...... Stroller access

POMPANO BEACH—1184 S FEDERAL HWY (AT SE 12TH ST); 954.545.1444; M-TH 11:30-10, F-SA 11:30-11, SU 11:30-10

Olive Garden

"...finally a place that is both kid and adult friendly... tasty Italian chain with lot's of convenient locations... the staff consistently attends to the details of dining with babies and toddlers—minimizing wait time, highchairs offered spontaneously, bread sticks brought immediately... food is served as quickly as possible... happy to create special orders... our waitress even acted as our family photographer..."

Children's menu......................... ✓	$$.. Prices
Changing station .... ✓	❹ ....Customer service
Highchairs/boosters.................... ✓	❹ .... Stroller access

WWW.OLIVEGARDEN.COM

FORT LAUDERDALE—5550 N FEDERAL HWY (AT NE 55TH ST); 954.776.3341; SU-TH 11-10, F-SA 11-11

FORT LAUDERDALE—807 S UNIVERSITY DR (AT SW 10 ST); 954.424.7201; SU-TH 11-10, F-SA 11-11

PEMBROKE PINES—11425 PINES BLVD (AT PEMBROKE LAKES MALL); 954.432.5529; SU-TH 11-10, F-SA 11-11; MALL PARKING

Original Pancake House ★★★★⯪

❝...consistently the best breakfast around... great flapjacks and appropriately-sized kids meals... food comes quickly... the most amazing apple pancakes ever... service is always friendly, but sometimes it can take a while to actually get the food... the highlight for my daughter is the free balloon when we leave... always a lot of families here with small children on the weekends, so you don't have to worry about being the only one... **❞**

Children's menu......................... ✓	$$.. Prices
Changing station .... ✓	❹ ....Customer service
Highchairs/boosters.................... ✓	❸ .... Stroller access

WWW.ORIGINALPANCAKEHOUSE.COM

CORAL SPRINGS—1840 UNIVERSITY DR (OFF 19TH ST); 954.255.8080; M-TH 7-2, F-SA 7-8, SU 7-4

FORT LAUDERDALE—2851 N FEDERAL HWY (OFF RT 816); 954.564.8881; M-TH 7-2, F-SA 7-8, SU 7-4

PLANTATION—8640 BROWARD BLVD (AT PINE ISLAND RD); 954.473.2771; DAILY 7-9

Rainforest Cafe ★★★⯪☆

❝...like eating in the jungle... the decor keeps the kids entertained and the food is decent... kids either love it or are terrified at first and need to ease into the wild animal thing... I get at least 20 extra minutes of hang time with my friends because my daughter is so enchanted by the setting... waiters tend to be very accommodating... they always give me (with my three kiddos) an extra-large table... watch the toy section chock full of 'but I want it' items... **❞**

Children's menu......................... ✓	$$$...................................... Prices
Changing station .... ✓	❹ ....Customer service
Highchairs/boosters.................... ✓	❹ .... Stroller access

WWW.RAINFORESTCAFE.COM

SUNRISE—12801 W SUNRISE BLVD (AT WHITE SEAHORSE WAY); 954.851.1015; M-TH 11-9:30, F-SA 11-10, SU 11-8:30

Red Lobster Restaurants ★★★★★

❝...better than I expected from the TV commercials... food was enjoyable, especially the garlic-cheese biscuits... sea-themed decor is popular with kids... friendly staff was terrific with our kids—they must all be parents... servers even offered to heat up the baby food we brought along from home... not the cheapest prices around... kids menu offers lots of appealing choices... a comfortable place to bring kids... **❞**

Children's menu......................... ✓	$$$...................................... Prices
Changing station .... ✓	❹ ....Customer service
Highchairs/boosters.................... ✓	❹ .... Stroller access

WWW.REDLOBSTER.COM

CORAL SPRINGS—2000 UNIVERSITY DR (AT NW 20TH ST); 954.752.6131; SU-TH 11-10, F-SA 11-11; PARKING LOT

FORT LAUDERDALE—5950 N FEDERAL HWY (AT 62ND ST); 954.491.3030;
SU-TH 11-10, F-SA 11-11

HOLLYWOOD—296 N UNIVERSITY DR (AT NW 3RD ST); 954.432.8500; SU-TH
11-10, F-SA 11-11; PARKING LOT

PLANTATION—803 S UNIVERSITY DR (AT SW 10TH ST); 954.424.0406; SU-TH
11-10, F-SA 11-11; PARKING LOT

Roadhouse Grill

"...delicious grilled steak, chicken and shrimp... pasta too... my kids
love that you can throw peanut shells on the floor... nice, simple
childrens' menu... they also give your child a balloon when you walk
in... reasonable prices and nice atmosphere—an easy choice for when
you want to take a break from cooking... **"**

Children's menu	✓	$$	Prices
Changing station	✓	❹	Customer service
Highchairs/boosters	✓	❹	Stroller access

WWW.ROADHOUSEGRILL.COM

CORAL SPRINGS—1580 N UNIVERSITY DR (AT ROYAL PALM BLVD);
954.346.6344; SU-TH 11-10, F-SA 11-11

DAVIE—1900 S UNIVERSITY DR (OFF RT 595); 954.370.3044; SU-TH 11-10,
F-SA 11-11

DEERFIELD BEACH—401 N FEDERAL HWY (AT RT 810); 954.428.9080; SU-TH
11-10, F-SA 11-11

FORT LAUDERDALE—3300 E COMMERCIAL BLVD (AT BAYVIEW DR);
954.772.3700; SU-TH 11-10, F-SA 11-11

PEMBROKE PINES—8525 PINES BLVD (AT 86TH AVE); 954.438.0599; SU-TH
11-10, F-SA 11-11

Roly Poly Sandwiches

"...kids sandwiches start at 99c, which is great... for adults, and older
kids, you can go with one of their combinations or select what you
want to go in your wrap... it's terrific if you are on any kind of diet
because you can choose exactly what goes in your wrap... **"**

Children's menu	✓	$	Prices
Changing station	✓	❺	Customer service
Highchairs/boosters	✓	❹	Stroller access

WWW.ROLYPOLYFLORIDA.COM

CORAL SPRINGS—2866 UNIVERSITY DR (AT NW 28TH ST); 954.341.6744; M-
F 10-9, SA 11-8, SU 11-7

PLANTATION—801 S UNIVERSITY DR (AT SW 10TH ST); 954.476.2356; M-F
10-8, SA-SU 11-6

Ruby Tuesday

"...nice variety of healthy choices on the kids' menu—turkey,
spaghetti, chicken tenders... you can definitely find something healthy
here... prices are on the high side, but at least everyone can find
something they like... service is fast and efficient... my daughter makes
a mess and they never let me clean it up... your typical chain, but it
works—you'll be happy to see ample aisle space, storage for your
stroller, and attentive staff... **"**

Children's menu	✓	$$	Prices
Changing station	✓	❹	Customer service
Highchairs/boosters	✓	❸	Stroller access

WWW.RUBYTUESDAY.COM

CORAL SPRINGS—9511 WESTVIEW DR (AT N UNIVERSITY DR); 954.757.0885;
SU-TH 11-11, F-SA 11-12

DAVIE—6405 NOVA DR (AT DAVIE RD); 954.476.0780; SU-TH 11-11, F-SA 11-
12

restaurants

DEERFIELD BEACH—3887 HILLSBORO BLVD (AT POWERLINE RD); 954.725.8151; M-TH 11-11, F-SA 11-12, SU 11-10

LAUDERHILL—7736 W COMMERCIAL BLVD (AT UNIVERSITY DR); 954.749.4242; M-TH 11-11, F-SA 11-12, SU 11-10

PEMBROKE PINES—11401 PINES BLVD (AT N HAITUS RD); 954.430.8911; SU-TH 11-11, F-SA 11-12

PLANTATION—8000 W BROWARD BLVD (AT UNIVERSITY DR); 954.473.1601; M-TH 11-11, F-SA 11-12, SU 11-10

POMPANO BEACH—POMPANO PKY (AT POMPANO PARK PL); 954.969.8082; M-TH 11-11, F-SA 11-12, SU 11-10

SUNRISE—12801 W SUNRISE BLVD (AT SATIN LEAF WY); 954.846.8267; M-TH 10:30-9:30, F-SA 10:30-10, SU 10:30-9

Scruby's Bar-B-Q ★★★★☆

"...delish BBQ... four kinds of sauces available... the beans are amazing... kids eat free with an adult... limited menu, but it's free... good value, great taste...**"**

Children's menu	✓	$$	Prices
Changing station	✓	❹	Customer service
Highchairs/boosters	✓	❹	Stroller access

WWW.SCRUBYS.COM

FORT LAUDERDALE—251 N UNIVERSITY DR (AT FASHION SQ MARKETPLACE); 954.987.1933; SU-TH 11-9:30, F-SA 11-10

Shorty's BBQ ★★★★★

"...incredible BBQ that's not too spicy for toddlers... beef sandwiches. and delicious sauces... we always end up well fed and happy... you can get as dirty as you want and nobody minds... totally casual and I love that my kids can eat with their hands—it makes it so much more fun for them...**"**

Children's menu	✓	$$$	Prices
Changing station	✓	❸	Customer service
Highchairs/boosters	✓	❸	Stroller access

WWW.SHORTYS.COM

DAVIE—5989 S UNIVERSITY DR (AT STIRLING RD); 954.680.9900; M-TH 11-10, F-SU 11-11

Smokey Bones BBQ ★★★★☆

"...reasonably healthy food for kids—not fried chicken fingers and fries... lots of TVs to entertain kids so adults can have a little time to talk... volume control at each table, stations often set to Nickelodeon... unique holders for car seats that cradle the seats...**"**

Children's menu	✓	$$$	Prices
Changing station	✓	❹	Customer service
Highchairs/boosters	✓	❹	Stroller access

WWW.SMOKEYBONES.COM

PLANTATION—809 S UNIVERSITY DR (AT SW 10TH ST); 954.474.3833; SU-TH 11-10, F-SA 11-11

Souplantation/Sweet Tomatoes ★★★★☆

"...you can't beat the price and selection of healthy foods... all you can eat—serve yourself soup and salad bar... lots of healthy choices plus pizza and pasta... great for picky eaters... free for 2 and under and only $3 for kids under 5... booths for comfy seating and discreet breastfeeding... helps to have another adult along since it is self serve... they always bring fresh cookies to the table and offer to refill drinks...**"**

Children's menu	✓	$$	Prices
Changing station	✓	❹	Customer service

participate in our survey at

Highchairs/boosters .... ✓ ❹ ....Stroller access

WWW.SOUPLANTATION.COM

CORAL SPRINGS—1850 UNIVERSITY DR (AT NW 19TH ST); 954.255.3800;
  SU-TH 11-9, F-SA 11-10; STREET PARKING

FORT LAUDERDALE—6245 N ANDREWS AVE (AT W CYPRESS CREEK RD);
  954.771.7111; SU-TH 11-9, F-SA 11-10; PARKING LOT

FORT LAUDERDALE—801 S UNIVERSITY DR (AT SW 10TH ST); 954.452.7364;
  SU-TH 11-9, F-SA 11-10

HOLLYWOOD—2906 OAKWOOD BLVD (AT N 26TH TER); 954.923.9444; SU-TH
  11-9, F-SA 11-10

PEMBROKE PINES—15901 PINES BLVD (AT DYKES RD); 954.441.3559; SU-TH
  11-9, F-SA 11-10

PLANTATION—801 S UNIVERISTY DR (OFF PETERS RD); 854.452.7364; SU-
  TH 11-9, F-SA 11-10

Tarpon Bend Food & Tackle ★★★★☆

❝...you feel like you are kickin' back in the Keys... stellar seafood as
well as the standard kids fare... sometimes they even have clowns to do
face painting and animal ballons... ❞

Children's menu .... ✓ $$$ .... Prices
Changing station......................... ✓   ❹ .... Customer service
Highchairs/boosters .... ✓   ❹ ....Stroller access

WWW.TARPONBEND.COM

FORT LAUDERDALE—200 SW 2ND ST (AT MOFFAT AVE); 954.523.3233;
  DAILY 11:30-1

WESTON—1630 BELL TOWER LN (AT TWN CTR CIR); 954.888.9118; DAILY
  11:30-1

TGI Friday's ★★★★☆

❝...good old American bar food with a reasonable selection for the
healthier set as well... I love that the kids meal includes salad... my
daughter requests the potato skins on a regular basis (which is good
because they are also my favorite)... moderately priced... cheerful
servers are used to the mess my kids leave behind... relaxed scene... I'd
steer clear on a Friday night unless you don't mind waiting and
watching the singles scene... ❞

Children's menu .... ✓ $$ .... Prices
Changing station......................... ✓   ❹ .... Customer service
Highchairs/boosters .... ✓   ❸ ....Stroller access

WWW.TGIFRIDAYS.COM

CORAL SPRINGS—855 UNIVERSITY DR (AT CORAL SQ MALL); 954.344.0884;
  DAILY 11-2

FORT LAUDERDALE—6200 N FEDERAL HWY (AT BAYVIEW DR);
  954.772.1390; DAILY 11-2

HOLLYWOOD—2940 OAKWOOD BLVD (AT SHERIDAN ST); 954.922.2771;
  DAILY 11-10

PEMBROKE PINES—90 N UNIVERSITY DR (AT PINES BLVD); 954.436.4716;
  M-SA 11-2, SU 11-1; PARKING LOT

PLANTATION—80 SW 84TH AVE (AT BROWARD BLVD); 954.472.5560; DAILY
  11-2

SUNRISE—13500 W SUNRISE BLVD (OFF 136TH AVE); 954.846.1210; DAILY
  11-2

Palm Beach County

★★★★★

"lila picks"

★Red Lobster Restaurant

American Cafe ★★★★☆

"...average food, but very kid-friendly... a back room which is convenient for moms and babies to meet up and have a bite... very easy to fit strollers... always great service..."

Children's menu	✓	$$$	Prices
Changing station	✗	❹	Customer service
Highchairs/boosters	✓	❹	Stroller access

WWW.AMERICANCAFE.COM

BOCA RATON—351 PLZ REAL (AT MIZNER PARK); 561.750.3580; SU-TH 11-10, F-SA 11-11

Applebee's Neighborhood Grill ★★★⯪☆

"...geared to family dining—they expect you to be loud and leave a mess... Macaroni & Cheese, Hot Dogs, and tasty grilled cheese... activity book and special kids cup are a bonus... service can be slow, but they will cover you with things to snack on... stay clear on Friday and Saturday nights... comfort food in a casual atmosphere... even though it's part of a very large chain you get the feeling it's a neighborhood-type place..."

Children's menu	✓	$$	Prices
Changing station	✓	❹	Customer service
Highchairs/boosters	✓	❸	Stroller access

WWW.APPLEBEES.COM

BOYNTON BEACH—1570 W BOYNTON BEACH BLVD (AT WINCHESTER PARK BLVD); 561.752.4339; M-TH 11-11, F-SA 11-12, SU 11-10

Baja Cafe Uno ★★★⯪☆

"...California style Mexican food... go before the 'bar' crowd arrives... the decor of lights and the music will amuse your kid... we actually get to finish our meal here..."

Children's menu	✓	$$	Prices
Changing station	✓	❹	Customer service
Highchairs/boosters	✓	❸	Stroller access

WWW.BAJACAFE.COM

BOCA RATON—201 NW 1ST AV (AT NE 2ND AVE); 561.394.5449; SU-TH 11-10, F-SA 11-11

Boston Market ★★★⯪☆

"...tons of locations makes it convenient... great for a nice, easy dinner... healthy side dishes available... reasonble prices... the chicken is always a crowd pleaser... when you buy a kids meal, you get a book, crayons and a coupon for a free kiddie meal..."

Children's menu	✓	$$	Prices

| Changing station | ✗ | ➍ | Customer service |
| Highchairs/boosters | ✓ | ➍ | Stroller access |

WWW.BOSTONMARKET.COM

BOYNTON BEACH—1797 N CONGRESS AVE (AT SAVANNAH LAKES DR);
  561.736.3393; M-TH 10:30-9:30, F-SA 10:30-10, SU 10:30-9:30

BOYNTON BEACH—9929 S MILITARY TR (AT W BOYNTON BEACH BLVD);
  561.731.4441; DAILY 10:30-10; STREET PARKING

Brio Tuscan Grille ★★★★☆

"*...kids menu with options for young children as well as selections for small adults... great food and service...* **"**

Children's menu	✓	$$$	Prices
Changing station	✓	➍	Customer service
Highchairs/boosters	✓	➌	Stroller access

WWW.BESTITALIANUSA.COM

PALM BEACH GARDENS—3101 PGA BLVD (AT CAMPUS DR); 561.622.0491;
  DAILY 11-10; FREE PARKING

California Pizza Kitchen ★★★★⯨

"*...you can't go wrong with their fabulous pizza... always clean... the food's great, the kids drinks all come with a lid... the staff is super friendly to kids... crayons and coloring books keep little minds busy... most locations have a place for strollers at the front... no funny looks or attitude when breastfeeding... open atmosphere with friendly service... tables are well spaced so you don't feel like your kid is annoying the diners nearby (it's usually full of kids anyway)...* **"**

Children's menu	✓	$$	Prices
Changing station	✓	➍	Customer service
Highchairs/boosters	✓	➍	Stroller access

WWW.CPK.COM

PALM BEACH GARDENS—3101 PGA BLVD (AT CAMPUS DR); 561.625.4682;
  M-SA 11-10, SU 11-7

Cheeburger Cheeburger ★★★⯨☆

"*...old time feel... classic 50's and 60's rock and roll on the radio... big, big burgers—salads too... you can choose whatever topping you want for your burgers and salads... great shakes... don't miss the clown on Friday nights—free face painting and my kids love it... good food and a very relaxed environment...* **"**

Children's menu	✓	$$	Prices
Changing station	✓	➍	Customer service
Highchairs/boosters	✓	➌	Stroller access

WWW.CHEEBURGER.COM

BOCA RATON—200 S FEDERAL HWY (AT SE 2ND ST); 561.392.1969; M-TH
  11-9, F-SA 11-10, SU 12-9; FREE PARKING

DELRAY BEACH—450 E ATLANTIC AVE (AT N FEDERAL HWY); 561.265.1959;
  M-TH 11-9, F-SA 11-10, SU 12-9; FREE PARKING

PALM BEACH GARDENS—5520 PGA BLVD (AT S CENTRAL BLVD);
  561.627.1793; M-TH 11-9, F-SA 11-11, SU 12-9

WEST PALM BEACH—760 S ROSEMARY AVE (AT CITYPLACE); 561.833.1997;
  M-TH 11-9, F-SA 11-11, SU 12-9

Cheeseburgers And More ★★★★☆

"*...a game room for kids... the play area is wonderful on an extremely hot or stormy day... lots of games that take tokens and a huge tunnel maze for older kids to climb and crawl around... the food is also very good, they have a good kids menu, but also a great adult menu including sandwiches and salads...* **"**

| Children's menu | ✓ | $ | Prices |

Changing station .... ✗   **❸** ....Customer service
Highchairs/boosters.................... ✓   **❹** .... Stroller access

JUPITER—6779 W INDIANTOWN RD (AT CENTRAL BLVD); 561.575.9490; SU-TH11-9 , F-SA TIL10 ; FREE PARKING

Cheesecake Factory, The ★★★★☆

"...although their cheesecake is good, we come here for the kid friendly atmosphere and selection of good food... eclectic menu has something for everyone... they will bring your tot a plate of yogurt, cheese, bananas and bread free of charge... we love how flexible they are—they'll make whatever my kids want... lots of mommies here... always fun and always crazy... no real kids menu, but the pizza is great to share... waits can be really long... **"**

Children's menu...........................✗ $$$...Prices
Changing station .... ✓   **❹** ....Customer service
Highchairs/boosters.................... ✓   **❸** .... Stroller access

WWW.THECHEESECAKEFACTORY.COM

BOCA RATON—5530 GLADES RD (AT PINEHURST LN); 561.393.0344; M-TH 11:30-11:30, F-SA 11:30-12:30, SU 10-11

WEST PALM BEACH—701 S ROSEMARY AV (AT CITYPLACE); 561.802.3838; M-TH 11:30-11:30, F-SA 11:30-12:30, SU 10-11

Chili's Grill & Bar ★★★⯨☆

"...family-friendly, mild Mexican fare... delicious ribs, soups, salads... kids' menu and crayons as you sit down... on the noisy side, so you don't mind if your kids talk in their usual loud voices... service is excellent... fun night out with the family... a wide variety of menu selections for kids and their parents—all at a reasonable price... best chicken fingers on any kids' menu... **"**

Children's menu.......................... ✓ $$...Prices
Changing station .... ✓   **❹** ....Customer service
Highchairs/boosters.................... ✓   **❹** .... Stroller access

WWW.CHILIS.COM

BOCA RATON—21078 ST ANDREWS BLVD (AT TOWN CTR AT BOCA RATON); 561.391.2300; M-TH 11-11, F-SA 11-12, SU 11-10

BOCA RATON—21769 STATE RD 7 (AT W PALMETTO PARK RD); 561.451.3771; SU-TH 11-11, F-SA 11-12

BOYNTON BEACH—2202 N CONGRESS AVE (AT GATEWAY BLVD); 561.735.0429; M-TH 11-11, F-SA 11-12, SU 11-10

JUPITER—65 US 1 N (AT INDIANTOWN RD); 561.575.6900; SU-TH 11-11, F-SA 11-12

WELLINGTON—2525 S STATE RD 7 (OFF FOREST HILL BLVD); 561.790.0062; SU-TH 11-11, F-SA 11-12

WEST PALM BEACH—4252 OKEECHOBEE BLVD (OFF RT 809); 561.689.9118; SU-TH 11-11, F-SA 11-12

Friendly's ★★★⯨☆

"...we love Friendly's because it's fast, fun and the food is pretty good... you may wait a bit for your service, but given the promise of a sundae most kids will persevere... colorful menu and M&M pancakes... desert and a drink are included with some kids meals... convenient if you have kids of varying ages—there's something good for everyone... burgers, sandwiches and more fries than you'll know what to do with... **"**

Children's menu.......................... ✓ $$...Prices
Changing station .... ✓   **❸** ....Customer service
Highchairs/boosters.................... ✓   **❸** .... Stroller access

WWW.FRIENDLYS.COM

ROYAL PALM BEACH—1001 N STATE RD 7 (AT BELVEDERE RD);
561.333.5757; SU-TH 7-11, F-SA 7-12

Longhorn Steakhouse ★★★★☆

"...for meat and seafood lovers... the staff totally gets 'the kid thing' here... they bring out snacks, get the orders going quickly, and frequently check back for things like new spoons and napkins... lots of things for baby to look at... get there early or call ahead to avoid the wait..."

Children's menu ✓	$$$ .... Prices	
Changing station ✓	❹ .... Customer service	
Highchairs/boosters ✓	❸ .... Stroller access	

WWW.LONGHORNSTEAKHOUSE.COM

BOYNTON BEACH—501 N CONGRESS AV (AT BOYNTON BEACH MALL);
561.737.4111; SU-TH 11-10, F-SA 11-11; MALL PARKING

Original Pancake House ★★★★½

"...consistently the best breakfast around... great flapjacks and appropriately-sized kids meals... food comes quickly... the most amazing apple pancakes ever... service is always friendly, but sometimes it can take a while to actually get the food... the highlight for my daughter is the free balloon when we leave... always a lot of families here with small children on the weekends, so you don't have to worry about being the only one..."

Children's menu ✓	$$ .... Prices	
Changing station ✓	❹ .... Customer service	
Highchairs/boosters ✓	❸ .... Stroller access	

WWW.ORIGINALPANCAKEHOUSE.COM

BOCA RATON—7146 BERA CASA WY; 561.395.2303

BOYNTON BEACH—1485 W GATEWY BLVD (AT CONGRESS AVE);
561.733.3306

DELRAY BEACH—1840 S FEDERAL HWY (OFF LINTON BLVD); 561.276.0769;
DAILY 7-9

ROYAL PALM BEACH—105 S STATE RD 7 (AT SOUTHERN BLVD);
561.296.0878; DAILY 7-9

Red Lobster Restaurants ★★★★★

"...better than I expected from the TV commercials... food was enjoyable, especially the garlic-cheese biscuits... sea-themed decor is popular with kids... friendly staff was terrific with our kids—they must all be parents... servers even offered to heat up the baby food we brought along from home... not the cheapest prices around... kids menu offers lots of appealing choices... a comfortable place to bring kids..."

Children's menu ✓	$$$ .... Prices	
Changing station ✓	❹ .... Customer service	
Highchairs/boosters ✓	❹ .... Stroller access	

WWW.REDLOBSTER.COM

BOCA RATON—3600 N FEDERAL HWY (AT 36TH AVE); 561.391.3529; SU-TH
11-10, F-SA 11-11; PARKING IN FRONT OF BLDG

Roadhouse Grill ★★★★☆

"...delicious grilled steak, chicken and shrimp... pasta too... my kids love that you can throw peanut shells on the floor... nice, simple childrens' menu... they also give your child a balloon when you walk in... reasonable prices and nice atmosphere—an easy choice for when you want to take a break from cooking..."

Children's menu ✓	$$ .... Prices	
Changing station ✓	❹ .... Customer service	
Highchairs/boosters ✓	❹ .... Stroller access	

restaurants

WWW.ROADHOUSEGRILL.COM

BOCA RATON—20455 SR 7 441) (OFF RT 808); 561.883.0828; SU-TH 11-10,
F-SA 11-11

GREENACRES—3887 JOG RD (AT LAKE WORTH RD); 561.963.7182; SU-TH
11-10, F-SA 11-11

WEST PALM BEACH—4201 OKEECHOBEE BLVD (OFF RT 809); 561.688.1027,
SU-TH 11-10, F-SA 11-11

Ruby Tuesday ★★★½☆

"...nice variety of healthy choices on the kids' menu—turkey,
spaghetti, chicken tenders... you can definitely find something healthy
here... prices are on the high side, but at least everyone can find
something they like... service is fast and efficient... my daughter makes
a mess and they never let me clean it up... your typical chain, but it
works—you'll be happy to see ample aisle space, storage for your
stroller, and attentive staff... **"**

Children's menu	✓	$$	Prices
Changing station	✓	❹	Customer service
Highchairs/boosters	✓	❸	Stroller access

WWW.RUBYTUESDAY.COM

BOCA RATON—409 PLAZA REAL (AT MIZNER PARK); 561.392.5705; SU-TH
11-11, F-SA 11-12

BOYNTON BEACH—801 N CONGRESS AVE (AT BOYNTON BEACH MALL);
561.737.3501; M-TH 11-10, F-SA 11-11, SU 11-9

PALM BEACH GARDENS—3101 PGA BLVD SPACE C (AT THE GARDENS);
561.694.7909; M-SA 11-10, SU 11-8

ROYAL PALM BEACH—1271 N STATE RD 7 (AT OKEECHOBEE BLVD);
561.383.8200; M-TH 11-10, F-SA 11-11, SU 11-9

WELLINGTON—10300 W FORREST HILL BLVD (OFF RT 441); 561.753.3300;
M-TH 11-9, F-SA 11-10, SU 11-8

Souplantation/Sweet Tomatoes ★★★★☆

"...you can't beat the price and selection of healthy foods... all you
can eat—serve yourself soup and salad bar... lots of healthy choices
plus pizza and pasta... great for picky eaters... free for 2 and under and
only $3 for kids under 5... booths for comfy seating and discreet
breastfeeding... helps to have another adult along since it is self serve...
they always bring fresh cookies to the table and offer to refill
drinks... **"**

Children's menu	✓	$$	Prices
Changing station	✓	❹	Customer service
Highchairs/boosters	✓	❹	Stroller access

WWW.SOUPLANTATION.COM

BOCA RATON—7110 BERACASA WY (AT W PALMETTO PARK RD);
561.750.3303; SU-TH 11-9, F-SA 11-10

TGI Friday's ★★★★☆

"...good old American bar food with a reasonable selection for the
healthier set as well... I love that the kids meal includes salad... my
daughter requests the potato skins on a regular basis (which is good
because they are also my favorite)... moderately priced... cheerful
servers are used to the mess my kids leave behind... relaxed scene... I'd
steer clear on a Friday night unless you don't mind waiting and
watching the singles scene... **"**

Children's menu	✓	$$	Prices
Changing station	✓	❹	Customer service
Highchairs/boosters	✓	❸	Stroller access

WWW.TGIFRIDAYS.COM

participate in our survey at

BOCA RATON—164 TOWN CTR AT BOCA RATON (AT NW 32ND ST);
  561.392.6656; DAILY 11:30-1:30

BOCA RATON—20465 STATE RD (OFF GLADES RD); 561.483.8443; DAILY 11-
  10

BOYNTON BEACH—382 N CONGRESS RD (AT BOYNTON BEACH BLVD);
  561.734.3400; DAILY 11:30-1:30

ROYAL PALM BEACH—580 N STATE RD (AT N TAMARIND AVE);
  561.795.8955; SU-TH 11-12, F-SA 11-2

WEST PALM BEACH—600 VILLAGE BLVD (AT PALM BEACH LAKES BLVD);
  561.471.5888; DAILY 11-10; PARKING LOT

The Keys

★★★★★

"lila picks"

★Benihana

Baskin Robbins and Subway

Children's menu...........................✗   ✗ ....Changing station
Highchairs/boosters......................✗

WWW.BASKINROBBINS.COM

KEY WEST—1800 N ROOSEVELT BLVD (AT TRUMAN AVE); 305.294.0001; SU-
  TH 9:30-12, F-SA 9:30-1

Benihana   ★★★★★

*"...stir-fry meals are always prepared in front of you—it keeps
everyone entertained, parents and kids alike... chefs often perform
especially for the little ones... tables sit about 10 people, so it
encourages talking with other diners... tend to be pretty loud so it's
pretty family friendly... delicious for adults and fun for kids..."*

Children's menu...........................✗ $$$...Prices
Changing station ....✓   ❹.........................Customer service
Highchairs/boosters......................✓   ❸............................Stroller access

WWW.BENIHANA.COM

KEY WEST—3591 S ROOSEVELT BLVD (AT FARALDO CIR); 305.294.6400; SU-
  TH 5:30-10, F-SA 5:30-10:30

Dairy Queen   ★★★☆☆

*"...you know Dairy Queen... always a great treat on the menu for the
little ones..."*

Children's menu...........................✗ $$...Prices
Changing station ....✗   ❸.........................Customer service
Highchairs/boosters......................✗   ❸............................Stroller access

WWW.DAIRYQUEEN.COM

TAVERNIER—92661 OVERSEAS HWY (AT GARDEN ST); 305.852.2219; SU-TH
  10-9:30, F-SA 10-10:30

Garden Cafe, The   ★★★★★

*"...great fresh foods, wholefoods, vegetarian and meats, gourmet
with great garden for kids to explore. outdoor cafe, but very safe and
fenced in..."*

Children's menu...........................✗ $$$...Prices
Changing station ....✗   ❺.........................Customer service
Highchairs/boosters......................✓   ❺............................Stroller access

ISLAMORADA—86700 OVERSEAS HWY (AT TREASURE HARBOR DR);
  305.852.6499

Haagen-dazs Ice Cream   ★★★☆☆

"...great ice cream... love the flavors..."

Children's menu...........................✗ $$$...Prices

Changing station..........................✗   ❸........................Customer service
Highchairs/boosters ....✗   ❸............................Stroller access

WWW.HAAGEN-DAZS.COM

KEY WEST—625 DUVAL ST (AT SOUTHARD ST); 305.294.3378; SU-TH 10-11,
  F-SA 10-12

Hard Rock Cafe   ★★★⯪☆

"...fun and tasty if you can get in... the lines can be horrendous so be
sure to check in with them first... a good spot if you have tots in tow—
food tastes good and the staff is clearly used to messy eaters... hectic
and loud... fun for adults as well as kids... **"**

Children's menu ....✓ $$$ .... Prices
Changing station..........................✓   ❹........................Customer service
Highchairs/boosters ....✓   ❸............................Stroller access

WWW.HARDROCK.COM

KEY WEST—313 DUVAL ST (AT CAROLINE ST); 305.293.0230; DAILY 11-12AM

Holiday Isle Ice Cream Trolley

Children's menu ....✗   ✗............................Changing station
Highchairs/boosters ....✗

WWW.HOLIDAYISLE.COM/TROLLEY.HTML

ISLAMORADA—84001 OVERSEAS HWY (AT WINDLEY KEY); 305.664.2321;
  OPEN F-SU

Mangoes Restaurant   ★★★☆☆

"...a varied menu for all tastes... you can sit outside and they have a
pizza oven so the kids are happy and entertained... **"**

Children's menu ....✗ $$ .... Prices
Changing station..........................✓   ❹........................Customer service
Highchairs/boosters ....✓   ❸............................Stroller access

WWW.MANGOESKEYWEST.COM

KEY WEST—700 DUVAL ST (AT ANGELA ST); 305.292.4606; CALL FOR HOURS

Monty's   ★★★★★

"...great outdoor dining on the water and easy to tote the kid along...
music on the weekends and a kid's menu to boot... **"**

Children's menu ....✓ $$$ .... Prices
Changing station..........................✗   ❺........................Customer service
Highchairs/boosters ....✓   ❺............................Stroller access

WWW.MONTYSSTONECRAB.COM

KEY WEST—951 CAROLINE ST (AT GRINNELL ST); 305.293.5123; SU-TH 11-
  10, F-SA 11-11

Morada Bay   ★★★★★

"...great food, view and beach for the kids... great beautiful
restaurant on the beach... kids can play in the sand while you leisurely
enjoy drinks and dinner... **"**

Children's menu ....✓ $$$$ .... Prices
Changing station..........................✗   ❺........................Customer service
Highchairs/boosters ....✓   ❺............................Stroller access

ISLAMORADA—81600 OVERSEAS HWY (AT PALM AVE); 305.664.0604; SU-TH
  11:30-10, F-SA 11:30-11

TGI Friday's   ★★★★☆

"...good old American bar food with a reasonable selection for the
healthier set as well... I love that the kids meal includes salad... my
daughter requests the potato skins on a regular basis (which is good
because they are also my favorite)... moderately priced... cheerful
servers are used to the mess my kids leave behind... relaxed scene... I'd

steer clear on a Friday night unless you don't mind waiting and watching the singles scene... **"**

Children's menu	✓	$$	Prices
Changing station	✓	❹	Customer service
Highchairs/boosters	✓	❸	Stroller access

WWW.TGIFRIDAYS.COM

KEY WEST—2710 N ROOSEVELT BLVD (AT GULFVIEW DR); 305.296.4093; SU-TH 11-11, F-SA 11-12

Tiki Beach Snowballs

★★★☆☆

"...*yummy snowballs... my kids love picking out their flavor...* **"**

Children's menu	✗	$$$	Prices
Changing station	✗	❸	Customer service
Highchairs/boosters	✗	❸	Stroller access

KEY WEST—1910 N ROOSEVELT BLVD (AT PALM AVE)

participate in our survey at

doulas &
lactation
consultants

Editor's Note: Doulas and lactation consultants provide a wide range of services and are very difficult to classify, let alone rate. In fact the terms 'doula' and 'lactation consultant' have very specific industry definitions that are far more complex than we are able to cover in this brief guide. For this reason we have decided to list only those businesses and individuals who received overwhelmingly positive reviews, without listing the reviewers' comments.

South FL Area

A Delivery With Love Birth Center

Labor Doula .... ✓   ✓ .... Postpartum doula
Pre & post natal massage .... ✗   ✗ .... Lactation consultant

WEST PALM BEACH—4550 IRIS ST (AT N MILITARY TRL); 561.687.7885

Association of Labor Assistants & Childbirth Educators (ALACE)

Labor doula .... ✓   ✗ .... Postpartum doula
Pre & post natal massage .... ✗   ✗ .... Lactation consultant

WWW.ALACE.ORG

MIAMI—617.441.2500

Birthing Center Of South Florida

Labor doula .... ✓   ✓ .... Postpartum doula
Pre & post natal massage .... ✗   ✗ .... Lactation consultant

WWW.BIRTHNATURALLY.COM

HOMESTEAD—646 W PALM DR (AT NW 7TH AVE); 305.245.3730; CHECK
  SCHEDULE ONLINE

Doulas of North America (DONA)

Labor doula .... ✓   ✓ .... Postpartum doula
Pre & post natal massage .... ✗   ✗ .... Lactation consultant

WWW.DONA.ORG

MIAMI—888.788.3662

Fit for a Mom

Labor doula .... ✓   ✗ .... Postpartum doula
Pre & post natal massage .... ✗   ✗ .... Lactation consultant

WWW.FITFORAMOMANDBABY.COM

DELRAY BEACH—310 SE 1ST AVE (AT 3RD ST); 561.504.9436; CHECK
  SCHEDULE ONLINE

La Leche League

Labor doula .... ✗   ✗ .... Postpartum doula
Pre & post natal massage .... ✗   ✓ .... Lactation consultant

WWW.LALECHELEAGUE.ORG

MIAMI—VARIOUS LOCATIONS; 847.519.7730

participate in our survey at

exercise

South Dade & Downtown

★★★★★
"lila picks"

★Baby Boot Camp   ★Prenatal Plus Yoga

Baby Boot Camp   ★★★★★

❝...a great, low-cost, outdoor mom and baby workout... I've met some really fun moms and babies at these classes... not only fun, but more importantly I got results... the first class is free so there's no excuse not to give it a try... instructors are well-trained physical therapists that really know their stuff... class sizes are limited... it's like a personal trainer and motivational system all in one... I do their exercises even when I'm on my own with my baby... ❞

Prenatal	✗	$$$	Prices
Mommy & me	✓	❸	Decor
Child care available	✗	❸	Customer service

WWW.BABYBOOTCAMP.COM

MIAMI—VARIOUS LOCATIONS; 786.208.9211; CHECK SCHEDULE ONLINE

Prana Yoga Center, The   ★★★★☆

❝...the best yoga instruction I've ever had... helped me connect with my growing baby and pending parenthood... classes offer exercise, spirituality, helpful preparation for birth and a great way to meet other future moms... a bit pricey, but great staff... ❞

Prenatal	✓	$$$$	Prices
Mommy & me	✗	❹	Decor
Child care available	✗	❹	Customer service

WWW.PRANAYOGAMIAMI.COM/

CORAL GABLES—247 MALAGA AVE (AT PONCE DE LEON BLVD); 305.567.9812; CHECK SCHEDULE ONLINE; STREET PARKING

Prenatal Plus Yoga   ★★★★★

❝...specializes in prenatal and post natal yoga... terrific classes... the main instructor is a doula and they focus on exercise for new moms... extremely knowledgeable staff... peaceful and calming environment... ❞

Prenatal	✓	$$$	Prices
Mommy & me	✓	❸	Decor
Child care available	✗	❸	Customer service

WWW.PRENATALPLUSYOGA.COM

CORAL GABLES—401 MIRACLE MILE (AT S LE JEUNE RD); 305.443.4533; CHECK SCHEDULE ONLINE

South Miami Hospital (Prenatal Yoga)   ★★★★☆

❝...the prenatal yoga class at South Miami Hospital is awesome... Michelle, the instructor, is incredibly knowledgeable, enthusiastic, *sweet and makes you feel great... the ending relaxation and guided imagery with Michelle's foot massage leave you feeling great...* **"**

Prenatal	✓	$$	Prices
Mommy & me	✗	❺	Decor
Child care available	✗	❺	Customer service

WWW.BAPTISTHEALTH.NET

SOUTH MIAMI—6200 SW 73RD ST (AT SW 62ND AVE); 786.662.4000; CALL FOR SCHEDULE

Umaa Tantra ★★★★★

"...*very helpful instructors... great with beginners as well as the more advanced... prenatal yoga very rewarding...* **"**

Prenatal	✓	$$	Prices
Mommy & me	✗	❸	Decor
Child care available	✗	❺	Customer service

WWW.UMAATANTRA.COM

MIAMI—12580 SW 88TH ST (AT UNIFIED MARTIAL ART ACADEMY); 305.595.2892; CHECK SCHEDULE ONLINE

YMCA ★★★★☆

"...*the variety of fitness programs offered is astounding... class types and quality vary from facility to facility, but it's a must for new moms to check out... most facilities offer some kind of kids' activities or childcare so you can time your workouts around the classes... aerobics, yoga, pool—our Y even offers Pilates now... my favorite classes are the mom & baby yoga... the best bang for your buck... they have it all—great programs that meet the needs of a diverse range of families...* **"**

Prenatal	✓	$$$	Prices
Mommy & me	✓	❸	Decor
Child care available	✓	❸	Customer service

WWW.YMCAMIAMI.ORG

HOMESTEAD—1034 NE 8TH ST (AT HARRIS FIELD); 305.248.5189; CHECK SCHEDULE ONLINE

MIAMI—16649 NE 19TH AVE (AT N GLADES DR); 305.944.1944; M-F 8-5

MIAMI—2370 NW 17TH AVE (AT ALLAPATTAH-COMSTOCK PARK); 305.635.1813; CHECK SCHEDULE ONLINE

MIAMI—401 NW 71ST ST (AT NW 4TH AVE); 305.759.3317; M-F 6:30-8, SA 9-2

MIAMI—4300 SW 58TH AVE (AT SW 42ND TER); 305.665.3513; M-F 7-9, SA-SU 10-2

MIAMI—450 SW 16TH AVE (AT SW 5TH ST); 305.643.2626; M-F 7-6

MIAMI—9355 SW 134 ST (ACROSS FROM FALLS SHOPPING CTR); 305.254.0310; CHECK SCHEDULE ONLINE

exercise

North Dade & Beaches

★★★★★

"lila picks"

★Prenatal Yoga With Mia Glick

Bay Harbor Fitness Center

Prenatal	✕	✕	Mommy & me
Child care available	✕		

WWW.LISA-RAY.COM/ISLANDFITNESS/ISLANDFITNESS.HTM

BAY HARBOR ISLANDS—1086 KANE CONCOURSE (AT BAY HARBOR TER); 305.865.4144

Island Fitness

Prenatal	✕	✕	Mommy & me
Child care available	✕		

WWW.LISA-RAY.COM/ISLANDFITNESS/ISLANDFITNESS.HTM

SURFSIDE—9448 HARDING AVE (AT 94TH ST); 305.725.2772

Nirvana Spa ★★★⯪☆

"...great yoga classes, given by Synergy yoga which is on South Beach... not a ton of classes and they change frequently, but great instructors in a lovely studio... also a gym and full spa offering pre natal massages... they sometimes often prenatal yoga... "

Prenatal	✓	$$$	Prices
Mommy & me	✕	❹	Decor
Child care available	✕	❸	Customer service

WWW.NIRVANASPAMIAMIBEACH.COM

MIAMI BEACH—8701 COLLINS AVE (AT 87TH ST); 305.867.4850; M-SA 11-11 SU 1:30-11; PARKING LOT

Prenatal Yoga With Mia Glick ★★★★★

"...Mia teaches an amazing prenatal class, on the body and soul level... pleasant, patient and knowledgeable teacher... a lot of stretching and meditative techniques... it takes place in a small room upstairs in a synagogue, so don't expect much in terms of decor, but it's a small, intimate class and a great way to do yoga and meet other expecting moms... "

Prenatal	✓	$$$	Prices
Mommy & me	✕	❸	Decor
Child care available	✕	❺	Customer service

WWW.YOGAWITHMIA.COM

MIAMI BEACH—VARIOUS LOCATIONS—CHECK ONLINE; 305.672.6537; CHECK SCHEDULE ONLINE

Umaa Tantra ★☆☆☆☆

"...very helpful instructors... great with beginners as well as the more advanced... prenatal yoga very rewarding... "

Prenatal	✓	$$$$	Prices

participate in our survey at

| Mommy & me | ✗ | ❶ | Decor |
| Child care available | ✗ | ❶ | Customer service |

WWW.UMAATANTRA.COM

MIAMI BEACH—1800 SUNSET HARBOUR DR (AT 18TH ST); 305.604.5988;
  CHECK SCHEDULE ONLINE

YMCA

"...the variety of fitness programs offered is astounding... class types
and quality vary from facility to facility, but it's a must for new moms to
check out... most facilities offer some kind of kids' activities or
childcare so you can time your workouts around the classes... aerobics,
yoga, pool—our Y even offers Pilates now... my favorite classes are the
mom & baby yoga... the best bang for your buck... they have it all—
great programs that meet the needs of a diverse range of families... **"**

Prenatal	✓	$$$	Prices
Mommy & me	✓	❸	Decor
Child care available	✓	❸	Customer service

WWW.YMCAMIAMI.ORG

HIALEAH—500 W 49TH ST (AT RED RD); 305.825.9622; CALL FOR SCHEDULE

exercise

Broward County

★★★★★
"lila picks"

★ Baby Boot Camp

Baby Boot Camp

"...a great, low-cost, outdoor mom and baby workout... I've met some really fun moms and babies at these classes... not only fun, but more importantly I got results... the first class is free so there's no excuse not to give it a try... instructors are well-trained physical therapists that really know their stuff... class sizes are limited... it's like a personal trainer and motivational system all in one... I do their exercises even when I'm on my own with my baby..."

Prenatal	✗	$$$	Prices
Mommy & me	✓	❸	Decor
Child care available	✗	❸	Customer service

WWW.BABYBOOTCAMP.COM

DAVIE—VARIOUS LOCATIONS; 561.350.3391; CHECK SCHEDULE ONLINE

PEMBROKE PINES—VARIOUS LOCATIONS; 561.350.3391; CHECK SCHEDULE ONLINE

Memorial Regional Hospital
Fitness & Rehab Center
Prenatal Yoga

"...terrific prenatal yoga classes... they don't require a gym membership and if you buy a card of multiple passes, it costs only $4/per class... what a steal!.. the gym is clean and the classes were helpful..."

Prenatal	✓	$	Prices
Mommy & me	✗	❺	Decor
Child care available	✗	❺	Customer service

WWW.MHS.NET

HOLLYWOOD—3501 JOHNSON ST (AT N 37TH AVE); 954.985.5800; M-W 5:30-10, TH 5:30-9, F 5:30-8, SA 6-6, SU 8-4

Mind Body & Baby

"...I thought it was expensive so I didn't go back after one prenatal yoga class, but I know several people who really love the staff and classes... offer mommy and me as well as prenatal classes which is nice... also has child care..."

Prenatal	✓	$$$$$	Prices
Mommy & me	✓	❺	Decor
Child care available	✓	❸	Customer service

FORT LAUDERDALE—519 E 26TH ST (AT MIAMI RD); 954.564.1577; CALL FOR SCHEDULE

Stroller Strides

★★★★⯪

" *...fantastic fun and very effective for losing those post-baby pounds... this is the greatest way to stay in shape as a mom—you have your baby in the stroller with you the whole time... the instructors are very professional, knowledgeable and motivating... beautiful, outdoor locations... classes consist of power walking combined with body toning exercises using exercise tubing and strollers... a great way to bond with my baby and other moms...* **"**

Prenatal	✗	$$	Prices
Mommy & me	✓	❺	Decor
Child care available	✗	❺	Customer service

WWW.STROLLERSTRIDES.NET

PLANTATION—VARIOUS LOCATIONS; 954.551.0145; CHECK SCHEDULE
ONLINE

exercise

Palm Beach County

★★★★★

"lila picks"

★ Baby Boot Camp

Baby Boot Camp ★★★★★

"...a great, low-cost, outdoor mom and baby workout... I've met some really fun moms and babies at these classes... not only fun, but more importantly I got results... the first class is free so there's no excuse not to give it a try... instructors are well-trained physical therapists that really know their stuff... class sizes are limited... it's like a personal trainer and motivational system all in one... I do their exercises even when I'm on my own with my baby..."

Prenatal	✗	$$$	Prices
Mommy & me	✓	❺	Decor
Child care available	✗	❸	Customer service

WWW.BABYBOOTCAMP.COM

BOCA RATON—VARIOUS LOCATIONS; 561.350.3391; CHECK SCHEDULE ONLINE

WEST PALM BEACH—VARIOUS LOCATIONS; 561.350.3391; CHECK SCHEDULE ONLINE

Boca Raton Community Hospital (One Family Place)

"...pre and postnatal workout classes... stretch and strengthening exercises... everything focused on and adjusted to the pregnant body... really helped me get in touch with my pregnant body..."

Prenatal	✓	$$	Prices
Mommy & me	✓	❺	Decor
Child care available	✗	❺	Customer service

WWW.BRCH.COM

BOCA RATON—800 MEADOWS RD (AT NW 7TH AVE); 561.955.5110; CHECK SCHEDULE ONLINE; PARKING LOT

participate in our survey at

parent education & support

South FL Area

A Birth Center

❝...as a midwife team, Deborah DiGiacomo and Mary Harris became part of our family... we really missed the wonderful staff after the baby came!.. by giving you options of a home, birth center or hospital birth you feel in control of your experience while being the care of wonderful practitioners... ❞

Childbirth classes	✓	$$$	Prices
Parent group/club	✓	❸	Class selection
Breastfeeding support	✓	❺	Staff knowledge
Child care info	✓	❺	Customer service

WWW.OBONCALL.COM

HALLANDALE—3001 W HALLANDALE BEACH BLVD (AT HWY 95); 954.456.4888; CHECK SCHEDULE ONLINE

A Delivery With Love Birth Center

❝...a comforting prenatal support group to learn about all of the childbirth options with other parents... insightful and interesting information... ❞

Childbirth classes	✗	$$$	Prices
Parent group/club	✗	❸	Class selection
Breastfeeding support	✗	❸	Staff knowledge
Child care info	✗	❸	Customer service

WEST PALM BEACH—4550 IRIS ST (AT N MILITARY TRL); 561.687.7885

America's Toddler Guard

❝...they have tons of safety equipment for your home and will help install it... will make your pools safe for kids... lots of information... they will tell you safety precautions you never would have thought of... useful... ❞

Childbirth classes	✗	$$$	Prices
Parent group/club	✗	❸	Class selection
Breastfeeding support	✗	❸	Staff knowledge

Child care info..............................✗　❸........................Customer service

WWW.TODDLERGUARD.COM

DEERFIELD BEACH—812 SE 8TH AV (AT S FEDERAL HWY); 954.418.0101;
CHECK SCHEDULE ONLINE

Baptist Hospital Of Miami (Healthy Beginnings) ★★★★☆

"...a special series of classes held for new expectant parents that really help relieve a lot of the nervousness and stress... wonderful nurse led the course... very informative... group was large, but we had lots of fun..."

Childbirth classes ....✓　$$ ....Prices
Parent group/club.........................✓　❹............................Class selection
Breastfeeding support ....✓　❺...........................Staff knowledge
Child care info..............................✗　❺...........................Customer service

WWW.BAPTISTHEALTH.NET

MIAMI—8900 N KENDALL DR (AT SW 89TH CT); 786.596.8748; CHECK
SCHEDULE ONLINE

Birthing Center Of South Florida

Childbirth classes ....✗　✓.................Breastfeeding support
Parent group/club.........................✗　✓.............................Child care info

WWW.BIRTHNATURALLY.COM

HOMESTEAD—646 W PALM DR (AT NW 7TH AVE); 305.245.3730; CHECK
SCHEDULE ONLINE

Birthroot Breastfeeding Support Group ★★★★☆

"...offers a unique variety of classes and workshops for the expectant mom, from birth preparation to breastfeeding... also offer doulas and midwife referrals... a nice community resource..."

Childbirth classes ....✓　$$$ ....Prices
Parent group/club.........................✗　❺............................Class selection
Breastfeeding support ....✓　❺...........................Staff knowledge
Child care info..............................✓　❺...........................Customer service

WWW.BIRTHROOT.COM

CORAL GABLES—1514 SAN IGNACIO AVE (AT YUMUNI ST); 305.582.5454;
CHECK SCHEDULE ONLINE

Boca Raton Community Hospital (One Family Place) ★★★★★

"...I was very pleased with the prenatal class I attended, it was informative and the nurse teaching the class was excellent... modern birthing awareness , birthing class, basic baby care, sibling class, prenatal breastfeeding, partner and baby massage, baby CPR just to name a few... huge selection... excellent class quality..."

Childbirth classes ....✓　$$ ....Prices
Parent group/club.........................✓　❺............................Class selection
Breastfeeding support ....✓　❺...........................Staff knowledge
Child care info..............................✗　❺...........................Customer service

WWW.BRCH.COM

BOCA RATON—800 MEADOWS RD (AT NW 7TH AVE); 561.955.5110; CHECK
SCHEDULE ONLINE

Bradley Method, The ★★★☆☆

"...12 week classes that cover all of the basics of giving birth... run by individual instructors nationwide... classes differ based on the quality

and experience of the instructor... they cover everything from nutrition and physical conditioning to spousal support and medication... wonderful series that can be very educational... their web site has listings of instructors on a regional basis... **"**

Childbirth classes	✓	$$$	Prices
Parent group/club	✗	❸	Class selection
Breastfeeding support	✗	❸	Staff knowledge
Child care info	✓	❶	Customer service

WWW.BRADLEYBIRTH.COM

MIAMI—VARIOUS LOCATIONS; 800.422.4784; CHECK SCHEDULE & LOCATIONS ONLINE

Children's Center For Therapy & Learning

"*...our 2-year-old was not talking at all and we have seen great progress since starting therapy here... a nice, spacious facility... a wonderful new therapy room has a great rock climbing wall and other exciting therapy tools... a warm loving environment with great therapists in speech, occupational and physical therapy, tutoring and more... one stop therapy center that is reasonable... will travel to your home or child's school in some cases...* **"**

Childbirth classes	✗	$$$	Prices
Parent group/club	✓	❺	Class selection
Breastfeeding support	✗	❺	Staff knowledge
Child care info	✗	❺	Customer service

WWW.THERAPYANDLEARNING.COM

NORTH MIAMI—2124 NE 123RD ST (AT SANS SOUCI BLVD); 305.895.0444

Easter Seals

"*...a great resource for special needs including speech, occupational and physical therapy... they work with mainstream children with minor issues as well as those in higher need... amazing, kind and patient group of professionals... Director Mary Inhoffer is absolutely wonderful....* **"**

Childbirth classes	✓	$	Prices
Parent group/club	✓	❸	Class selection
Breastfeeding support	✗	❺	Staff knowledge
Child care info	✓	❺	Customer service

WWW.MIAMI.EASTERSEALS.COM

MIAMI—1475 NW 14TH AVE (AT NW 14TH TER); 305.325.0470; CHECK SCHEDULE ONLINE

Esther L Grossman Women's Health & Resource Cente

"*...this center offers classes and has tons of resources for new moms and parents... hey have hospital breast pumps and are affiliated with Memorial Regional Hospital... the perinatal and lactation services are informative and the teachers are warm and loving...* **"**

Childbirth classes	✓	$$$	Prices
Parent group/club	✗	❺	Class selection
Breastfeeding support	✓	❸	Staff knowledge
Child care info	✓	❺	Customer service

WWW.MEMORIALREGIONAL.COM/WOMENSSERVICES/ESTHERL.GROSSMANWOMENSHEALTHANDRESOURCECENTER.ASPX

HOLLYWOOD—4320 SHERIDAN ST (AT N 40TH AVE); 954.966.2611; CHECK SCHEDULE ONLINE

participate in our survey at

Family Central Inc

"...they have an awesome resource library with educational books, games, toys, music, videos, and resources... the parenting classes, referrals for child care providers and child and family services are real helpful... they make parenting a bit easier..."

Childbirth classes	✗	$$	Prices
Parent group/club	✗	❹	Class selection
Breastfeeding support	✗	❹	Staff knowledge
Child care info	✓	❹	Customer service

WWW.FAMILYCENTRAL.ORG

NORTH LAUDERDALE—840 SW 81ST AVE (AT 8TH ST); 954.720.1000; M 7-6, T-F 8-6

Fit for a Mom

★★★☆☆

"...a range of prenatal, new parenting and baby classes that are magical and wonderful... a definite place to utilize especially if you are a new parent... these wellness programs are one of a kind..."

Childbirth classes	✓	$$$	Prices
Parent group/club	✗	❸	Class selection
Breastfeeding support	✓	❸	Staff knowledge
Child care info	✗	❸	Customer service

WWW.FITFORAMOMANDBABY.COM

DELRAY BEACH—310 SE 1ST AVE (AT 3RD ST); 561.504.9436; CHECK SCHEDULE ONLINE

Holistic Maternity Center

★★★★☆

"...a beautiful center and an amazing place to give birth—I highly recommend it... an underwater birth is an incredible experience, especially with their guidance... they offer a great selection of pregnancy and childbirth classes with wonderful teachers..."

Childbirth classes	✓	$$	Prices
Parent group/club	✓	❺	Class selection
Breastfeeding support	✓	❺	Staff knowledge
Child care info	✗	❺	Customer service

WWW.H2OBIRTH.COM

NORTH MIAMI BEACH—16801 NE 6TH AVE (AT NE 167TH AVE); 305.249.2229; CALL FOR SCHEDULE

Hollywood Birth Center

★★★★☆

"...prenatal through postnatal classes... water births in your home or at the center... compassionate care... they offer breastfeeding and doula support plus so many other wonderful resources..."

Childbirth classes	✓	$$$	Prices
Parent group/club	✓	❸	Class selection
Breastfeeding support	✓	❷	Staff knowledge
Child care info	✗	❷	Customer service

WWW.HOLLYWOODBIRTHCENTER.COM

HOLLYWOOD—2316 HOLLYWOOD BLVD (AT S 24TH AVE); 954.925.4499; CHECK SCHEDULE ONLINE

Jackson South Community Hospital (Childbirth Education)

★★★★☆

"...great childbirth class and free too... instructor is friendly, well-informed and a pleasure... from nutrition, breastfeeding and relaxation this class hits all the hot spots..."

Childbirth classes	✓	$	Prices
Parent group/club	✓	❺	Class selection
Breastfeeding support	✓	❺	Staff knowledge
Child care info	✗	❺	Customer service

WWW.UM-JMH.ORG

MIAMI—9333 SW 152ND ST (AT SW 93RD AVE); 305.256.5071; CALL FOR
SCHEDULE

Lamaze International

"...thousands of women each year are educated about the birth
process by Lamaze educators their web site offers a list of local
instructors... they follow a basic curriculum, but invariably class quality
will depend on the individual instructor... in many ways they've set the
standard for birth education classes... **"**

Childbirth classes	✓	$$$	Prices
Parent group/club	✗	❸	Class selection
Breastfeeding support	✗	❸	Staff knowledge
Child care info	✗	❸	Customer service

WWW.LAMAZE.ORG

MIAMI—VARIOUS LOCATIONS; 800.368.4404; CHECK SCHEDULE AND
LOCATIONS ONLINE

Memorial Hospital West (Family Birthplace) ★★★★★

"...a tremendous resource for new moms and dads... a great selection
of classes from childcare to CPR... variety of classes to choose from in
both English and Spanish... reasonably priced... schedules are flexible,
offering evening and weekend classes... accommodating and helpful...
knowledgeable staff... **"**

Childbirth classes	✓	$$	Prices
Parent group/club	✗	❺	Class selection
Breastfeeding support	✗	❺	Staff knowledge
Child care info	✗	❹	Customer service

WWW.MEMORIALWEST.COM

PEMBROKE PINES—703 N FLAMINGO RD (AT PINES BLVD); 954.433.7110;
CALL FOR SCHEDULE

Mercy Hospital (Lactation Center)

"...every type of class a new and expecting parent could need... the
classes answer all the questions you may have about childbirth and
beyond... helpful lactation consultant... it's a wonderful way to bond
with your baby and to meet other parents... **"**

Childbirth classes	✓	$$	Prices
Parent group/club	✓	❺	Class selection
Breastfeeding support	✓	❺	Staff knowledge
Child care info	✗	❹	Customer service

WWW.MERCYMIAMI.COM

MIAMI—3659S MIAMI AVE (AT MERCY WAY N); 305.446.2229; CALL FOR
SCHEDULE; GARAGE LOCATED AT VISITOR

Miami Beach Maternity Center ★★★★★

"...excellent center for classes and a holistic birth experience... staff is
incredibly comforting and knowledgeable... the head midwife is more
knowledgeable than almost all of the OB's in Miami... a spiritual and
wonderful experience before and during childbirth... a friendly relaxing
atmosphere which was perfect for my child's birth... my wife and I were
very happy with the maternity classes we attended here and they were
FREE... **"**

Childbirth classes	✓	$$$	Prices
Parent group/club	✗	❺	Class selection
Breastfeeding support	✓	❺	Staff knowledge
Child care info	✗	❺	Customer service

participate in our survey at

WWW.MIAMIBIRTH.COM

MIAMI BEACH—1259 NORMANDY DR (AT RUE NOTRE DAME); 305.754.2229;
CHECK SCHEDULE ONLINE

Miami Maternity Center ★★★★★

"...an excellent center for classes and a holistic birth experience... staff is incredibly comforting and knowledgeable... the head midwife is more knowledgeable than almost all of the OB's in Miami... a spiritual and wonderful experience before and during childbirth... a friendly relaxing atmosphere which was perfect for my child's birth... my wife and I were very happy with the maternity classes we attended here and they were FREE..."

Childbirth classes	✓	$	Prices
Parent group/club	✗	❹	Class selection
Breastfeeding support	✓	❺	Staff knowledge
Child care info	✗	❺	Customer service

WWW.MIAMIBIRTH.COM

MIAMI—140 NE 119TH ST (AT NE 2ND AVE); 305.754.2229; PARKING LOT ON
PROPERTY

Mind Body & Baby ★★★½☆

"...a nice parenting education and fitness studio... they offer a variety of classes for expectant and new parents and children, ages birth to five years... great environment for mommy and me, prenatal yoga, and mommy and baby fitness..."

Childbirth classes	✓	$$$	Prices
Parent group/club	✗	❸	Class selection
Breastfeeding support	✓	❸	Staff knowledge
Child care info	✓	❸	Customer service

FORT LAUDERDALE—1000 SEMINOLE DR (AT E SUNRISE BLVD);
954.564.1577; CALL FOR SCHEDULE; GARAGE AT SITE

Mocha Moms ★★★★½

"...a wonderfully supportive group of women—the kind of place you'll make lifelong friends for both mother and child... a comfortable forum for bouncing ideas off of other moms with same-age children... easy to get involved and not too demanding... the annual membership dues seem a small price to pay for the many activities, play groups, field trips, Moms Nights Out and book club meetings... local chapters in cities nationwide..."

Childbirth classes	✗	$$$	Prices
Parent group/club	✓	❸	Class selection
Breastfeeding support	✗	❸	Staff knowledge
Child care info	✗	❸	Customer service

WWW.MOCHAMOMS.ORG

MIAMI—VARIOUS LOCATIONS

MOMS Club ★★★★☆

"...an international nonprofit with lots of local chapters and literally tens of thousands of members... designed to introduce you to new mothers with same-age kids wherever you live... they organize all sorts of activities and provide support for new mothers with babies... very inexpensive for all the activities you get... book clubs, moms night out, play group connections... generally a very diverse group of women..."

Childbirth classes	✗	$$$	Prices
Parent group/club	✓	❸	Class selection
Breastfeeding support	✗	❸	Staff knowledge
Child care info	✗	❸	Customer service

WWW.MOMSCLUB.ORG

SOUTH DADE & DOWNTOWN—VARIOUS LOCATIONS

parent education & support

Mothers and More

"...a very neat support system for moms who are deciding to stay at home... a great way to get together with other moms in your area for organized activities... book clubs, play groups, even a 'mom's only' night out... local chapters offer more or less activities depending on the involvement of local moms..."

Childbirth classes	✗	$$$	Prices
Parent group/club	✓	❸	Class selection
Breastfeeding support	✗	❸	Staff knowledge
Child care info	✗	❸	Customer service

WWW.MOTHERSANDMORE.COM

MIAMI—VARIOUS LOCATIONS; CHECK SCHEDULE & LOCATIONS ONLINE

Mount Sinai Medical Center (Maternal-child Center)

"...we took a six week breastfeeding and childbirth prep classes which was very helpful in preparing for the birth of our first child... would have liked more time on Lamaze, but felt overall, the class was worthwhile... they offer a variety of child preparedness and breastfeeding classes in a convenient location..."

Childbirth classes	✓	$$$	Prices
Parent group/club	✗	❸	Class selection
Breastfeeding support	✓	❸	Staff knowledge
Child care info	✗	❸	Customer service

WWW.MSMC.COM

MIAMI BEACH—4300 ALTON RD (AT SULLIVAN DR); 305.674.2229; CALL FOR
SCHEDULE

Palm Beach Moms

"...this is an email-based mothers' support group that helps you feel connected to other new moms... the group meets for frequent playdates and monthly Moms' Nights Out... I have developed lasting friendship through this group... very supportive ..."

Childbirth classes	✗	$$$	Prices
Parent group/club	✓	❸	Class selection
Breastfeeding support	✗	❸	Staff knowledge
Child care info	✗	❸	Customer service

PALM BEACH—VARIOUS LOCATIONS

Palmetto General (Tenet)

Childbirth classes	✗	✓	Breastfeeding support
Parent group/club	✓	✗	Child care info

WWW.PALMETTOGENERAL.COM/CWSCONTENT/PALMETTOGENERAL

HIALEAH—2001 W 68TH ST (AT W 20TH AVE); 800.522.5292; CHECK
SCHEDULE ONLINE

Plantation General Hospital (Lactation Center)

"...great information regarding childbirth and parenting... plenty of help and support for before and after baby... lots of resources to choose from... a very convenient resource for all things related to having a baby and breastfeeding..."

Childbirth classes	✗	$	Prices
Parent group/club	✓	❺	Class selection
Breastfeeding support	✓	❺	Staff knowledge
Child care info	✗	❺	Customer service

WWW.PLANTATIONGENERAL.COM

PLANTATION—401 NW 42ND AVE (AT N HOSPITAL DR); 954.587.5010; CALL
FOR SCHEDULE

participate in our survey at

South Miami Hospital (Birth-Day School)

★★★★★

"...friendly, caring, smart people teach the classes here... most of them have kids so they know what you're thinking before you even open your mouth... thorough and in-depth coverage of topic... helpful for first time parents... baby massage class is great..."

Childbirth classes .... ✓
Parent group/club .... ✗
Breastfeeding support .... ✓
Child care info .... ✗

$$ .... Prices
❹ .... Class selection
❹ .... Staff knowledge
❺ .... Customer service

WWW.BAPTISTHEALTH.NET

SOUTH MIAMI—6200 SW 73RD ST (AT SW 62ND AVE); 786.662.5026; CALL FOR SCHEDULE

parent education & support

pediatricians

Editor's Note: Pediatricians provide a tremendous breadth of services and are very difficult to classify and rate in a brief guide. For this reason we list only those practices for which we received overwhelmingly positive reviews. We hope this list of pediatricians will help you in your search.

South Dade & Downtown

Arango, Claudia MD
MIAMI—8525 SW 92ND ST BLG B (AT SW 87TH AVE); 305.279.8491; M-T TH-F 9 5.30

Dominguez, Luis DO
WWW.DRLUISDOMINGUEZ.COM
MIAMI—9220 SW 72ND ST (AT SW 92ND AVE); 305.279.6502; M-F 9-5; STREET PARKING

Edelstein, Jaime MD
CORAL GABLES—400 UNIVERSITY DR (AT S LE JEUME RD); 305.444.6882; M-F 9-5 SA 8:30-12; PARKING LOT

Eye Care For Kids
MIAMI—1555 SUNSET DR (AT 72ND ST); 305.662.2990; T-F 10-6 SA 11-5

Hershorin, Eugene MD
MIAMI—18469 S DIXIE HWY (AT EUREKA DR); 305.259.3005; M W F 8:30-5, T TH 8:30-8, SA 9-12; MALL PARKING

Jimenez, Joaquin MD
CORAL GABLES—400 UNIVERSITY DR (AT S LE JEUME RD); 305.444.6882; M-F 9-12 & 1-5, SA 8:30-12; PARKING LOT

Kaszovitz, Barbara MD
MIAMI—7001 SW 87TH AVE (AT SW 70TH ST); 305.271.8222; M-F 8:30-5, SA 8:30-12; PARKING LOT

Key Biscayne Associates In Pediatrics
KEY BISCAYNE—240 CRANDON BLVD (AT EAST DR); 305.361.6232; M-F 8:30-1 2-5

Kings Bay Pediatrics
MIAMI—8750 SW 144TH ST (AT SW 88TH AVE); 305.253.5585; M-F 8:30-4:30, SA 8:30-11

Miami Pediatrics
MIAMI—4300 ALTON RD (AT NW 17TH CT); 305.532.3378; M-F 9-5

My Doctor's Pediatrics
MIAMI—137 KENDLE DR (AT SW 147TH AVE); 305.383.1902; M-F 9-5

Pediatric Professionals
MIAMI—7001 SW 87TH AVE (AT SW 70TH ST); 305.271.8222

Rub Pediatrics MD PA
WWW.RUBPEDIATRICS.COM
MIAMI—1190 NW 95TH ST (AT NORTHSHORE MEDICAL CTR); 305.696.9490; M-W F 9-5, TH 9-12; FRONT OF BLDG

South Florida Pediatric Partners
MIAMI—7000 SW 97TH AV (AT SW 70TH ST); 305.595.3225; M-F 9-5

TLC Medical Center

WWW.TLCMEDICALCENTER.COM

MIAMI—10621 N KENDALL DR (AT SW 107TH AVE); 305.412.0071; M-T TH-F
9-5, W 12-8,; PARKING LOT

University of Miami Pediatric Accociates

WWW.MED.MIAMI.EDU/

MIAMI—11150 NW14TH ST (BTWN 12TH AVE & 14TH ST NW); 305.243.7570;
M-F 9-5; GARAGE

North Dade & Beaches

Aventura Children's Center

AVENTURA—19030 NE 29TH AVE (AT CONCORDE CENTRE DR);
305.932.5933; M-F 9-5

Beachside Pediatrics

BAY HARBOR ISLANDS—1145 KANE CONCOURSE (AT E BAY HARBOR DR);
305.865.5439; M-F 8:30-5:30, SA 9-11; STREET PARKING

BAY HARBOR ISLANDS—745 KANE CONCOURSE (AT BAL BAY DR);
305.865.5439; M-F 8:30-5:30, SA 9-12; STREET PARKING

Miami Beach Pediatrics

MIAMI BEACH—524 41ST ST (AT ROYAL PALM AVE); 305.672.7337; M TH-F
9-5, T-W 9-8, SU 9-12; STREET PARKING

Roger, Vicente MD

BAY HARBOR ISLANDS—1069 KANE CONCOURSE (AT BAY HARBOR TER);
305.868.5181; M 9-8, T-F 9-6

Rub Pediatrics MD PA

WWW.RUBPEDIATRICS.COM

AVENTURA—21110 BISCAYNE BLVD (AT NE 209TH ST); 305.696.9490; M-W F
9-5, TH 9-12; FRONT OF BLDG

Siegel, Steven MD

BAY HARBOR ISLANDS—1160 KANE CONCOURSE (AT W BAY HARBOR DR);
305.865.9861; M-F 9-5

participate in our survey at

Broward County

Children's Medical Association
FORT LAUDERDALE—8430 W BROWARD BLVD (AT NW 84TH AVE);
954.473.1101; M W F 8-5, T TH 8-7

Children's Medical Center
HOLLYWOOD—1051 N 35TH AV (AT JOHNSON ST); 954.989.6000; M-F 8-5

Coconut Creek Pediatrics
COCONUT CREEK—4400 W SAMPLE RD (AT LYONS RD); 954.978.6130; M-TH
9-5, F 9-12, SA 9-12

Dixon, Donald MD
PEMBROKE PINES—7942 PINES BLVD (AT N UNIVERSITY DR); 954.985.0774;
M-T F 9-5, W 9-6:30, TH SA 9-1

East West Pediatrics
FORT LAUDERDALE—1319 SE 2ND AV (AT HAM FORMAN'S WAY);
954.467.3053; M-F 9-5 SA 9-12

Family Health Place At Rio Vista
WWW.BROWARDHEALTH.ORG
FORT LAUDERDALE—789 S FEDERAL HWY (AT 8TH ST); 954.462.8323; M-F
8:30-5 SA 9-12

Halle, Michael MD
SUNRISE—12651 W SUNRISE BLVD (AT PURPLE PARROT PL); 954.835.2111;
M-F 8:30-5, SA 8:30-12

Holy Cross Medical Group
FORT LAUDERDALE—1900 E COMMERCIAL BLVD (AT HOLY CROSS
HOSPITAL); 954.351.5840; M-F 9-5

Lwin, Khin MD
FORT LAUDERDALE—300 NW 70TH AV (AT NW 68TH AVE); 954.581.3100; M-
F 8:30-5

Pediatric Associates
WWW.PEDIATRICASSOCIATES.COM
WESTON—1835 N CORPORATE LAKES BLVD (AT N COMMERCE PKWY);
954.389.7000; M-F 8-5 SA 8-12

Personal Care Pediatrics
MARGATE—2825 N STATE RD 7 (AT COLONIAL DR); 954.974.3006; M-TH 8-
6:30, F 8-5, SA 8-12

West Broward Pediatrics
PLANTATION—220 SW 84TH AVE (AR 2ND ST); 954.423.2300; M-T TH-F 8-5,
W 8-8, SA 8-12

pediatricians

Palm Beach County

Boca Pediatric Group

BOCA RATON—5458 TOWN CTR RD (AT BOCA RATON); 561.391.6210; BY
APP

Childrens Physicians

PALM BEACH GARDENS—3365 BURNS RD (AT GARDEN EAST DR);
561.626.4000; M-F 8:30-5; PARKING LOT

ENT Consultants Of Palm
Beaches

WEST PALM BEACH—927 45TH ST (AT ST MARY'S HOSPITAL); 561.848.5579;
M-F 8:30-5

Infants And Children

WWW.DOH.STATE.FL.US/CHDPALMBEACH/CENTERS/DELRAYBEACH.HTML

WEST PALM BEACH—5205 VILLAGE BLVD (AT 45TH ST); 561.242.0505; M-F
8-5

Pediatric Associates

WWW.PEDIATRICASSOCIATES.COM

BOYNTON BEACH—10301 HAGEN RANCH RD (AT VENTURA CTR WAY);
561.733.4400; M-F 8-8, SA 8-8, SU 2-8

breast pump
sales & rentals

South FL Area

"lila picks"

★ Babies R Us
★ Faith Ploude (Mercy Outpatient Center)

Babies R Us ★★★★★

❝...Medela pumps, Boppy pillows and lots of other breastfeeding supplies... staff knowledge varies from store to store, but everyone was friendly and helpful... clean and well-stocked... not a huge selection, but what they've got is great and very competitively priced...❞

Customer Service .... ❹ $$$ .... Prices

WWW.BABIESRUS.COM

BOCA RATON—21697 STATE RD 7 (AT CENTRAL PARK BLVD); 561.477.3337; M-SA 9:30-9:30; SU 11-7; PARKING IN FRONT OF BLDG

LAUDERHILL—7350 W COMMERCIAL BLVD (AT UNIVERSITY DR); 954.749.2229; M-SA 9:30-9:30, SU 11-7; PARKING IN FRONT OF BLDG

MIAMI—15625 N KENDALL DR (AT SW 157TH AVE); 305.382.4060; M-SA 9:30-9:30; SU 11-7; PARKING IN FRONT OF BLDG

MIAMI—8755 SW 24TH ST (AT SW 87TH AVE); 305.226.8334; M-SA 9:30-9:30, SU 11-7; PARKING IN FRONT OF BLDG

NORTH MIAMI—2745 NE 193RD ST (AT BISCAYNE BLVD); 305.705.9893; M-SA 9:30-9:30, SU 11-7 ; PARKING LOT

PEMBROKE PINES—11930 PINES BLVD (AT PEMBROKE LAKES MALL); 954.441.8600; M-SA 9:30-9:30, SU 11-7; MALL PARKING

WEST PALM BEACH—4895 OKEECHOBEE BLVD (AT HAVERHILL RD N); 561.478.9400; M-SA 9:30-9:30, SU 11-7; PARKING LOT

Baptist Hospital Of Miami (Parent Education)

WWW.BAPTISTHEALTH.NET

MIAMI—8900 N KENDALL DR (AT SW 89TH CT); 305.596.1960

Baptist Medical Plaza At Palmetto Bay

WWW.BAPTISTHEALTH.NET

MIAMI—8750 SW 144TH ST (OFF RTE 1); 786.596.2671

Breastfeeding Boutique

WWW.BREASTFEEDINGBOUTIQUE.COM

BOCA RATON—1575 SW 4TH CIR (AT SW 15TH AVE); 561.338.3322; M-F 8-3; NA

Faith Ploude (Mercy Outpatient Center)

"...Faith is a genius... she spends a tremendous amount of time with you... afterhours phone number if you need help... her consultations are very reasonable and my health insurance reimbursed me..."

Customer Service........................ ❺ $$ .... Prices

WWW.FLCA.INFO/ID27.HTM

MIAMI—3659 S MIAMI AVE (AT MERCY WY); 305.663.9763; M-T TH-F 10-5, W 10-12; FREE PARKING

La Ideal Baby Store

WWW.IDEALBABY.COM

HIALEAH—1170 W 49TH ST (AT W 12TH AVE); 305.826.2021; M-SA 10-9, SU 11-6

PEMBROKE PINES—12151 PINES BLVD (AT N FLAMINGO RD); 954.620.2229; M-SA 10-9, SU 11-6

Memorial Hospital (Lactation Center)

"...carry the Medela breast pump at a reasonable price... wonderful lactation support from knowledgeable staff..."

Customer Service........................ ❺ $$ .... Prices

WWW.MEMORIALPEMBROKE.COM

PEMBROKE PINES—801 N FLAMINGO RD (AT JOHNSON ST); 954.430.6880

Mercy Hospital

"...rents Medela pumps... they also sell other useful products for breastfeeding... my insurance company covered the consultation... daily classes are only $5... they have a scale where you can weigh your baby...."

Customer Service........................ ❺ $$ .... Prices

WWW.MERCYMIAMI.COM/

MIAMI—3659 S MIAMI AVE (AT MERCY WY); 305.446.2229

Pill Box Pharmacy

"...a wonderful pharmacy that carries great, hospital-grade pumps... they showed me how to use it and even answered questions over the phone once I got home... rates are around $20 per week or $50 per month for the Medela Lactina... they also carry a large inventory of things for other 'new mom' ailments... they make the process hassle free..."

Customer Service........................ ❹ $$$ .... Prices

WWW.PILLBOX123.COM

PEMBROKE PINES—1700 NW 122 TERRACE (AT N FLAMINGO RD); 954.432.7455; CHECK SCHEDULE ONLINE; FREE PARKING

PEMBROKE PINES—601 N FLAMINGO RD (AT PEMBROKE LAKES MALL); 954.437.7455

WESTON—1932 WESTON RD (AT N CORPORATE LAKES BLVD); 954.389.7455

Surfmed Pharmacy

"...easy rental of Ameda or Medela pumps... knowledgeable staff..."

Customer Service........................ ❹ $$ .... Prices

WWW.SURFMED.COM

MIAMI BEACH—4302 ALTON RD (AT W 44TH ST); 305.672.3660

MIAMI BEACH—7430 COLLINS AVE (AT 74TH ST); 305.866.2427; M-F 9-7, SA 9-1

diaper delivery

USA Baby

HOLLYWOOD—4923 SHERIDAN ST (AT N 52ND AVE); 954.985.6464; M TH SA 10-8, T-W 10-5:30, F 10-6, SU 11:30-6

participate in our survey at

Online

amazon.com

"...I'm always amazed by the amount of stuff Amazon sells—including a pretty good selection of pumps... Medela, Avent, Isis, Ameda... prices range from great to average... pretty easy shopping experience... free shipping on bigger orders..."

babycenter.com

"...they carry all the major brands... prices are competitive, but keep in mind you'll need to pay for shipping too... the comments from parents are incredibly helpful... excellent customer service... easy shopping experience..."

birthexperience.com

"...Medela and Avent products... great deal with the Canadian currency conversion... get free shipping with big orders... easy site to navigate..."

breast-pumps.com

breastmilk.com

ebay.com

"...you can get Medela pumps brand new in packaging with the warranty for $100 less than retail... able to buy immediately instead of having to bid and wait... wide variety... be sure to check for shipping price... great place to find deals, but research the seller before you bid..."

express-yourself.net

healthchecksystems.com

lactationconnection.com

"...Ameda and Whisper Wear products... nice selection and competitive prices... quick delivery of any nursing or lactation product you can imagine... the selection of mom and baby related items is fantastic..."

medela.com

"...well worth the money... fast, courteous and responsive... great site for a full listing of Medela products and links to purchase online... quality of customer service by phone varies... licensed lactation specialist answers e-mail via email at no charge and with quick turnaround..."

mybreastpump.com

"...a great online one-stop-shop for all things breast feeding... you can purchase hospital grade pumps from them... fast service for all you breastfeeding needs..."

diaper delivery

haircuts

South FL Area

★★★★★

"lila picks"

★Cartoon Cuts

Be Young & Aveda Concepts Salon

❝...although this is not a place for kids, they give great kids haircuts for about seventeen dollars... the staff is very friendly and great with the little ones and the store is very clean and pleasant... I would not take kids under 3 years, but it's great for 4 year olds and bigger... ❞

Customer Service .... **❺** $$$ .... Prices

NORTH MIAMI—12780 BISCAYNE BLVD (AT NE 127TH ST); 305.891.2003; T-F 10-8, SA 9-6, SU 12-6

Cartoon Cuts
★★★★★

❝...if your tot squirms at the thought of getting his hair cut, then you might want to try Cartoon Cuts... cartoons and toys catch your kid's attention while the cutters do their job... the staff is patient and friendly... cuts vary depending on the staff, so once you've found someone good I'd suggest coming back to her... lollipops are an extra added bonus... a fun waiting area and TV's at each station to keep the little ones happy... kids seem to love it... ❞

Customer Service .... **❸** $$ .... Prices

WWW.CARTOONCUTS.COM

CORAL SPRINGS—9481 W ATLANTIC BLVD (AT N UNIVERSITY DR); 954.341.4221; M-SA 10-9:30, SU 11-6; MALL PARKING

HIALEAH—9300 NW 77TH AVE (AT W OKEECHOBEE RD); 305.231.9006; M-SA 10-9:30, SU 11-6; MALL PARKING

MIAMI—8412 MILLS DR (AT SHERI LN); 305.270.2325; M-F 10-8, SA 9-8, SU 11-6; MALL PARKING

PEMBROKE PINES—11401 PINES BLVD (AT N HAITUS RD); 954.435.7166; M-SA 10-9, SU 11-6; MALL PARKING

WELLINGTON—10300 W FOREST HILL BLVD (AT HWY 441); 561.383.6500; M-F 9-9, SA 9-8, SU 11-6; MALL PARKING

Champs Haircuts

Customer Service .... **❹** $$ .... Prices

BOYNTON BEACH—143- 1/2 CONGRESS AVE (AT SW GOLFVIEW TER); 561.736.1416; M-F 9-9, SA 9-6

Coco's Day Spa & Salon

❝...Danny gives my kids the best haircuts ever... he is kind, patient and has a following of entire families.... it 's amazing to get a professional haircut for my children for only a couple dollars more than kids' salons... ❞

Customer Service .... **❺** $$$ .... Prices

WWW.COCOSDAYSPA.COM

AVENTURA—AVENTURA MALL (AT BISCAYNE BLVD); 305.931.1411; M-SA 9-9:30; FREE PARKING

Cut N Play

"...kids can get their haircut in a fire truck or a Porsche while watching a video... girls can even get a mini-manicure... my son is sometimes happier with his haircut than I am... they e-mail you a photo of the first haircut... each chair is equipped with a TV/VCR and many videos... sometimes the cuts aren't so fashionable... pick a good stylist..."

Customer Service...................... ❹ $$ .... Prices

AVENTURA—18787 BISCAYNE BLVD (AT NE 187TH ST); 305.932.1947; M 1-6:30, T-F 10:30-6:30, SA 10-6

Deerfield Buzz

"...fun place to get your haircut... they even do baby's first haircut and give you a piece of their hair and a certificate..."

Customer Service...................... ❺ $$ .... Prices

WWW.DEERFIELDBUZZ.COM

DEERFIELD BEACH—3708 W HILLSBORO BLVD (AT N POWELINE RD); 954.698.6367; CALL FOR APPT

Just Kids

"...it's been around for over 30 yrs... very friendly staff, great prices, and reliable service... you can also set up an appointment via email..."

Customer Service...................... ❸ $$$ .... Prices

WWW.JUSTKIDSHAIR.COM

MIAMI—10910 W FLAGLE ST (AT NW 109TH AVE); 305.554.0667; T-SA 10-5; FREE PARKING

Just Kids Hair Styling

"...limited hours, but hard to beat the price... lots of toys to play with, including computer games, and videos to watch... cute haircuts, and great with toddlers..."

Customer Service...................... ❸ $$$ .... Prices

CORAL SPRINGS—7544 WILES RD (AT E LEITNER); 954.755.8580; T-F 9-11 2-5, SA 8-12

Kids Cut

"...the car seats, toys and videos ease a fussy toddler (try to find a car with a steering wheel)... the special enticements are well worth a couple extra bucks... the haircuts range from acceptable to excellent..."

Customer Service...................... ❹ $ .... Prices

HIALEAH—11300 NW 87TH CT (AT NW 114TH ST); 305.819.3839; CALL FOR APPT

Kids Haircut Station

MIAMI—8765 SW 24TH ST (AT SW 88TH AVE); 305.227.4248; CALL FOR APPT

Kids Haircuts

"...the decor is outdated, but the service is very good..."

Customer Service...................... ❹ $$$ .... Prices

MIAMI—8765 CORAL WY (AT SW 87TH AVE); 305.227.4248; CALL FOR APPT

Kids Magic Cuts

"...this is an ok place to go to get a child's hair cut... it is very reasonable, they have fun car seats and cartoons... the staff is friendly,

haircuts

but it is not as clean as I would like and it can be a zoo on the weekend... **"**

Customer Service ....**4** $$ .... Prices

SUNRISE—15912 W STATE RD 84 (AT E WATERSIDE CIR); 954.385.2329; CALL FOR APPT

Kids' Only Place Inc ★★★★☆

"*...bilingual (Spanish) stylists... never a bad cut and always fun... staff is very patient, and very professional... for baby's first cut, they have certificates for keepsake...* **"**

Customer Service ....**4** $ .... Prices

MIAMI—2712 SW 137TH AVE (AT SW 26TH ST); 305.551.9155; T-F 10-7, SA 9-6

Kids Or Not ★★★★☆

"*...great offer for first haircut includes strand of babies hair, certificate and picture... great keepsakes... cute decorations...* **"**

Customer Service ....**4** $ .... Prices

MIAMI—11865 SW 26TH ST (AT SW 25TH TER); 305.223.1877; CALL FOR APPT

Kool Klips ★★★★☆

"*...a great touch that the children can watch videos... the first place my daughter let anyone cut her hair... call for an appointment or just drop in... waiting area with toys available, but sometimes dirty... staff works well with kids... service is quick, friendly and patient ...* **"**

Customer Service ....**3** $$ .... Prices

WWW.CARTOONCUTS.COM

MIAMI—8888 SW 136TH ST (AT FALLS SHOPPING CENTER); 305.278.1211; CALL FOR APPT

WEST PALM BEACH—4375 BELVEDERE RD (AT N MILITARY TRL); 561.616.7366; CALL FOR APPT

Manely It's A Jungle In Hair ★★★☆☆

"*...the quality of the haircut is variable depending on stylist, but the kids stations are great... the toddlers sit in cars instead of regular chairs, and there is always a video for them to watch while getting their haircut... the staff is friendly and used to working with toddlers...* **"**

Customer Service ....**4** $$ .... Prices

JUPITER—6779 W INDIANTOWN RD (AT CENTRAL BLVD); 561.743.8887; M-SA 10-5; FREE PARKING

Pete's Suniland Barber Shop ★★★★☆

"*...love the old-time barber shop feel... don't miss the first haircut certificate and photo... walk-ins welcome... they also provide lollipops and gum...* **"**

Customer Service ....**4** $ .... Prices

MIAMI—11505 S DIXIE HWY (AT KILLIAN DR); 305.251.5893; CALL FOR APPT

Salon Trio ★★★★☆

"*...one stop haircutting for you and your kids... Nancy is the best... everyone's great with children and it's generally a fun outing...* **"**

Customer Service ....**5** $$$ .... Prices

PINECREST—12515 S DIXIE HWY (AT CHAPMAN FIELD DR); 305.251.9115; T-W 9-7, TH-F 9-5, SA 9-5

Sport Clips ★★★☆☆

"*...a sports-themed haircutter with TVs at every station... staff is friendly and they do a good job... the price is reasonable at about $12*

per cut... it's not a specialty kids salon, but it's fun coming here and the cuts generally turn out pretty good... **"**

Customer Service........................ **❸** $$ .... Prices

WWW.SPORTCLIPS.COM

PEMBROKE PINES—18247 PINES BLVD (AT NW 184TH AVE); 954.435.6089;
CALL FOR APPT

Supercuts ★★★⯪☆

"...*results definitely vary from location to location... they did their best to amuse my son and an okay job with his hair... cheap and easy, with decent results... some locations have toys for kids to play with... walk-ins welcome, but make an appointment if you are going on the weekend... ask for the cutter who's best with kids... great cut for the price... fast and easy...* **"**

Customer Service........................ **❹** $$ .... Prices

WWW.SUPERCUTS.COM

HOLLYWOOD—1831 N FEDERAL HWY (AT HARDING ST); 954.925.8771; M-F
9-9, SA 9-7, SU 10-5

MIAMI—13909 SW 88TH ST (AT SW 124TH AVE); 305.385.5090; M-F 9-9, SA
9-7, SU 10-6

NORTH MIAMI—12567 BISCAYNE BLVD (AT KEYSTONE BLVD); 305.892.0508;
M-F 9-9, SA 9-7, SU 10-6

PEMBROKE PINES—18371 PINES BLVD (AT NW 184TH AVE); 954.450.8778;
M-F 9-9, SA 9-7, SU 10-5

haircuts

nanny & babysitter referrals

South FL Area

Family Central Inc ★★★★☆

"...a free resource and referral agency for all childcare needs... information available online, by phone, or in person... expect long phone waits, but they do try to respond to every call..."

Baby nurses	✗	$	Prices
Nannies	✗	❸	Candidate selection
Au pairs	✗	❺	Staff knowledge
Babysitters	✓	❸	Customer service

Service AreaBroward & Palm Beach Counties

WWW.FAMILYCENTRAL.ORG

NORTH LAUDERDALE—840 SW 81ST AVE (AT SW 8TH ST); 954.721.3525

First Choice Nannies, Inc

Baby nurses	✗	✓	Nannies
Au pairs	✗	✗	Babysitters

Service Area .... Southern Florida

JUPITER—561.575.1011

Florida Atlantic University (Student Employment Babysitting List) ★★★★★

"...call the student employment center and they email or fax you a list... you contact the babysitter directly and take it from there..."

Baby nurses	✗	$	Prices
Nannies	✗	❺	Candidate selection
Au pairs	✗	❶	Staff knowledge
Babysitters	✓	❺	Customer service

Service AreaDade & Broward Counties

DAVIE—2912 COLLEGE AVE (AT SW 30TH ST); 561.297.3680

LIttle Angels Nanny Service

Baby nurses	✗	✓	Nannies
Au pairs	✗	✓	Babysitters

Service Area .... places statewide

LAKE WORTH—802 COCHRAN DR; 561.586.5936

Nannies And More ★★★★☆

"...they'll get the job done... even though it didn't work out the first time around, they were great about working with us to find a replacement quickly... good, but a little pricey... if your budget will accomodate, I wouldn't hesitate to use them..."

Baby nurses	✓	$$$	Prices
Nannies	✓	❸	Candidate selection
Au pairs	✗	❸	Staff knowledge
Babysitters	✗	❸	Customer service

Service AreaNationwide (focus on East Coast)

WWW.NANNIESANDMORE.COM

BOCA RATON—2255 GLADES RD (AT N MILITARY TRL); 888.466.4525; CALL FOR APPT

Nannies N' More

Baby nurses	✗	✓	Nannies
Au pairs	✗	✗	Babysitters

Service AreaDade, Broward and Palm Beach Counties

WWW.NANNIES-N-MORE.COM

participate in our survey at

Nanny Network Inc

Baby nurses	✗	✓	Nannies
Au pairs	✗	✗	Babysitters

Service Area.................Miami area

WWW.NANNYNETWORKINC.COM

MIAMI—20145 NE 25TH AVE; 305.932.5335

Nanny On The Net, A ★★★⯪☆

"...a national agency that places experienced (at least three years) nannies... easy to use and efficient... detailed background checks... all prospects are trained in CPR... legal, financial, and practical help for first-time 'employer' families... about $75 for the application fee and then additional placement fees when you succeed in finding a nanny... **"**

Baby nurses	✓	$$$	Prices
Nannies	✓	❺	Candidate selection
Au pairs	✗	❺	Staff knowledge
Babysitters	✗	❺	Customer service

Service Area................. Dade County

WWW.ANANNYONTHENET.COM

MIAMI—305.667.5099; M-F 9-5

Palm Beach Atlantic University ★★★★☆

"...this Christian-based college keeps a list of students interested in babysitting... call them and ask them to send you the Babysitters Club list... you will get a list of students' names, phone numbers, answers to questions such as do they have transportation, smoke, drink, certified in CPR and lifeguard, as well as a short personal comment... the babysitter we found is fantastic... **"**

Baby nurses	✗	$$$	Prices
Nannies	✗	❹	Candidate selection
Au pairs	✗	❹	Staff knowledge
Babysitters	✗	❹	Customer service

WWW.PBA.EDU

WEST PALM BEACH—901 S FLAGLER DR (AT OKEECHOBEE BLVD); 561.803.2060

nanny & babysitter referrals

Online

★★★★★
"lila picks"
★craigslist.org

4nannies.com

Baby nurses	✗	✓ Nannies
Au pairs	✗	✗ Babysitters
Service Area	nationwide	

WWW.4NANNIES.COM

aupaircare.com

Baby nurses	✗	✗ Nannies
Au pairs	✓	✗ Babysitters
Service Area	International	

WWW.AUPAIRCARE.COM

aupairinamerica.com

Baby nurses	✗	✗ Nannies
Au pairs	✓	✗ Babysitters
Service Area	International	

WWW.AUPAIRINAMERICA.COM

babysitters.com

Baby nurses	✗	✗ Nannies
Au pairs	✗	✓ Babysitters
Service Area	nationwide	

WWW.BABYSITTERS.COM

craigslist.org

★★★★★

❝...you can find just about anything on craigslist... good starting point, especially if you don't want to spend a lot of money and are willing to do your own screening... we received at least 50 responses to our 'nanny wanted' ad... helped me find very qualified baby-sitters... includes all major cities in the US...❞

Baby nurses	✓	✓ Nannies
Au pairs	✗	✓ Babysitters

WWW.CRAIGSLIST.ORG

enannysource.com

Baby nurses	✗	✓ Nannies
Au pairs	✗	✗ Babysitters
Service Area	nationwide	

WWW.ENANNYSOURCE.COM

findcarenow.com

Baby nurses	✗	✗ Nannies
Au pairs	✗	✓ Babysitters
Service Area	nationwide	

participate in our survey a

get-a-sitter.com

Baby nurses	✗	✗	Nannies
Au pairs	✗	✓	Babysitters
Service Area	nationwide		

WWW.GET-A-SITTER.COM

householdstaffing.com

Baby nurses	✓	✓	Nannies
Au pairs	✗	✗	Babysitters

WWW.HOUSEHOLDSTAFFING.COM

interexchange.org

Baby nurses	✗	✗	Nannies
Au pairs	✓	✗	Babysitters
Service Area	International		

WWW.INTEREXCHANGE.ORG

nannies4hire.com

Baby nurses	✗	✓	Nannies
Au pairs	✗	✗	Babysitters

WWW.NANNIES4HIRE.COM

nannylocators.com

★★★★☆

"...many listings of local nannies available... I have found that the listings are not always up to date... $100 subscriber fee to respond and contact nannies that have posted... different regions have varying amounts of listings available...**"**

Baby nurses	✗	✓	Nannies
Au pairs	✗	✗	Babysitters
Service Area	Nationwide		

WWW.NANNYLOCATORS.COM

sittercity.com

★★★★☆

"...wonderful online resource... an online baby-sitter database filled with mostly college and graduate students looking for baby-sitting and nanny jobs... candidates are not prescreened so you must check references... Fee to access the database is $35 plus $5 per month... tends to be be more useful for baby-sitters than regular daytime nannies...**"**

Baby nurses	✗	✗	Nannies
Au pairs	✗	✓	Babysitters
Service Area	nationwide		

WWW.SITTERCITY.COM

student-sitters.com

Baby nurses	✗	✗	Nannies
Au pairs	✗	✓	Babysitters

WWW.STUDENT-SITTERS.COM

nanny & babysitter referrals

photographers

South FL Area

"lila picks"

★ Janine Stone Photography
★ Kiddie Kandids

Allison Langer Photography ★★★★☆

❝...stunning beach pictures... a natural with kids... she gives you the negatives!.. she shoots mainly outside in the Coral Gables area... color and b/w... ❞

Customer service........................**5** $$$..Prices

WWW.ALLISONLANGER.COM

CORAL GABLES—1526 SARRIA AVE (AT ALHAMBRA CIR); 305.665.1171; CALL FOR APPT

Amy Kratish Photography ★★★★½

❝...we've gone back for more... brilliant pictures at a reasonable price... she charges by the roll and lets you keep all the negatives... we loved the pictures taken by her outside pool area... fun to work with for the whole family—including your pets... ❞

Customer service........................**4** $$...Prices
Service Area ....Dade and Broward

COOPER CITY—5200 SW 115TH AVE (AT SW 52ND ST); 954.434.1625; CALL FOR APPT

Amy Stone Photography ★★★★★

❝...I had such a great experience working with Amy and the pictures came out great... I plan to use her for all my future photoshoots in the future... reasonably priced... a true professional that creates wonderful candid and studio shots... she can be very creative and artsy, if you want that... ❞

Customer service........................**5** $ ....Prices

WWW.AMYSTONEPHOTOGRAPHY.COM

COCONUT GROVE—305.439.7397

Birth Naturally ★★★★★

❝...stunning pictures that capture the childbirth experience... a special photographer that really captures the emotions of bringing a baby into the world... ❞

Customer service........................**4** $$...Prices

WWW.BIRTHNATURALLY.COM

MIAMI—305.498.2575

Indigo Images ★★★★★

❝...Sandy will takes beautiful natural looking prenatal and baby shots in either black and white or color... Sandy is very flexible and easy going and her prices are very reasonable.... ❞

participate in our survey at ▇

Customer service .... ❺ $$ .... Prices

Service Area........Miami-Dade County

WWW.INDIGOIMAGES.SMUGMUG.COM

COCONUT GROVE—3173 MCDONALD ST (AT DAY AVE); 786.390.7322; CALL
  FOR APPT

Janine Stone Photography   ★★★★★

❝...Janine has chronicled our kids from pregnancy to preschool...
timeless wonderful photographs and she's a pleasure to work with...
beautiful black and whites... we take advantage of her seasonal spring
and fall photo shoots sales... she sees the essence of your children and
puts it down on paper for years to come... **❞**

Customer service .... ❺ $$ .... Prices

WWW.JANINESTONEPHOTOGRAPHY.COM

SOUTH MIAMI—10170 N KENDALL DR (AT SW 102ND AVE); 305.903.5126;
  CALL FOR APPT

JCPenney Portrait Studio   ★★★⯪☆

❝...don't expect works of art, but they are great for a quick wallet
photo... photographers and staff range from great to not so good... a
quick portrait with standard props and backdrops... definitely join the
portrait club and use coupons... waits are especially long around the
holidays, so consider taking your Christmas pictures early... the e-
picture option is a time saver... wait time for prints can be up to a
month... look for coupons and you'll never have to pay full price... **❞**

Customer service .... ❹ $$ .... Prices

WWW.JCPENNEYPORTRAITS.COM

PLANTATION—8000 W BROWARD BLVD (AT N UNIVERSITY DR);
  954.472.0566; M-SA 10-6, SU 11-4

Kiddie Kandids   ★★★★★

❝...good quality photos for all occasions... they made a big effort to
get a smile out of my grumpy son... you don't need to make a
reservation, just pop in and have the pictures taken... no sitting fee...
photographers take the extra time necessary to get a great shot and
they have the cutest props... lots of items to buy with your pictures on
them—cups, bags, mouse pads... buy the CD of pictures rather than
buying the prints... pictures are available right after the sitting... **❞**

Customer service .... ❹ $$$ .... Prices

WWW.KIDDIEKANDIDS.COM

BOCA RATON—21695 STATE RD 7 (AT CENTRAL PARK BLVD N);
  561.470.3551

KENDALL—15625 N KENDALL DR (AT SW 157TH CT); 305.383.9449; M-SA
  9:30-8, SU 11-6

LAUDERHILL—7350 W COMMERCIAL BLVD (AT N UNIVERSITY DR);
  954.578.3233; M-SA 9:30-8:30, SU 11-6

MIAMI—8755 SW 24TH ST (AT SW 87TH AVE); 305.554.7040; M-SA 9:30-
  9:30, SU 11:30-6

PEMBROKE PINES—11930 PINES BLVD (AT SW 118TH AVE); 954.450.0923;
  M-SA 9:30-8, SU 11-6

Mercy Photo   ★★★★★

❝...incredible pictures paired with unbeatable customer service... a
little expensive for those on a budget, but awesome pictures to last a
lifetime... strictly studio photography, not a natural setting... **❞**

Customer service .... ❺ $$$ .... Prices

HIALEAH—3960 W 16TH AVE (AT W 39TH PL); 305.887.3751; M-F 9-5, SA 9-4

photographers

Photography By Mia

"...unique photography with lots of props, costumes, framing and flowers... she has a great baby's first year package... the pictures look like greeting cards, very whimsical... **"**

Customer service..........................**5** $$............................,,,   ., Prices

WWW.PORTRAITSBYMIA.COM

MIAMI—1425 SW 107 AVE (AT NW 13TH ST); 305.229.5714; CALL FOR APPT

Sadies

"...a mall-based studio that takes great pictures that are ready in an hour... we have been there twice and will continue to go back... they take a whole roll of pictures to choose from... great staff that is always happy, even when baby isn't... creative photography with props, costumes and funky digital effects... **"**

Customer service..........................**4** $$$...Prices

WWW.SADIESONLINE.COM

CORAL SPRINGS—9085 W ATLANTIC BLVD (AT RIVERSIDE DR);
  954.757.2248; M-SA 10-9, SU 11-6

Sears Portrait Studio

"...the price is right, but the service and quality are variable... make an appointment to cut down on the wait time... bring your coupons for even better prices... perfect for getting a nice wallet size portrait without spending a fortune... I wish the wait time for prints wasn't so long (2 weeks)... the quality and service-orientation of the photographers really vary a lot—some are great, some aren't... **"**

Customer service..........................**3** $$...Prices

WWW.SEARSPORTRAIT.COM

BOCA RATON—5900 W GLADE RD (AT TOWN CTR AT BOCA RATON);
  561.338.1190; M-F 10-8, T SA SU 10-6

CORAL SPRINGS—9565 W ATLANTIC BLVD (AT N UNIVERSITY DR);
  954.345.1354; SA-SU T 10-6, M W TH-F 10-8; PARKING IN FRONT OF BLDG

FORT LAUDERDALE—901 N FEDERAL HWY (AT NE 9TH AVE); 954.779.1366;
  M 10-8, T 10-6, W-F 10-8, SA 10-6, SU 10-5; PARKING IN FRONT OF BLDG

HIALEAH—1625 W 49TH ST (AT WESTLAND MALL); 305.364.3884; M-SA 10-8,
  SU 11-5; PARKING IN FRONT OF BLDG

MIAMI—1625 NW 107TH AVE (AT MIAMI INTERNATIONAL MALL);
  305.470.7854

MIAMI—19505 BISCAYNE BLVD (AT AVENTURA MALL); 305.937.7551; M-SA
  10-8, SU 11-5; PARKING IN FRONT OF BLDG

MIAMI—20701 S ALLAPATTAH DR (AT CUTLER RIDGE MALL); 305.378.5198;
  M-F10-8, SA 9-8, SU 11-5; PARKING IN FRONT OF BLDG

MIAMI—3655 SW 22ND ST (AT S DOUGLAS RD); 305.460.3465; M-SA 10-8,
  SU 11-6; PARKING IN FRONT OF BLDG

PEMBROKE PINES—12055 PINES BLVD (AT PEMBROKE LAKE MALL);
  954.704.4197; M-SA 10-6, SU 11-4:30; PARKING IN FRONT OF BLDG

PLANTATION—8000 W BROWARD BLVD (AT BROWARD MALL); 954.370.2866;
  M-F 10 6, SA 10-8, SA 10-6, SU 11-6; PARKING IN FRONT OF BLDG

POMPANO BEACH—2251 N FEDERAL HWY (AT POMPANO SQUARE);
  954.783.1166; M-F 10-8, SA 9-8, SU 11-6

Touch Of Class Photograhy, A

WWW.GIANCARLOFOTO.COM

NORTH MIAMI BEACH—2100 NE 164TH ST (AT NE 21ST AVE); 305.949.8480;
  CALL FOR APPT

Unique Design Studios

"...*very talented photographer... works with you to create pictures which capture your child's moods and inclinations... I'm a satisfied customer... creative pictures in a natural setting enhanced with props... great family photos, will even include your dog!...* **"**

Customer service .... ❺ $$$ .... Prices

Service Area....................on location

WWW.UDSPHOTO.COM

MIAMI—4990 SW 72ND AVE (AT SW 48TH ST); 305.668.7171; M-F 10-6, SA-SU BY APPT

photographers

Online

clubphoto.com
WWW.CLUBPHOTO.COM

dotphoto.com
WWW.DOTPHOTO.COM

flickr.com
WWW.FLICKR.COM

kodakgallery.com

"...the popular ofoto.com is now under it's wings... very easy to use desktop software to upload your pictures on their site... prints, books, mugs and other photo gifts are reasonably priced and are always shipped promptly... I like that there is no limit to how many pictures and albums you can have their site... **"**

WWW.KODAKGALLERY.COM

photoworks.com
WWW.PHOTOWORKS.COM

shutterfly.com

"...I've spent hundreds of dollars with them—it's so easy and the quality of the pictures is great... they use really nice quality photo paper... what a lifesaver—since I store all of my pictures with them I didn't lose any when my computer crashed... most special occasions are take care of with a personal photo calendar, book or other item with the cutest pictures of our kids... reasonable prices... **"**

WWW.SHUTTERFLY.COM

snapfish.com

"...great photo quality and never a problem with storage limits... we love their photo books and flip books—easy to make and fun to give... good service and a good price... we have family that lives all over the country and yet everyone still gets to see and order pictures of our new baby... **"**

WWW.SNAPFISH.COM

indexes

alphabetical

by city/neighborhood

alphabetical

participate in our survey at

participate in our survey a ▶

by city/neighborhood

participate in our survey at

participate in our survey at

Wilton Manors

Notes

Notes

Notes

Notes

Notes

Notes

....

....

....

....

....

....

....

....

....

....

....

....

....

....

....

....

Notes

YOUR RECOMMENDATIONS MAKE THE LILAGUIDE BETTER!
PLEASE SHARE YOUR NOTES WITH US AT WWW.LILAGUIDE.COM

Notes

Notes

Notes

Notes

Notes